Beyond Money

'Outstanding ... a highly original and incisive analysis of the crippling role that money plays in today's global capitalist world.'

—Mike Berry, author of *Justice and Democracy*

'A fascinating portal into arguments about why we need to get beyond money.'

—Harry Cleaver, author of *33 Lessons on Capital: Reading Marx Politically*

'A book for our time. Anitra Nelson takes us from theory to praxis in clear steps. Nelson's turn towards a materialist ecofeminist analysis is pure joy.'

—Ariel Salleh, editor of *Eco-Sufficiency & Global Justice: Women Write Political Ecology*

'Takes monetised economies head-on, demonstrating how they exacerbate ecological devastation and socio-economic inequality, and provides examples and pathways towards non-monetary economies based on real values. Does a great service to movements seeking social and ecological justice for all humans and other life forms.'

—Ashish Kothari, founder of Kalpavriksh and co-editor of *Pluriverse*

'Challenges and inspires – a spur to action.'

—Helena Norberg-Hodge, author of *Ancient Futures* and winner of the Alternative Nobel prize

'It is easier to imagine the end of capitalism than the end of money. Anitra Nelson's book challenges us to think what viable postcapitalisms without money could look like.'

—Professor Giorgos Kallis, University of Barcelona

'If you had to choose one book to read on making the next political economy it should be this one. It will have you bristling with political energy.'
— Professor Adam David Morton, Department of Political Economy, University of Sydney

'An accessible and important book. If you want an alternative to economic and environmental disasters, you need to engage with her arguments.'
— Jeff Sparrow, writer, editor and broadcaster

'A passionate critique of money as the root cause of our many problems, presenting a clear vision of what life without money could look like. Inspiring.'
— Matthias Schmelzer, Friedrich-Schiller-University Jena and author of *The Hegemony of Growth* and *The Future is Degrowth*

'With a compelling narrative, Nelson lays out the unavoidable question of today's anti-capitalist, ecological politics – the question of money. Grounded in long-term political experience, her answer is at once elaborate and unequivocal: a wonderful tool for radical imagination and praxis.'
— Stefania Barca, author of *Forces of Reproduction* and *Workers of the Earth*

'An exciting, original book that, in exploring the ritual structure of assets, capital, money and profit, helps open a way for more powerful, creative resistance.'
— Larry Lohmann, founding member of the Durban Group for Climate Justice

'Can capitalism be overcome without challenging money? In this thought-provoking book, Anitra Nelson argues that moving beyond money is necessary for addressing inequalities and environmental unsustainability and shows what a non-monetary postcapitalist world might look like.'
— Ekaterina Chertkovskaya, researcher in degrowth and critical organisation studies, Lund University

'Alternatives to capitalism, price-making markets and monetary values are essential for social-ecological transformation. Going well beyond typical economic discourse she opens the door of human potentiality to a different way of life.'
— Clive L. Spash, Professor of Public Policy and Governance at WU, Vienna University of Economics and Business

Beyond Money

A Postcapitalist Strategy

Anitra Nelson

Foreword by John Holloway

PLUTO PRESS

First published 2022 by Pluto Press
New Wing, Somerset House, Strand, London WC2R 1LA

www.plutobooks.com

British Library Cataloguing in Publication Data
A catalogue record for this book is available from the British Library

ISBN   978 0 7453 4012 8   Hardback
ISBN   978 0 7453 4011 1   Paperback
ISBN   978 1 786807 80 9   PDF eBook
ISBN   978 1 786807 81 6   EPUB eBook

This book is printed on paper suitable for recycling and made from fully
managed and sustained forest sources. Logging, pulping and manufacturing
processes are expected to conform to the environmental standards of the
country of origin.

Typeset by Stanford DTP Services, Northampton, England

Simultaneously printed in the United Kingdom, United States of America and
Australia

Contents

List of Abbreviations and Symbols

°C	Degree/s Celsius
A$	Australian dollar/s
ACT	Australian Capital Territory
BBC	British Broadcasting Corporation
BCE	Before the common era
CES	Community Exchange System
CIC	*Cooperativa Integral Catalana* (Catalan Integral Cooperative)
CNT	*Confederación Nacional del Trabajo* (Spain) (National Confederation of Labour)
ETS	Emissions Trading System
EZLN	*Ejército Zapatista de Liberación Nacional* (Zapatista Army of National Liberation)
FaDA	Feminisms and Degrowth Alliance
FAO	Food and Agriculture Organization
FILAC	Fund for the Development of the Indigenous Peoples of Latin America and the Caribbean
IASC	International Association for the Study of the Commons
IFAD	International Fund for Agricultural Development
IUCN	International Union for Conservation of Nature
LETS	Local (or labour) exchange trading system, or local energy transfer system
M	Money
M′	Money plus monetary increment, or profit (′)
MDB	Murray–Darling Basin
MMT	Modern monetary theory
NACLA	North American Congress on Latin America
NAFTA	North American Free Trade Agreement
NEF	New Economics Foundation
NRM	Natural resource management
NYDF	New York Declaration on Forests
OECD	Organisation for Co-operation and Development
P2P	Peer-to-peer

REDD+   Reducing Emissions from Deforestation and Forest Degradation (incorporating conservation, sustainable forest management and improving developing countries' stocks of forest carbon)

SITA   Subsistence is the alternative

SUV   Sports utility (or 'special use') vehicle

TINA   There is no alternative

UGT   *Unión General de Trabajadores* (Spain) (General Union of Workers)

WFP   World Food Programme

WHO   World Health Organization

XR   Extinction Rebellion (movement)

ZAD/Zad   *Zone à Défendre* (France) – deferred development area

Glossary

Carbon emissions: a somewhat misleading but standard shorthand that stands not only for carbon dioxide but also five other major greenhouse gases – methane, nitrous oxide, hydrofluorocarbons, perfluorocarbons and sulphur hexafluoride.

Collective sufficiency: self-provisioning performed collectively, co-governing, working together or as delegated, and sharing the total output on the basis of various needs.

Commodity: a good or service created to sell; a result of production for trade.

Commoning: practices of shared use, benefit, responsibility and co-governance.

Community mode of production: the essential characteristic of post-capitalism whereby community-oriented commoning and production based on real values enable everyone's needs to be met – including needs for healing and conviviality – while sustainably using Earth and sensitively caring for Earth, including regeneration.

Compact: a nonmonetary arrangement to exchange made between, say neighbouring communities.

Earth: a sense of nature integrating human and nonhuman nature.

Ecotat: truncation of 'eco-habitats' – peculiarly appropriate environs for human communities in that the local ecosystem is substantively capable of meeting their needs and they, in a mutual way, are able to care for its needs.

Ecotone: a region of transition, that is both integrative and distinctive, between two ecological communities.

Ejidos (Mexico): lands that operate via communal (or individual) use rights with potential for collective forms of self-provisioning and co-governance.

Exchange value: refers to an abstract general societal relationship, and practical processes of exchange, wherein money represents future worth to be redeemed via the market.

Gift economy: nonmonetary modes or forms of production and exchange, characterised in various ways by different theorists, and of particular interest to anthropologists, i.e. in economic anthropology.

Good: a material object potentially offering a benefit for someone or something.

Horizontalism, horizontalist relations and organisation: mutually respectful, non-hierarchical relations; sharing power as in *power-with* and based in skills and knowledge sharing; assemblies, networks and self-organising working groups with accountability and transparency in activities and relations.

Late stage capitalism: the final stage of capitalism within which we now live.

Real values: actual and potential diverse values of living things, plant, animal and rock in landscapes and the atmosphere relevant to actual and holistic human and ecological needs.

Real value studies: investigations focusing on actual and potential real values in the context of likely and optimum social and ecological outcomes (totally distinct from exchange value).

Real valuism: arguments and theories pertaining to nonmonetary economies based on real values.

Real valuist: as a noun, a supporter and/or advocate of nonmonetary economies based on real values; as an adjective, associated with non-monetary economies based on real values.

Rentier: one who derives income from investments, including property.

Service: an act aiming to produce a benefit for someone or something.

Trade: exchange using money; monetary exchange.

Universal equivalent: the essential character of money, to reduce and project a singular market-based (exchange) value, as in prices – the key term of monetary exchange and accounting.

Use right: a right of use often bounded in time and by type of use.

Use value: the qualities, functions and purposes of anything with respect to satisfying specific needs or wants.

Yenomon: a fictionalised but, arguably, plausible and feasible non-monetary postcapitalist local–global commons, based on commoning and a community mode of production.

Zad: a zone to defend (zone à défendre), a physical occupation by activists to block a development project.

Foreword

John Holloway

Strike at the heart of the beast! Kill money!

That is my own crude formulation of Anitra Nelson's argument in this book, an argument that I fully share. Her presentation is far from being crude, but it is very clear. In the opening words of the first chapter, she states her purpose: 'Money as we know it is capitalism's *sine qua non*, its essence. We cannot describe or define either capitalism or capitalist management and capitalist work without recourse to money'. You might respond, 'Just because capitalism relies on money, money might not always lead to capitalism', or state that the real problem is 'capital' and/ or 'commodification'. Indeed, these positions typify leftists, environmentalists and anti-capitalist theorists and movements today. Consequently, modified forms of money and markets are included or inferred in practically all visions of postcapitalism. So, if you're thinking money is not really that much of a problem, that we could mould money to progressive ends, consider this book my answer to you.'

The book is very much an intervention in a debate or, better, in a series of debates. This is perhaps true of all political books, but in this case it is very explicit. 'The desired use value of this book is to act as a key intervention in these contemporary discourses to point out that we can neither address inequalities and unsustainability nor establish postcapitalism without moving beyond money.' Anitra examines different movements for radical change, especially the environmental, feminist and indigenous movements, and argues that these movements are weakened to the extent that they do not address the central issue of money. As long as money exists, the central social problems of inequality and the unsustainability of life will continue to be generated.

I find it helpful to think of money in relation to the metaphor of the hydra of capitalism proposed by the Zapatistas. It is very difficult to defeat capitalism because every time we succeed in cutting off one of the monster's heads, other heads sprout up to attack us. We defeat fascism, for example, and then find that it springs up in a variety of authoritarian and racist forms. We win shorter working hours through various forms of factory legislation and then find that in practice the hours become longer and longer, so that the very idea of 'nine-to-five' becomes a joke. We achieve recognition of the weekend and then find it invaded by pressures to work. We defeat discrimination against women and find that femicides are increasing. Sometimes it seems like an endless struggle to defend human dignity, in which any gains we make are always threatened with reversal.

If we think of the different heads of the monster as different forms of oppression – sexism, racism, exploitation of labour, destruction of other forms of life and of the environment, and so on – then it is clear that resistance takes the form of a multiplicity of struggles against these different heads. This seems to me both inevitable and desirable. Such struggles can lead to real changes that affect and often improve people's lives profoundly. The different struggles also relate to one another, often recognise a common cause and develop relations of mutual support. But there is an often unspoken question in these struggles. Are the different heads just an array of nasty oppressions or is there some unseen or only dimly seen body that not only connects them but continually generates new forms of oppression? If we really want to transform society, to create a society based on the mutual recognition of human dignities, do we not have to reach beyond the heads and defeat this generator of oppressions? The danger is that in the necessary and important battles against the heads, this question gets lost. Although she does not use the hydra metaphor, Anitra argues that it is important that this question should not get lost and that it is money that is the generator of these oppressions: money, such an essential part of our lives in capitalism that we do not even see it, such a ubiquitous force that the very idea or abolishing it seems nonsensical, beyond the bounds of rational discourse. For this reason, it is necessary to intervene in these different discussions to say 'aren't you forgetting about the heart of the beast, money? Don't you see that to achieve our aims, we must create a society without money?' In this I agree with her completely.

This is not a dogmatic position. There is a sense in which we will be able to understand the importance of abolishing money only after it is actually achieved, that the owl of Minerva can indeed fly only at dusk. For us now, there is an element of betting here, but we can give strong and reasoned arguments for seeing money and therefore capital and its unceasing pursuit of profit as the key generator of the destruction that is pointing us towards our possible extinction. It is urgent, therefore, that we should abolish money and create a society in which social relationships are not mediated through money.

The argument is not dogmatic in the old sense of trying to establish a hierarchy of struggle. Anitra poses her argument as an intervention in the different debates that are going on. Possibly the abolition of money can be understood only as an overflowing from the different visible struggles. Perhaps the only way of reaching the heart or body of the hydra is if the struggles against the distinct heads break through their own definitions, their own identities. It is hard to imagine 'abolish money' as a slogan that would attract support in the same way as, say, 'Black Lives Matter': much better to argue that the only way of creating a non-racist society of mutual recognition is through the abolition of money with its logic of identity and death. The particular struggles can be seen as possible gateways to the abolition of money, but for this to happen they must overflow their own starting-point. Precisely for this reason, it is enormously important that Anitra frames her argument as an intervention in the more particular 'head-centred' debates and seeks to draw out the overflowings that are already present in those debates.

Life against money: this is a central theme of the current Zapatista Voyage for Life and it is a slogan that should be taken up in all forms of radical struggle for a better world. Anitra sings out this theme in *Beyond Money*. I also intend to take it up myself, in a slightly different direction, in a forthcoming book.*

I hope that this book of Anitra's will put the abolition of money where it belongs, at the centre of radical, rebellious hope.

Puebla
October 2021

---

* Due in 2022 from Pluto Press.

Preface

Every author has a beginning. I was born at the end of 1952 in an inconspicuous rural town in Australia's south-eastern state of Victoria. At that point of history, Heyfield owed its existence to three timber mills. It had emerged as a rest place for diggers in the gold rushes of the 1850s and 1860s; the Heyfield post office was established in 1870. At this time, state-issued monies in many parts of the world were based on a metallic standard and gold was a resplendent symbol of money. Like most Antipodean outposts, Heyfield was a node in state and national economies that, since white settlement just 165 years earlier, were intricately linked within a capitalist world system based on production for trade, for money.

Australia was settled by the British, who invaded and colonised an ancient continent covered with hundreds of distinctive tribes of Aboriginal and Torres Strait Islander peoples living off their local lands and waters using multifarious ecologically respectful practices. The area that the settlers named East Gippsland Forests, east of Heyfield, stretched from the highest peaks to coastal ecotones, offering complex ecologies and bioregions to sustain the Indigenous Gunnaikurnai, Monero and Bidawel peoples. Initially, these forests proved a haven to resist and defend themselves from murderous and exploitative settlers. Subsequently, the timber industry was a preferred worksite for Indigenous men. Aboriginal and Torres Strait Islander peoples as a whole were unable to vote until 1968. They still suffer all the worst ignominies of peoples throughout the world who are entangled in systemic class and racial prejudice.

As a far-flung settler colony, Australia's twentieth-century economy was characterised by a fair degree of independent individualism and authoritarianism counterposed to cultural practices of 'mateship', equality and fairness and, historically, a relatively strong union movement. Small businesses, foreign-owned companies and mainly agricultural cooperatives operated alongside self-provisioning from expansive public land and river systems where people could fish, hunt, forage, gather wood and, in their ample backyards they grew vegetables and fruit trees. During the depression years, my grandfather and mother's maternal uncle would leave home for days, even weeks, at a time to eke out a living for my mother's family – arriving home with, say, rabbits, fish and a bit of cash.

Initially, Australia's export income relied on wheat and meat, similar to Argentina at that time. Later, agriculture was overtaken by mining as the major economic sector. Australia's economy was a beguiling hybrid of developed and developing countries' economic and political structures. Divided internally and cut off externally by the 'tyranny of distance' – a descriptor coined by Melbournian historian Geoffrey Blainey – Australia remained an exotic other-worldly land 'down under' while expanding on the basis of immigration.

At 30 years of age, having completing a civil engineering degree after service in the Second World War, my Welsh father immigrated to Australia for work and a new life. He met my mother in Heyfield where they worked for the State Rivers and Water Supply Commission. He caused a deal of humour because he could neither sing – an attribute for which Welsh are known worldwide – nor pronounce 'rivers' without it sounding like 'livers'. He became subject to the 'tall poppy syndrome' in a land where people contradictorily revered and hated anything British.

A singularly important memory of my childhood, which benefitted from my Welsh grandfather living with us from when I was age 6 till 10, related to the concept 'money'. He was a well-known mining engineer who spent most of his time at his desk writing engineering-related articles and books so he was an endless source of scientific knowledge. I loved reading and getting him to set me arithmetic exercises.

One day he picked up some coins, which he regularly used when explaining how to add and subtract, multiply and divide. This day he picked up one florin and four sixpenny bits. This florin, he said, is only worth four sixpences because people say it is. This seemed curious. I was aware of standard measures for weight and distance, presented like laws of physics by my father and grandfather. An inch was an inch and 12 inches equalled one foot – presented as more reliable facts than any religious nonsense they might teach me at the Anglican school that I attended.

After a while I understood Gramps as saying that these coins measured something that was both social and malleable. My grandfather had been through two world wars and associated depressions. He had seen inflation, deflation, financial crises, national debt blowouts and morato-riums, and stock booms and busts. So, he was saying money was different from maths. It was an uncertain, unreliable, unstable measure because its base was social. I have always wondered whether this doubt, seeded in me so young meant that, later in my life, I was unusually prepared to challenge the concept of money, perceptions of money and monetary practices. While many saw economics and trade as legitimate, and in terms of sophisticated algebraic formula and quasi-laws, I interpreted our monetary economies as illogical, full of flaws and system failures.

If my grandfather was mildly conservative, my father was fundamentally so, a nobleman, who could truck no ideas beyond his own. For instance, as an 8-year-old, when we listened to the radio commentary on the 1961 federal elections, I asked him, 'What's "right" and what's "left"?' He retorted, 'All you need to remember is that right is right.' Neither my father nor grandfather had much time for the vagaries of money or economics. My father's personal imaginary was more feudal and aristocratic than capitalist and commercial.

From all this, and the mind-blowing cultural and political developments emerging in the mid-to-late 1960s – when I found my bearings as a radical women's liberationist, environmentalist, anarchist and socialist – I would continue to wonder how and why money existed and whether we needed it at all. When I came to do a doctoral thesis, I chose an interdisciplinary study of Karl Marx's concept of money. This was really a cover for a grand investigation into as many theories of money as I could digest. After all, you really need to understand something thoroughly before you dismiss it – especially money, the secular quasi-god of the world I had been forced to inhabit, capitalism.

In the 1990s, I discovered 'nonmarket socialist' thinking and I was set. I had not so much found a home or ideology as a thread of heretical questioners of my own ilk. Nonmarket socialists argue that socialism cannot be achieved in a society based on a market economy. Money is the main source of social inequity in capitalism, and the values and care (management) of nature cannot be reduced to prices and costs. The environmental crises of the early twenty-first century – of which out-of-control carbon emissions have emerged as the mere tip of the iceberg – starkly reveal that the market economy is inadequate and inappropriate for establishing and maintaining fair and sustainable means of producing and consuming – the main challenge we face today.

This book is not simply an analysis of why this is so. More significantly, it is about a world beyond money – a really existing postcapitalism – which is already emerging in enclaves and practice. Moreover, I present the case for numerous distinctive social and environmental activists

– and local and global movements – to embrace a position beyond money that might inform visions, discourse and strategies for action in deeply significant ways. In the course of writing this manuscript I have re-defined my nonmarket socialist position in more positive and constructive terms as 'real valuism'.

ACKNOWLEDGEMENTS

I did not develop the ideas in this book in either a practical or an intellectual vacuum; various and numerous experiences, relationships, discussions and analyses contributed to my thoughts. I have cut down references to a minimum for readability. Similarly, acknowledgements of those who supported the development of this manuscript follow that brief.

I acknowledge that various chapters have drawn on material already published, as indicated in endnotes, specifically as follows:

- A short version of a paper presented in the Green Agenda Panel at the Historical Materialism Australasia 2015: Reading Capital, Class & Gender Today conference at University of Sydney (17–18 July) – Anitra Nelson, 'New and green materialism', 29 July 2015 at *Progress in Political Economy* (www.ppesydney.net/).
- Anitra Nelson, '"Your money or your life": Money and socialist transformation', *Capitalism Nature Socialism* 27(4), 2016: pp. 40–60.
- A short version of a paper presented at the 9th Australian International Political Economy Network (AIPEN) Workshop, 8–9 February 2018 at Monash University, Melbourne – Anitra Nelson, 'The political economy of space and time in Eduardo Galeano', 20 February 2018 at *Progress in Political Economy* (www.ppesydney.net/).

I duly thank editors of *Capitalism Nature Socialism* (Salvatore Engel-Di Mauro, SUNY New Paltz, New York, United States) and *Progress in Political Economy* (Adam David Morton and Gareth Bryant, University of Sydney, Sydney, New South Wales, Australia).

I illustrated the book, thanks to Central Victorian artist and art teacher Karen Ward.

xviii · BEYOND MONEY

My deepest thanks are extended to Mike Berry, Pluto Press's editorial director David Castle, Harry Cleaver, Friederike Habermann, Jeff Sparrow, the late Frans Timmerman and, especially for his detailed review of the penultimate draft, Terry Leahy. Still, of course, I am responsible for all the faults herein.

Most importantly, I respectfully acknowledge Elders past, present and future of the Kulin Nation on whose unceded lands I wrote this work, specifically the Dja Dja Wurrung, also known as the Jaara, people. This land always was, is, and always will be, theirs.

1
Capital and Crises

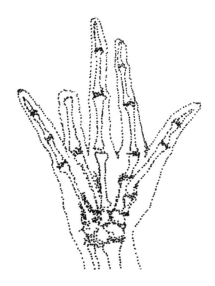

Money as we know it is capitalism's *sine qua non*, its essence. We cannot describe or define either capitalism or capitalist management and capitalist work without recourse to money. You might respond, 'Just because capitalism relies on money, money might not always lead to capitalism', or state that the real problem is 'capital' and/or 'commodification'. Indeed, these positions typify leftists, environmentalists and anti-capitalist theorists and movements today. Consequently, modified forms of money and markets are included or inferred in practically all visions of postcapitalism. So, if you're thinking money is not really that much of a problem, that we could mould money to progressive ends, consider this book my answer to you.

INEQUALITY

Today, production for trade – which requires monetary calculations, relations and exchanges from start to finish – supplies most of our basic needs and wants. Monetary practices are so widespread that they construct our everyday relations. We work for, and with, people in order to get money to buy our means of existence. We make purchases of goods and services made by lots of other people whom we will never know, just as we cannot know the terms on which, and conditions in which, they work. Similarly, we do not know the ecological implications of the techniques used to make such commodities. Living in market-based economies means that we are alienated from, cut out of, making decisions over what is produced and how it is produced.

This omnipotence of monetary practices tends to obscure, suffocate, or sideline those nonmonetary social and environmental values, relations and activities that we hold dear as marks of friendship and solidarity. We enjoy sharing, caring and receiving others' care and attention, both in slow time and convivial contexts. Such relationships offer us a deep sense of security. In contrast, it is only money that offers the ultimate security within capitalism and, even then, we are vulnerable to the hand-to-mouth culture of just-in-time supply chains as many have experienced in the context of coronavirus (COVID-19) restrictions.

Beyond being a standard of value in price and medium of exchange in cash, money creates and re-creates our social substance and being in subtle and complex ways. Significantly, money operates to *compare* and *contrast*: it is *divisive*. We are surrounded by winners and losers. If some profit and save, others lose. Our monetary system patterns and generates inequality. We might feel angst about diminishing such inequity and advocate for redistribution or develop policies to address disadvantage, but inequity is generated by capitalism and achieved in the first and final instance by money.

The 1% and the 99%

Today, most people right across the globe live in societies that are inequitable within their borders and in comparison with other countries, due to inequitable work and living conditions and unequal exchange. We witness flagrant overconsumption, massive waste and obesity alongside food shortages, starvation, famine and absolute poverty both within and between nations. The Occupy Wall Street protests starkly portrayed the '99%' who cannot enjoy the full benefits of their everyday work and have little say in how they live or work. There are deep inequities within this 99%, with people at one end of the spectrum living in comfortable overconsumption while marginalisation, precarity and poverty characterise those at the other end. Still, all those within the 99% share a low level of substantive, real, democracy.

Beginning in 2011, the Occupy movement spread rapidly in the United States (US) 'where inequality has soared in recent decades'.[1] Using data from the late stage capitalist states of the US, the United Kingdom (UK) and his home country France, economist Thomas Piketty has argued that 'global inequality of wealth in the early 2010s appears to be comparable in magnitude to that observed in Europe in 1900–1910.' That first decade of the twentieth century was a period of notoriously stark distinctions between wealth and poverty, as described in novels by E.M. Forster and John Steinbeck. But Piketty estimates that even in the early 2010s, the elite '1%' owned around *half* of total global wealth. That left around 50 per cent to be, unequally, shared amongst the remaining 99 per cent. In fact, half of the world's population do not even own 5 per cent of total global wealth. Similarly, while the top 10 per cent monopolise 80–90 per cent of global wealth, an extraordinarily tiny elite within that elite – the top 0.1 per cent – enjoy 20 per cent of total global wealth.[2] Moreover, the '1%' comprise an international bourgeoisie from which many of our political leaders are drawn. Piketty is no anti-capitalist, yet he has argued that 'it is an illusion to think that something about the nature of modern growth or the laws of the market economy ensures that inequality of wealth will decrease and harmonious stability will be achieved.'[3]

Furthermore, there is a global divide referred to variously as developed versus un(der)developed countries, First World versus Third World, global North versus global South and, most recently, the minority world versus the majority world. From a world-systems perspective of regions categorised as centre, periphery and semi-periphery, such spatial distinctions highlight an uneven and inequitable operation of global capitalism.[4] As such, Piketty points out that while global per capita income increased more than ten-fold between 1700 and 2012, wealthy country per capita income increased much more than twenty-fold.[5] Moreover, financial globalisation means 'that every country is to a large extent owned by other countries', which undercuts any sense of substantive democratic state-based citizen control and supports the concept of an international bourgeoisie.[6] Inequalities of material well-being and political power are replicated within states spatially, with cities typically dominating and marginalising regional hinterlands even as the city is demarcated by advantaged and disadvantaged zones.

Another book, based on widely acknowledged international data by Californian Seth Donnelly, reveals 'the epidemic of poverty that is the real and persistent fruit of capitalist development' in flagrant contradiction to widespread propaganda of 'a dramatic decline in global poverty'.[7] Donnelly unpacks spurious concepts and dubious practices underlying World Bank data by drawing, instead, on the UK Multidimensional Poverty Index. Significantly, this index is based on real social values not monetary or monetised data, to show that 1.45 billion people (almost half of them children) experience seriously poor health, educational and/or living standards.[8] Is this 'just' relative or comparable poverty? No, it is *absolute poverty* in terms of people's basic needs. In fact, 1.5 billion go hungry and yet another 1 billion do not eat enough food to enable 'intense activity'.[9] We are talking undernourishment of around one-third of Earth's people.

Money generates inequality

The data on inequalities at every scale strongly challenge the politico-cultural messages and assumptions iterated by the mainstream media that global capitalism represents the best of all possible worlds, and that all we need to do is to tweak the system to overcome its weaknesses.

Many of us have lived in capitalist societies for generations and have no other point of comparison except for analyses of certain national experiments with communism, such as the Soviet Union, Cuba and China in the twentieth century. Such experiments never represented ideally functioning socialism because they were ruled by elites who continued production for the market, even if in modified, state-planned, ways. Money remained a tool of control. By maintaining money and markets, or some kind of substitute indicator/s enabling calculation, such elites undermined efforts to achieve real and direct democracy and the real sharing of responsibilities for satisfying our collective and individual needs that are essential principles of both socialism and communism. For reasons made clear in Chapter 6, the initial adaptation of capitalist technologies was determining and such 'revolutionary' elites increasingly adopted capitalist ways of operating.[10]

Capitalist dynamics produce inequities. In terms of enterprises, the carrots and rewards of competition play out as either more or less profits, even bankruptcy, all based on a firm's monetary efficiency. There is more downward pressure on wages the more one is supervised; those most controlled tend to be paid the least. Similarly, at the top of the pecking order, owners and managers tend to put upward pressure to increase their absolute incomes as well as their share of total incomes. Having higher or lower incomes means either more or less access to the market, the main source of basic needs and non-essential wants. Haggling, calculating over whether to buy or sell and at what price, is a metaphor for life in which 'more' and 'less' are intrinsic points of reference. These social, cultural and economic dynamics of 'more' and 'less' all rotate around money that, by its very nature, compares, contrasts and divides.

Moreover, a citizen's 'social' contract with the capitalist state is a profoundly monetary one. Strong tensions arise because, although the national government is often regarded as *apart from* the market, it is actually *a part of* the market.

THE STATE OF CAPITAL

Within mainstream capitalist cultures, trading and producing for trade, working for money, and making goods and offering services to sell are all considered natural and normal. Everyday practices and legal, regulatory and political structures coalesce around production for trade. Capitalism reduces to a socio-political system centred on markets, structured on private property, the dynamics of working for money and a general reliance on the market to operate and live. Negotiable private property is synonymous with market economies.

As such, capitalism spawns a unique political system with its own ideology of 'freedom', characterised simply as freedom of speech and freedom of choice, and associated concepts of an individual citizen's rights and responsibilities, and representative parliamentary governance. Governments (states) and many and various state agencies operate on monetary principles of accounting, taxes and subsidies, and monetary calculations of so-called costs and benefits. Under neoliberalism – better referred to as late stage capitalism – the capitalist state is a structure formed by, as well as forming and reforming, capitalist ideals and efforts.

A planet of trading states

Global capitalism relies on international trade laws and conventions, on trading policies, relations, agreements and activities between and within states that are overwhelmingly capitalist. These international structures have evolved over centuries so that capitalist forces can operate across the planet, establishing and legitimating trade. The creation and upholding of universal human rights and environmental standards have struggled against such trade and investments, along with the commercial cultures and political structures that sustain them.

The rationale and functions of 'exchange value' – which refers to monetary value, prices, producing for markets and trade – oppose and undermine social values of mutual respect and sharing on the basis of need, expressed in terms of use values. In production for trade, the 'use value' of a commodity specifically refers to its qualities and purposes for users, in contrast to the commodity's exchange value, as in its price. As they created an entire societal paradigm to produce for trade, capitalist forces derided pre-existing Indigenous peoples' forms of production and exchange as well as women's extra-market roles and perspectives, issues taken up in Chapter 7 and Chapter 5, respectively.

This capitalist world system, characterised by marked inequalities of power and influence between nation states, has led to the familiar periodisation of world history into stages of hegemonic power, for instance British domination in the nineteenth and early twentieth century giving way to US dominance during the twentieth century. In both periods, the dominant state's currency became the international monetary currency and standard par excellence. British and US political, military and monetary influence facilitated economic advantages that, in turn, raised their political and military might. They ignited cultures of planetary grandness, dominance and extermination riddled with racial, patriarchal, violent and anti-environmental perspectives and practices.

Today, most nations are formal capitalist states based on some type and degree of representative democracy easily dominated by those with wealth, who have clear interests in perpetuating the capitalist system of private property and trade. The state develops policies that normalise and facilitate production for trade through financial incentives and policies, as well as economic regulations. States are critical for supporting bankers, manufacturers, farmers and retailers during endemic economic crises, such as the global financial crisis of 2007–08 and consequent national depressions and recessions. With the COVID-19 pandemic, a crisis associated with health sectors already weakened by neoliberalism met restrictions of movements that limited work and trade to induce classic conditions for a generic economic crisis. As such, states came into their own, typically creating stimulus packages as shock-absorbers for certain inherent failings of markets.

The state as a bulwark against the market

Even if long just-in-time supply chains were quickly revealed as systemic weaknesses in the context of a pandemic, most shortcomings of the market have so consistently found a bulwark in the state that both consumers and producers readily blame governments for economic consequences of market failings. Through welfare payments, nation states have tended to offer minimal financial support to those permanently or temporarily marginalised from earning an income. Even if capitalists do not provide enough work, this means the unemployed continue to fulfil their means of existence as consumers from markets – ensuring the baseline demand for capitalist producers. COVID-19 economic stimulus measures have been designed in similar ways.

As a support of first and last resort, the state alternates between saviour and, more often than not, an incompetent failure. This explains to some extent why, in the twenty-first century, as inequalities have increased, a range of competitive, isolationist, quasi-patriotic, anti-democratic, patriarchal and protectionist ideas of securing national borders have also increased. The state remains a space where magical promises are sought and hopes dashed. Simultaneously, social categories of 'them' and 'us' are inspired and fuelled by competitive relations of trade and by capitalist relations of credit and debt.

Still, we do not live in a black box of capitalism, even if capitalist forces strive to make it look and feel like that, and declare that 'there is no alternative' (TINA). Anti-capitalist resistance has resurged in a plethora of distinctive movements initially from the 1960s that have burgeoned in various ways during the twenty-first century. The character of anti-capitalist resistance to contemporary economic and political systems can only be fully understood within the context of the other great challenge facing us today: the existential threat of multiple ecological crises.

UNSUSTAINABILITY

By 1970, the environmental demands on Earth of our human species' productive, trading and consumptive activities were already at full capacity. Since then, the total impact on Earth of human activities has increasingly outpaced its natural regenerative capacities.[11] Degradation is evident in environmental crises associated with various sectors, from mining and industrial agriculture to overfishing of oceans and polluted rivers. Most of this damage has been a direct result of the growth impetus of capitalist economies, as state and powerful capitalist forces frame systemic inequality, marginalisation and poverty as challenges demanding growth rather than concluding that we all need to share and live modestly instead.

Ecological footprints

According to the Global Footprint Network, in 2020, the total global impact of human activities assumed a regenerative capacity of around 1.75 Earths.[12] In other words, we have been using Earth to a *severely* unsustainable extent. All the more so the richer we are – the more we use and consume Earth. This ecological footprint indicator is a necessary, but inadequate, measure of sustainability. Beyond the impossibility of collecting data for all consumption, ecological footprint accounting does not account for the degradation of Earth through current activities, which means it will 'underestimate the actual biocapacity deficit of countries, or overestimate their biocapacity reserves'.[13] Still, the ecological footprint remains a highly visible and useful suite of indicators of our dire predicament as a species.

Country comparisons are generally made using an ecological footprint measure of a one-planet footprint, which means living within Earth's regenerative capacities with respect to resource use and absorption of waste. According to this measure, in 2016, North Americans, Danes and Australians were treating Earth as if it had *four* times the potential resources, regenerative and waste absorption capacity than actually existed. In contrast, one-third of the world's countries for which there was data – countries such as India, South Korea and Indonesia – had a per capita average showing that they were living within a one-planet footprint.[14] Yet, this country-focused data and associated averages hide very real inequalities in levels of consumption between individuals and households within each country. Some individuals who live in the most extravagant countries live one-planet (or less) footprints; some wealthy individuals in the least extravagant countries have footprints that assume several planets.

When we examine inequalities in abuse of Earth in such ways, those of us in late stage capitalist societies are the worst contributors and often those least immediately impacted by climate changes caused by carbon emissions. The Stockholm Environment Institute has calculated that there was a 60 per cent rise in global carbon emissions from 1990 to 2015, with the richest 10 per cent of the global population responsible for half those emissions and the poorest 50 per cent accounting for just 7.5 per cent of emissions.[15] By the late 2010s, impacts of climate change threatened the livelihoods and security of almost 1 billion people residing in vulnerable regions – regions over-exposed to climate hazards and with relatively low capabilities (say infrastructure) to deal with more intense and greater frequencies of droughts, hurricanes and floods, rising sea levels and extremes of temperature.[16]

Climate change and other ecological crises

Climate change is just the tip of the iceberg, a symptom, of more profound and extensive environmental crises. If global heating was our only environmental problem, it would be bad enough. That's because, even if we manage to fulfil the goals of the United Nations Framework Convention on Climate Change 2016 Paris Agreement to address out-of-control carbon emissions through mitigation and adaptation, our activities are likely to contribute to at least 3.3°C climate heating.[17] Just 3°C would make us prone to tipping points that will deliver more immediate impacts and unexpected impacts.[18] A useful metaphor is a human experiencing a fever with an internal temperature raised from a normal of around 37°C to a life-threatening 40°C or so; it's a medical emergency, and no one is certain of the outcome even if some symptoms and risks are predictable. Could there be any more compelling demonstration that *we are Earthly beings*?

Entering a state of climatic heating is not a temporary phenomenon, as is a fever. James Hansen wrote over a decade ago about the path we seem to be on: 'There will be no return within the lifetime of any generation that can be imagined, and the trip will exterminate a large fraction of species on the planet.' The conditions that we're heading towards include melting ice sheets, permafrosts and glaciers, droughts, ocean rises of 25 metres, and mega-fires in massive rainforests such as the Amazon precipitating further and more rapid climate temperature rises.[19] The situation is dire, making the need for action urgent.

The state of Earth's forests is one example of various environmental crises associated with capitalist activities, all multiplying in expansive and intensive ways. A 2020 Climate Focus report revealed that, between 2014 and 2018, gross tree cover loss all over the world had increased by 43 per cent, with the extent of average annual deforestation in the tropics approximating the land cover of the UK. This tropical deforestation mostly occurred in order to produce agricultural commodities and for urban expansion.[20] Forests are rich biomes capable of directly satisfying all humans' basic needs. At the same time, they are critical carbon sinks for absorbing carbon emissions, potentially reversing climate change. In a dual hit, deforestation generates carbon emissions and reduces carbon sinks.

During 2014–18, tropical deforestation was responsible for an average of 4.7 gigatonnes of CO_2 per annum, increasing to a greater amount than all greenhouse gas emissions resulting from the European Union. In line with other poor performances in trying to reduce carbon emissions and reverse climate change, the five-year assessment report on goals of the New York Declaration on Forests (NYDF), which was signed by around two hundred parties, including governments, concluded that 'achieving the 2020 NYDF targets is likely impossible.' In summary, restoration efforts were minimal and often in less than ideal places with conversion of forestlands to commercial uses overriding conservation and restoration efforts.[21]

Similar sustainability assaults and struggles ensue in all types of lands and waters, such as oceans close to coasts impacted by chemical run-off, warming waters and over-fishing; remote areas with open cut and deep underground mines causing erosion, disrupting groundwater and natural river systems and generating other impacts due to vehicles and other infrastructure; degrading mangrove swamps, which leave coastlands more exposed to damage by cyclones; woodlands denuded for mining, timber, residential settlements, or other novel uses; river systems subject to over-use of water and fish, and polluted by wastes; and farming land degraded through growing mono-crops, use of chemical fertilisers and grazing animals. Wherever people live, they face dramatic results of such 'development' in their locales and regions more generally.

We in the Anthropocene are experiencing the start of a mass extinction caused by our own activities, a level of biodiversity loss that scientists estimate to be upwards of a thousand times greater than if human practices did not exist. Depending on estimates of the total number of species on Earth, this translates from hundreds to tens of thousands of species extinctions per annum.[22] We're talking particular types of leopards and tigers, gorillas, turtles, orangutans and rhinoceros becoming extinct. Moreover, specific frogs and corals, penguins, butterflies and bears are endangered by climate change.[23] In another indicator of ecosystem integrity and ill-health of the environments in which they live, long-term surveys of total *abundance* of 529 species of birds show losses of 2.9 billion in the US and Canada alone, with a loss by 2018 of 29 per cent of 1970 abundance – representing 'a pervasive and ongoing avifaunal crisis'.[24]

Responses to ecological crises

When one examines mainstream responses to this unfolding cataclysm, two aspects of capitalism are thrown into sharp relief. First, promoted as the most successful way to satisfy people's daily needs, capitalism is also referred to as the best form of society imaginable. Yet, we find generalised political impotence and delays in responding to environmental crises within capitalism's ideal political structure of representative democracy. Indeed, we seem to experience 'freedom' tenuously and narrowly as freedom of opportunity and choice in an uncertain and competitive world of seriously limited options, especially in terms of for whom and for what we can vote. Similarly, we only get to select from what is available and in our price range in markets and do not have any say in what is produced. Despite massive disquiet and calls for action in terms of inequity and unsustainability, business as usual continues.

Second, environmental 'solutions' are saturated with confidence in 'green', technological versions of growth, finance, trading and production for the market. Even many so-called alternatives are market-oriented – from local economies, fair trading and market-based cooperatives through to water and carbon trading, pricing ecosystem services (say, of forests) and ethical investment. The weak assumption of market-oriented models is that social and environmental values can be integrated within capitalist practices and that market-based processes are capable of fulfilling social and environmental goals.

Such approaches delay real solutions because capitalist practices are based, instead, on monetary values and tend to produce anti-social and anti-environmental outcomes at every scale, as outlined in Chapter 4. It suffices here to point out that not only neoliberals believe that market mechanisms are more efficient but also numbers of socialists and anarchists retain albeit modified markets in their visions of 'postcapitalism', just as certain environmentalists support market-based solutions. The late American sociologist Erik Olin Wright was typical in embracing a 'democratic market socialism, understood as a radical form of economic democracy' – in other words, 'a market economy that is effectively subordinate to the exercise of democratic power'.[25] But is it possible, in fact, to control a market democratically? Exactly how would you do that?

Market-oriented reforms

Reformist approaches assume that markets could operate in more equitable and environmentally reasonable ways, and that a market is the most efficient option available. Yet the logic of market efficiencies generally rotates on *purely monetarily* calculations, effectively reasoning in a hall of mirrors and marginalising real social and environmental values. Familiar examples are conventional food retailers, such as supermarkets, which purchase fruit and vegetables as cheaply as possible. Inexpensive produce might be grown using soil- and water-damaging fertilisers, by poorly paid illegal migrant workers, and transported long distances using more cheap labour and environmentally damaging practices. However, organic farmers can only follow ecologically sound practices and make sure they pay their workers fair wages if the food costs more, meaning supply for an elite demand. By its very nature, one never manages to escape the conundrums that production for trade entails. Real social and environmental values involved in caring for people and Earth highlight the inequities and damage of market-oriented activities.

Still, reformists persist in believing that markets can be restructured, that capitalists can be re-formed and state managers could be persuaded to make more socially desirable and environmentally sustainable decisions. Such arguments are increasingly dubious, as a range of market-based 'green' measures such as electric cars have suffered from a slow take-up by entrepreneurs and, once they are pursued, still exploit Earth in terms of materials and infrastructure costs. Despite decades of talk and even certain action, what substantial improvements have been made? Most environmental achievements have required voluntary labour by environmentalists and thus advances have been made *despite* capitalism not because of it. Indeed, systemic anti-social and anti-environmental capitalist tendencies have reached a critical conjunctural crisis.

Perversely, even if a rich elite is most influential within the market economy, in reality no one in particular manages any market. The market is a free-wheeling and all-encompassing set of flows and activities stitched together by price signals and other monetary relations. In this market-based wonderland, money is a quasi-god. Even the power of multi-billionaires and monopolies is limited to being simply more influential in, rather than driving, the system.

In short, we have all handed over control of our livelihoods to money, to monetary calculations that are irrational in terms of social and ecological values and outcomes. As such, the universal equivalent, money, is fatally implicated in inequalities and unsustainability. The existential threat of contemporary environmental crises suggests that we might commit species suicide if we don't immediately get into the driver's seat and collectively move away from monetary practices.

MONEY IN ACTION

Examining the main functions of money is not simply a technical exercise. As in learning basic knitting stitches in order to make a garment with a complex pattern, or simple and discrete rules to develop artful tactics in any sport, a few functions of money are key elements of complicated processes and patterns that form capitalist societies. Using money is a wholly social practice with a variety of assumptions and implications.

Simple monetary exchange

In a simple monetary exchange, when purchasing or selling, money functions as a 'unit of account'. When you buy some fruit juice for the price of $2, here the dollar is the unit in which the price is expressed, the unit of account. The vendor expects payment in this unit, which is referred to as state 'legal tender'. Examples of units of account are currencies like the euro (€), which is used by a series of nation states, and the US dollar (US$) or British pound (£, GBP), currencies issued and managed by one nation (but sometimes used in other territories). Your taxation and other invoices and accounts show payments and receipts in this unit of account, which is sometimes referred to as a standard of value.

A simple monetary exchange, say a purchase, is a fleeting interaction with another person, often a mere retailer, even a casual salesperson, who didn't make the product. In all exchanges, money functions not only as a unit of account but also as a means of exchange, most visibly if the payment takes the form of cash, i.e., paper or coins. Of course we can often pay using a credit card or debit card in which case the money is transferred to the vendor less visibly but with money still functioning as the medium of exchange.

We're continuously involved in trade, using money that we got for doing work to buy some bread or to pay for our Internet service. Holding money for purchases embraces us in a general societal relationship, as we trust money for its potential to make future purchases in the market. Most significantly, *holding money* gives us a vested interest in future production for trade.

Money and exchange value

Given the implied and expected continuity of the market, money held in our purses, wallets and bank accounts between exchanges, becomes a temporary 'store of value'. Still, both the qualitative and quantitative value of any such store is contingent on market conditions when you use it. For instance, house prices might rise so much over the years spent saving for a deposit that it seems like your store has lost value. This special monetary value that evolves from, and is peculiar to, market exchange is referred to generically as 'exchange value'. Exchange value is frequently contrasted to use value, as in the price of a banana if you sold it (exchange value) compared to its use as food for you or a friend (use value).

In conceptual terms, *exchange value refers to an abstract societal relationship, and practical processes of exchange, wherein money represents future worth to be redeemed via the market*. In short, the value of money is dependent on a series of market processes and the value of your money alters as, and if, these productive or trading processes develop and change. In everyday transactions, we accept that we have no control over quantitative meanings of the unit of account, in terms of the amount of produce we can purchase with one hundred dollars from one year to the next. But *we do expect money to maintain its quality as a trusted medium of exchange to access markets* – to buy food and make rental or mortgage payments.

In general, it suits consumers, workers and producers if the prices of essentials remain relatively constant or predictable. Because the value of money reflects what it can purchase, money itself seems solid and sound.

In fact, it is key to the smooth running of market-based societies that our unit of account – whether a euro, dollar, or pound – remains a relatively reliable reference point, with minimal inflation and deflation.

However, in times of upheaval, it is not uncommon for money to either lose value as prices inflate, so we have to spend more for the same goods, or to seem super-valuable as things become cheaper, say, because of low demand. In late stage capitalism, we have become used to at least a low level of inflation related to systemically pressured growth, discussed in Chapter 2, where we also return to qualitative and quantitative issues around the variability of the value of money as a unit of account.

Saving money, lending money and capital

Any idle sum of money can be 'saved' as a quasi-permanent store of value provided it is lent, rather than simply held (or hoarded). For the lender, money that is lent exists as if stored out of reach. Meanwhile, the borrower only uses this credit for a set period of time. Loan contracts include specific terms and conditions, namely a repayment date, consequences if the borrower fails to repay by the agreed time, and a particular rate of interest, often paid at regular intervals while lent. The interest rate is a percentage of the sum loaned per annum, whether paid over a number of years or for a fraction of a year. In the case of house mortgages, for instance, the loan is often amortised (meaning the capital starts to be repaid) very soon after the loan has been made. In other cases, such as commercial loans, repaying the loan and interest might take place at the end of the contract, and conclude it.

Lending money involves an asymmetrical relation between at least two parties or agents and, perhaps most significantly, has the embryonic *form* of 'capital'. The processes and relations of lending are entirely monetary but sketch out the formal characteristics of capitalist activities as 'money making more money'. As if they were a person acting solely as a lender, a capitalist investor uses their money – or, through contractual arrangements, other people's money – in ways that return as more money. This is represented as $M \rightarrow M'$, where M (money) purchases a range of inputs for producing goods or services that, once sold, return as M', the invested money plus profit. All this is recorded in double-entry bookkeeping with costs of inputs to production in one column and income from sales of products in the other.

As such, production for trade is premised on a continuously expanding M→M′→M″ and so on. This formula hides a complex underbelly of activities achieved by workers, who expend various forms of effort in exchange for money. Workers are supervised by managers who oversee that their combined activities result in a product that sells for more money than initially invested. In short, profit and growth occur via successful sales of the outputs from production. Clearly, all capitalists rely on these functions of money to *constitute* and *maintain* this whole array of capitalist activities. Money is lent. Goods are produced and then sold at a higher price than the costs of producing them. So, the loan is paid back and available to lend out to start another cycle, reproducing the cycle as a veritable system.

But systemic crises, such as the global financial crisis of 2007–08 and any hiatuses in production – such as those caused by restrictions associated with the COVID-19 pandemic – evolve regularly, with domino effects in the market. Whatever their sources, such crises inevitably involve an interruption in the smooth flow of expected incomes and debt repayments, upsetting monetary relations and values – i.e., trade and prices – and disturbing our necessary security in money as a solid and reliable 'universal equivalent'.

THE UNIVERSAL EQUIVALENT, BARTER AND OTHER 'MONIES'

A 'universal equivalent' is money as we know it – functioning as a unit of account, a medium of exchange and store of (exchange) value held or lent, borrowed and repaid. It is very familiar to us in our everyday capitalist practices, relations and processes – so familiar that American economist Randall Wray observes that 'Orthodox economists see exchange, markets and relative prices wherever they look.'[26] Indeed, gift economy theorist Genevieve Vaughan goes one step further to remark that 'the logic of market exchange, like God, makes everything in its own image.'[27] One consequence is the mistaken identity of 'money' with numerous objects and forms of exchange in various noncapitalist and nonmarket societies, as well as confusing barter with monetary exchange.

When I refer to nonmonetary exchange, people often say, 'Oh, you mean barter.' No, I don't. Barter tends to refer to a person making an ad hoc exchange of a good or service with another person without use of money but with material interests uppermost and some kind of notion of 'equivalence'. Economists, in particular, infuse 'barter' with a sense of a balanced exchange, which implies that the transactors estimate prices for such in markets familiar to the exchangers, as in commercial forms of barter today. Another example would be if you swapped a bicycle for a second-hand washing machine, knowing that they have a similar price in markets in which you engage. Certain monetary theorists argue that barter pre-empts, conceptually precedes, or is even characteristic of money circulating within commodity exchange. Yet, if barter incorporates calculative logic, by definition, it would seem to require pre-existing market-based monetary reference points.[28]

Anthropologists have made rich studies of exchange in noncapitalist economies to show unique patterns, meanings and implications in every case. The key point to be made here is that nonmonetary exchange is distinct from monetary exchange or trade as we know it and often means giving or taking without any direct simultaneous swap. As such, in Chapter 3, a real value model of a nonmonetary economy is presented without any recourse to barter. Similar to confusing barter with monetary exchange is confusing objects such as shells and beans regularly passed between people within noncapitalist exchanges as 'monies'. Points about alternative 'monies' are dealt with in various parts of this book; suffice to say here that exchanges within a noncapitalist society tend to follow conventions and rules associated with values and relations that are distinctive to that society.

Different 'monies'?

A popular view formulated by the Austro-Hungarian economic anthropologist and substantivist Karl Polanyi distinguishes certain forms of exchange in noncapitalist societies as facilitated by 'special-purpose' monies, compared with capitalist 'unicentric' and 'general-purpose' money'.[29] It is quite possible that he applies this framework because, even within capitalism, Polanyi sees our 'modern' money functioning essentially as a means of exchange, making all its other functions secondary.[30] In fact, this is the way that many mainstream economists see money, primarily as a *medium of exchange* in the present, similarly with a past and future use as a *means of payment* in relations of debt and credit.

Following a Polanyian perspective, any social object and exchange system within a noncapitalist system that appears similar to any monetary function within capitalism today is classified as a 'special-purpose money'. As such, a special-purpose money might be a string of beads, signifying a debt. However, detailed ethnographic accounts of such objects, and the relations and protocol they represent, so often reveal such sharp distinctions from money as we know it that I position myself among those who question whether such objects and practices can be usefully referred to as monies at all.

Money as we know it, as a universal equivalent within capitalist relations and processes of production, functions in various distinctive but multifunctional ways which impinge on and co-influence one another. For instance, if significant numbers of people hold on to their money, meaning it is neither used in trade nor for lending for some time, this would impact on production for trade, market prices and sales and, ultimately, the qualitative and quantitative value of money as a unit of account. Contra Polanyi, I am among those theorists who tend to see the main, primary, function of money as a standard of value, a *unit of account*. Moreover, it stands resplendent as the multifunctional *universal equivalent*.

Acknowledging that noncapitalist objects and terms of exchange are incomparable with money in capitalism undercuts the popular idea that money has existed almost forever and, consequently, that it is a neutral, 'natural', and useful 'tool' in almost any type of economy and society. In fact, even Polanyi has shown that, in as much as monetary exchange seems to have existed in noncapitalist history, it was marginal to any such society's dominant mode of production, instead typifying either exchanges with other societies, or minor roles and activities within a society.[31] In short, as an object and term of social exchange, money is not a tool as is a spade or a gun. Rather money as-we-know-it refers to codes of conduct that structure social relations critical to the operation and reproduction of capitalism.

In particular, capitalism is characterised by people who exchange human effort, skills and knowledge for monetary remuneration, who work for managers and owners who, in turn, make the decisions about what is produced, how it is produced, where it is produced and for whom – decisions all made with reference to the market. A worker's income is typically spent on essential needs and wants purchased in the market. Money, in this society, is the standout defining principle of what constitutes 'work' within capitalism. 'I don't have any work', generally means 'I can't find a paid job' rather than 'I can't be purposively active.'

BOOK STRUCTURE

This book addresses two closely associated questions – why should we, and how could we, develop societies without money? This first chapter has problematised money in the context of the two key challenges facing peoples across the globe today: divisive economic, social and political inequalities and planetary environmental unsustainability. Chapter 2 has an even stronger focus on the character of monetary practices and reasons why we need to move beyond a world developed around monetary values and production for trade. Chapter 3 sketches out how a nonmonetary postcapitalist local–global commons might operate, feel and look like. Having contrasted capitalist and postcapitalist models, the chapters that follow focus on some key movements and associated campaigns to outline monetary stumbling blocks to their success.

Chapter 4 examines key concerns of the environmental movement, such as responses to global heating and water scarcity, the fatal weaknesses of market-based approaches, and the in-kind economy *in natura* of Otto Neurath, a socialist who was very influential between the two world wars of the twentieth century. Chapter 5 reviews select developments within women's liberation – mainly ecofeminist thought and action around capitalist and subsistence economies, work, exchange value and human liberation – and identifies a determinedly nonmonetary activist tendency. Chapter 6 offers original perspectives on capitalist technology, appropriate technology and omnipotent capitalist debt, significant topics in contemporary social and environmental movements as well as in postcapitalist analyses and experimentation.

Indigenous peoples' movements continue in their struggle against capitalist forces to practice collective provisioning. Chapter 7 argues that a community mode of production based on substantive direct democracy and decision making focusing on real, social and ecological values is most appropriate for postcapitalist futures. Political assemblies and other forms of horizontal organising in locales are critical to practical efforts for achieving livelihoods through commoning. Chapter 8 argues that such intellectual, practical, political and cultural shifts already under way would benefit from focusing on nonmonetary futures.

While my arguments loosely align with the heterogenous 'nonmarket socialist' current, my thinking was initially prompted and developed by experiences in, and reading about, many revolutionary currents, such as women's liberation, nonviolence, political ecology, ecofeminism, Indigenous perspectives and ecosocialism.[32] I kept observing, thinking about, testing and revising my arguments in order to gain confidence in practising contemporary nonmonetary activities and economies. I engaged in alternative exchange networks and lived in partially self-provisioning intentional communities. Avidly following developments by those forging democratic autonomy as practiced by contemporary Zapatistas and democratic confederalism in the Rojava Revolution (see Chapter 7), I concluded that key distinctions between capitalist and ideal post-capitalist practices is collective decision making based on real values and human relationships, in contrast to money-oriented decision making and monetary relationships in capitalism where money is the central value.

REAL VALUES

Moving beyond money allows us to build a world based on social and environmental values appropriate for humanity and planetary sustainability. Material and conceptual keystones of capitalist practices, monetary value and monetary relations block system change in a post-capitalist transition. Monetary value and relations offer capitalist forces a strong practical base and discursive frame of reference. Given that capitalist practices, ideology and institutions require money in order to exist, acts of nonmonetary production and exchange have the potential to disable and dismantle capitalist forces.

Instead of a world built on 'exchange value', monetary value and prices, we can create a world based on 'real values'. I use this term advisedly, given that in economics 'real' has an established use as in 'real value' as distinct from 'nominal value', and 'real analysis' as distinct from 'monetary analysis'. The meaning I give 'real value' here is unique. The concept of 'real values' has certain similarities with the concept 'use value', in as much as both relate to qualities and purposes of things. Yet, real values go beyond mere use values to refer to actual and potential diverse values of living things, plant, animal and rock in landscapes and the atmosphere relevant to actual and holistic human and ecological needs.

An infinity of real values fill the entire space of a nonmonetary economy or world. A forest is perceived as a plethora of real values, as in potential values for us and other species and is, therefore, sacred. We call a spade a spade, its uses are what we can do with it, and its values involve its whole material constitution, inclusive of what that means for Earth. Moreover, most real values relate to specific communities within their residential ecological locales so the valuation is contextual both ecologically and socially. This concept, even philosophy, of real values can be better appreciated in the world of Yenomon sketched out in Chapter 3.

CONCLUSION

We face two great crises, two massive challenges, this century: divisive economic, social and political inequalities, and local- to planetary-scale environmental unsustainability. Indeed, climate change represents an existential threat to the future of our species. Inequity and unsustainability are intrinsic, if not endemic, to capitalism – phenomena driven by and expressing the everyday workings of capitalism, in particular its prerogative of infinite growth. As such, many anti-capitalist activists and scholars align with and discuss 'postcapitalist' visions and strategies.

The desired use value of this book is to act as a key intervention in these contemporary discourses to point out that we can neither address inequalities and unsustainability nor establish postcapitalism without moving beyond money. As a first step in making this intervention, this chapter has argued that money is best understood as a universal equivalent with the defining function of a unit of account. Its generic role is contingent both qualitatively and quantitatively on a diverse variety of constituent processes that mean the sum is greater than its parts.

Money and capital are simultaneously, and interchangeably, chicken and egg.

2
Money: The Universal Equivalent

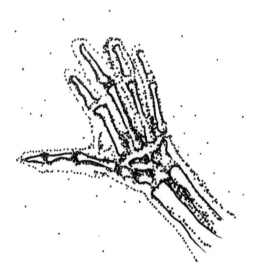

In producing for trade, capitalist enterprises use money to make more money, to make a profit. Their activities drive economic growth in market societies, epitomised as a nation's gross domestic product (GDP). Within this socio-political system, money represents absolute, as well as relative, poverty. Those with money can access markets offering essential needs and wants and those lacking money cannot access markets. Effectively a two-sided set of scales continuously generating and comparing inequalities money has become a socio-political generator of globally rampant inequities. Indeed, historical analyses of the appearance of money in Egypt in the third millennium BCE suggests that money accompanied the rise of a stratified class society out of an egalitarian tribal one.[1] Moreover, today, expanding production to make profits and grow the economy collides with the necessity for us to live within Earth's limits, to stabilise economies and to reduce unnecessary consumption.

Given that no market-based models have succeeded in directly fulfilling everyone's essential needs in practice, welfare states and nonmarket welfare, as well as relative poverty, have become characteristic features of capitalism. Proposals for cooperative enterprises producing for trade, community-based or public banks, guaranteed minimum incomes and community-controlled currencies all indicate faith in market-oriented production and exchange to meet the needs of people and planet. Reformers still imagine that they can alter capitalism in various ways to enable us to meet the challenges of socio-economic inequalities, marginalisation and hierarchies that have increasingly made a mockery of democracy.

Underlying many reformers' misconceptions is the assumption that monetary exchanges embody an ideal of 'equal exchange', a notion that informs their search for ways to represent diverse social and environmental values within an imagined marketplace characterised by equitability, effectiveness and efficiency. This chapter argues against such simplistic ideas of equivalence and faith that production for trade and markets could be restructured to offer a balanced matrix of prices for goods and services that would fulfil everyone's needs (no more, no less), especially while not breaching Earth's regenerative limits.

Instead, familiar market-based rituals create exchange value, money and capital as complex social products. Given that these practices simultaneously re-create inequalities and marginalisation, the notion of 'equal exchange' fulfilling the common good is bizarre. Moreover, production for trade forces us to neglect or underestimate ecological limits and planetary balance, which leads to ever-increasing unsustainability. While fleshing out essential characteristics of money, this chapter aims to show how this happens and, most significantly, why these processes are not amenable to transformation to greater equality or sustainability.

THE UNIVERSAL EQUIVALENT

We experience money functioning in several ways within our everyday lives, as outlined in the previous chapter, including as a unit of account in price and medium of exchange in transactions. This section explores the curious conception of money as a 'measure of value'; explains why – in its composite role as the universal equivalent – money is best understood as a *claim to future goods and services that have been produced for, and are available in, the market*; and reflects on the omnipotence of the universal equivalent in capitalist societies.

A 'measure' of value

Whether a pound, euro, or dollar is used to price things that we sell and buy, this unit of account is often referred to as a standard of value, and money is seen as a 'measure of value'. However, unlike measures of weight, distance and time that represent specific, permanent and standard units of measure, the monetary unit of account is neither a precise nor a constant standard. Indeed, the economic state of the market is the basic source of money's generic worth. The market is composed of a vast range of complex human and nonhuman forces, factors and relations extending to the political stability of the nation. As such, the market value of a unit of account at any particular time is often represented by reference to a basket of commonly needed goods and services. So the unit of account varies, with $100 buying a different basket of goods and services at different points in time. In other words, a standard basket of specific goods and services can cost different amounts from year to year.

In short, this measure of value, money, is such a peculiar 'measure' in terms of *quantity* that we have mainly been content if it simply fulfils its role as a *quality* par excellence, as *the* unit of account in which we express prices and, therefore, use in accounting records and commercial agreements and contracts. As such, contemporary governments sanction and support this legal tender as their 'universal equivalent'. Still, given that capitalism is a global system, the value of any particular unit of account such as the UK pound oscillates in a comparative way, via exchange rates, with other currencies. Such exchange rates are subject to certain national policies and regulatory measures but are most strongly influenced by market-based activities.

It is not surprising that these peculiarities of money as an apparent, even reliably unreliable, measure of value have been of particular interest to theorists of money.

A claim theory of money

State-supported currency facilitates production for trade, and trade is the basis of national economies. The capitalist state operates with money, relying on its legal tender and unit of account as a means of payment, a means of taxing citizens, a means of purchase and redistribution. It is a thoroughly capitalist state, inspiring state theories of money.[2] However, I prefer credit theories of money where money acts as a *claim*, as distinct from either a commodity theory of money, typically grounded by, say, gold, or a state theory of money.[3] In credit theories of money, whether we use a metal coin, plastic card, or paper legal tender as our means to trade, all simply represent or symbolise the quality of being a socio-political *claim* on future marketed goods and services. Money has no necessary physical being but is an entirely social construct and practical force arising specifically as a claim to marketed goods and services in a particular set of social relations and rituals that we call capitalism – a market society. In short, if the market is viewed as a wheel, money is its hub.

Once identified with precious metals such as gold and silver, with the qualities of divisibility and accumulation as well as seemingly intrinsic exchange value, the appearance of this social claim on the market has grown increasingly closer to its pure abstract form in online transfers. In other words, when you have money in a market society, you hold a generic credit from society as a whole. Society redeems this generic debt when you use the money to buy a certain amount of goods and services. As capitalist relations of production became omnipotent across the world, money was bound to lose its false association with gold or silver, a fabulous association suggesting that the value of money ultimately related to a specific physical substance, typically gold (or the work required to produce it), rather than intimately associated with generic activities comprising production for trade.[4]

As a claim essential to both market exchange and all financial transactions associated with capitalist production, it is crucial to understand money as a symbol of a social relation, a relation between the individual holder and a societal promise of access to an ongoing social creation: 'the market'. Without that market, our money has no value at all, which is why it simply *symbolises* exchange value and relies in perpetuity on future market conditions for its value to be realised. This essential role as a claim to marketed goods and services exists as *an holistic socio-political relation of credit between the individual and society*, a relation distinct from individual credit–debt relations.

This characteristic as a *claim on future goods and services* means that the unit of account has a value contingent on a social imaginary, social trust and the very material fact that the intentions and plans of all those sets of relations and activities that comprise production for trade will be realised. As long as this is more or less the case, our cash or liquid funds can be readily exchanged in the future for needs and wants, and our assets will retain their value (unless, of course, factors peculiar to particular assets force their depreciation).

The omnipotence of the universal equivalent

All the functions of money as a unit of account, means of exchange, store of value and delayed means of payment or loan are co-dependent dimensions of capital that amalgamate with totalising, isolating and marginalising effects. These aspects of money are consolidated in calculations integral to production for trade and revealed in accounting, implying a series of powerful consequences, including an inextricable impetus to economic growth, inequity, competition and systemic risks of crises.

Indeed, umpteen cycles of production routinely boom and bust associated with private and fragmented management of the supply of goods and services under competitive conditions for a public market of consumers, many with limited incomes and options. At the same time, opportunities and aspirations for personal advance in such an insecure system mean that trading and producing for trade mesmerise and entrap. In fully fledged capitalism, money – and its seemingly magical substance, exchange value – is supreme, akin to a god.[5]

Money is like an almighty god of the Old Testament, to be admired, revered and feared. All capitalist production starts with investments evaluated using money or bought with money; all enterprises operate on the basis of monetary calculations, exchanges and transfers, and accounting is central to every commercial arrangement and transaction. In capitalist societies, children get pocket-money and are taught to save money; most work is for money and, conversely, work that is not remunerated in money, such as voluntary caring for others, appears secondary and less worthy (even if it is essential); most needs and wants are created specifically for markets; fulfilling most dreams requires money; monetary punishments and rewards are commonplace, while taxes are paid and even gifts made in (or with reference to) money.

Monetary practices and monetary logic are ingrained in citizens of market societies. To question the legitimacy of money, monetary practices and monetary logic is akin to questioning the meaning of a religious god and the wholesomeness of a capitalist society.

THE IMPERATIVES OF PROFITMAKING AND ECONOMIC GROWTH

Acting as the grand comparator, the universal equivalent is a central enabler of capitalist dynamics of competition, efficiency, profit and growth. Money is the hub of the capitalist wheel. As a result of competitive dynamics, capitalist managers negotiate to minimise inputs and maximise outputs of production, by accounting using prices. They include wages for work – for the effort, skills, knowledge and passion workers apply to their job. Calculations solely using this unit of account guide capitalist financiers and managers as they optimise their chances of meeting their $M \rightarrow M'$ goal. The name of this game is maximising profit.

Profitmaking

Making a profit is a very necessary aim of operators in a market-based system, irrespective of whether they succeed in profitmaking or not. Individuals, companies and countries can and do sustain losses or negative growth for certain, even extended, periods of time, but only by drawing on savings, arranging to borrow money, delaying payments or having debts forgiven. Otherwise they go bankrupt or simply close down. If profitmaking is an operational requirement at the scale of an individual capitalist, the generic result at the scale of a nation is systemic economic growth.

While it is reasonable to criticise capitalists for focusing on making money and celebrating big profits, the capitalist's approach is more complex than a simple expression of personal greed and power, and protecting self-interests. Production for trade forces capitalists to act in ways that perpetuate and exaggerate the expansion of capitalism both intensively and extensively. Production for the market is so uncertain that the *only* way of maximising security as a capitalist is to seek as much money and lose as little money as possible at every point in your financial, productive and commercial practices. From the point of view of the individual capitalist, or the capitalist firm, this is the (in)famous bottom line.

Private companies compete with one another in the market to make the most profit and enjoy a competitive advantage by gaining more money to reinvest. In short, the competitiveness and secrecy of capitalist firms pressures them all to sell as much as possible, demand as high a price as consumers can bear, and expand their market. Cutting any cost of production such as wages, materials, equipment, or workspace is seen to optimise sales and profits because consumers tend to purchase the cheaper options among commodities with similar use values. Introducing technologies or other techniques to minimise production time or save money also aims to produce comparatively cheaper commodities. Of course, strategies such as improving the quality and increasing the cost of a product for a niche market of those with the capacity to pay can also lead to impressive sales and profitmaking. Still, if a capitalist departs from the basic principle of cutting costs and selling as much as they can at as high a price level as consumers can bear, they heighten their risks of losing money (capital) and going bankrupt. Reducing production or even keeping production stable without reinvestment in another profitable activity carries risks of loss of capital and economic suicide.

Productive activities integrate with various chains and networks supplying inputs and buying outputs. Businesses operate in an insecure, privatised and competitive environment when it comes to prices, supplies and markets for their goods and services. This is where capitalism is a game and, like all games, it involves skill, knowledge, experience and luck. The profit imperative is associated with uncertainties around input and output prices, especially future prices. Because of all these uncertainties, managers are circumstantially forced to set an asking price that they estimate will be the maximum current price that purchasers are likely to be prepared to pay. Consequently, there is an incessant focus on trade, making profits and expanding production for trade, which escalates private ownership and the social reproduction of monetary values, all of which constitutes generic economic growth.

In short, *profitmaking is an essential buffer systemically created within production for trade to enable enterprises and associated individuals to operate.* Even if certain capitalist managers scrupulously seek to expand their profit margin while others do not, all capitalists need to make some profit over the long term. Unless underwritten or funded in some other way, even so-called not-for-profit enterprises must operate in the market to make a profit. As distinct from for-profit firms, their profit is generally invested or spent in 'ethical' ways. Not-for-profit worker cooperatives produce for trade and aim to make a profit, even if that profit is generally dispersed in ways beneficial to the cooperative, the workers and wider community. Moreover, under shareholder capitalism where even workers' superannuation or old-age pension funds are invested in capitalist activities, there is a legal expectation that responsible management aims to make reasonable profits. In late stage capitalism, many agencies of the state are expected to balance their books so that even governments regard a surplus as ideal. For all these reasons, *profitmaking and growth are not optional but rather mandatory in the ordinary daily operation of capitalism.*

Economic growth

Universalising each capitalist's goals ($M \rightarrow M' \rightarrow M''$), economic growth expresses the total result of individual and sectoral profitmaking. The challenge for all capitalist investors and managers is to reinvest money gained as profit so as to maintain or, better, increase it. This explains the imperialist drive that has become characteristic of capitalism, incorporating new lands, resources and new workers. Profitmaking has driven capitalist practices and the compulsion to expand, as in colonialism and neo-colonialism, resulting in underdevelopment and advanced economies in an uneven modern world system.[6]

Money has been used as a beacon, carrot and stick as capitalists ply Indigenous and other peoples involved in noncapitalist production and exchange to engage in capitalist practices and logic through working for money, or selling land and goods for money. Capitalist cultures have notoriously treated noncapitalists as 'undeveloped' heathens and continue to do so. They deride nonmonetary production and exchange, asserting the superior logic, efficiency and effectiveness of capitalist production for trade.

Since the 1960s, the combined effect of increasingly breaching planetary limits, immense population growth, ecologically destructive practices and hyper-consumerism – making human life on Earth increasingly unsustainable – has led to calls to stabilise and rationalise market production to conform to people's basic needs. Chapter 4 deals with the strengths and weaknesses of common strategies to make capitalism more environmentally effective, respectful and efficient. It suffices here to emphasise that *capitalism is impossible without profitmaking and its twin, economic growth,* so imaginaries of reforming market activities to operate without profitmaking or growth are doomed to fail. Profitmaking and growth are essential aspects of monetary economies.

Market-based societies are characterised by conflicts between capitalists and workers. Yet, perversely, their clearly opposed interests both appear to be satisfied under conditions of strong growth. Economic growth is attractive to capitalists as their normal mode of operation, and appears to offer more job opportunities and the potential for rising wages. This seeming coincidence of workers' and capitalist financiers' and managers' interests is, in turn, another systemic pressure to make profits and grow the economy.

These insights throw our conjunctural crisis into sharp relief as we return to addressing the two key contemporary challenges of growing inequity and environmental unsustainability – by meeting everyone's basic needs but limiting production to simply satisfying such modest needs for the sake of the planet and the future of our species. In this context, the compulsive M→M′→M″→M‴ dynamic of capitalism, which drives both the individual capitalist and capitalism as a generic whole, can be appreciated as a critical, indeed fatal, deficiency. *Capitalism has no operating processes to either stabilise or reduce production: the compulsion to reproduce beyond itself is a systemic necessity.* Thus, the key barrier to necessary change is that market-based economies not only *will not*, but actually *cannot*, allow production to wax and wane according to people's and Earth's needs. Today, at the end of capitalism's reign, we can clearly see that these systemic failings beget societies characterised by inequality and unsustainability.

In short, the impetus to growth is innate to the simplistic monetary formula of capitalism, implying expansive and intensive drives to increasingly incorporate and manage people either as managers and owner-capitalists, or as workers and consumers, and to artificially transform nonhuman nature. This amounts to an assault not only on Earth but also on most of us, who are simply cogs in the wheels of capitalism or marginalised by it. The lack of collective control over, and secrecy surrounding, privatised production, competition and associated marketing and waste, together with uncertainties around sufficiency of private monetary savings, all contribute to anxiety around each of us having as much money, commodities and assets as we can.

In summary, capitalism is the epitome of a monetary economy; growth is not only a goal, tendency, or achievement of capitalism but an essential requirement that makes capitalist processes incapable of delivering socially and environmentally appropriate production. Paradoxically, pro-capitalist ideologies such as neoliberalism convincingly promote growth as capitalism's strength. In fact, especially apparent in the current conjuncture, growth is capitalism's critical weakness; if we are to preserve a place for ourselves as a species on this planet, then *capitalism has no future.*

PRODUCTION FOR PEOPLE AND PLANET,
OR PRODUCTION FOR TRADE?

The long history of anti-capitalist resistance has generated many visions that identify key reforms for progressive change. Within such visions and strategies, money takes more than its fair share of the limelight. The early nineteenth-century French anarcho-federalist Pierre-Joseph Proudhon advocated establishing workers' cooperatives along with a bank offering low-interest credit and credit notes rather than gold or silver state-backed legal tender as current at that time.[7] Other ideas popular today include guaranteed minimum income (or services) schemes, local community-based currencies (alongside formal legal tender) and modern monetary theory ('MMT').[8]

However, the nineteenth-century German political philosopher Karl Marx, who wrote much of his classic work in London, roundly critiqued monetary proposals for remedying the ills of capitalism.[9] Marx believed that the ideal society was one in which each person contributed to fulfilling communal needs to the extent of their abilities, and took what they needed from the communal product. In this practice and discourse 'equity', which is a preoccupation within monetary societies, has little meaning. Rather than everyone receiving an equal amount of money, a just approach recognises multi-various contributions, diverse needs and various ways of satisfying them.

Moreover, Marx understood and respected the limits of nature, arguing that:

> From the standpoint of a higher socio-economic formation, the private property of particular individuals in the earth will appear just as absurd as the private property of one man in other men. Even an entire society, a nation, or all simultaneously existing societies taken together, are not the owners of the earth. They are simply its possessors, its beneficiaries, and have to bequeath it in an improved state to succeeding generations.[10]

He was deeply aware of our need to conserve Earth and of our reliance on Earth, writing: 'Man *lives* on nature – means that nature is his body, with which he must remain in continuous interchange if he is not to die. That man's physical and spiritual life is linked to nature means simply that nature is linked to itself, for man is a part of nature.'[11] This position and other works by Marx support ecosocialist interpretations of his work and the ecosocialist movement that has gained ground in the last few decades.[12]

Even if Marx's vision ultimately means the dissolution of money and state, only a minority of Marxist-influenced scholars, activists and politicians have proposed dispensing with money as key to achieving a transition to socialism.[13] Indeed, many socialists and anarchists seem to overstate the potential of markets in both their visions of, and strategic proposals for, transitioning to postcapitalism. A majority of democratic socialists believe that markets are amenable to state regulation and direction, and that a modest version of the market would be useful within a fairer and more sustainable future. Like Karl Polanyi, they imagine that, by reducing the scope of the market, market exchange can be kept within manageable bounds.[14]

Yet the arguments made here regarding profitmaking and economic growth challenge such ideas for regulating the market to simply satisfy people's basic and diverse needs, especially given that consumers have so little influence over the production of commodities. However, proposals in Chapter 3 show how the state might wither in favour of networked, localised economies operating under direct democracy. In this model, *people re-appropriate all the current functions of money by directly making decisions over what is produced, how it is produced, in what quantities and for whom*; in other words, people institute a nonmonetary economic model. But, before exploring that very real alternative, let's examine some more market-based processes and concepts, such as so-called free trade and equal exchange, private property, assets and debts.

MONETARY CONUNDRUMS: EXCHANGE VALUE AND REAL VALUES

A metonym for trade in general, for capitalists and for capitalist activities, money is the unit of calculation that distinguishes capitalist production and trade from other modes of societal reproduction. Money is full of ambiguities related to its critical role in production for trade, which produces antagonistic relations as its central dynamic, and due to its centrality to power and status in market societies more generally. Money grows out of, is central to, and reproduces reductive ways of thinking. Money becomes the hub, form, seed and product of capital as a system, a social system, a productive system. Marx quoted writers, such as the celebrated English playwright William Shakespeare, to illustrate the incongruities and paradoxes of monetary practices.[15] Decades later, German philosopher Georg Simmel would take a phenomenological, even essentialist, position to highlight contradictory aspects of money.[16] Here I raise just a few conflicts between the rhetoric and reality, the ideals and practices, of monetary relationships and dynamics.

Free trade, free will?

Trade is often referred to as a voluntary act, subject to free will, yet engaging in monetary exchange is frequently experienced as forced, even violent.[17] This is as true for individual acts as it is for the international, colonial and neo-colonial relations in which companies have forged global capitalism.[18] Most of us cannot live without *buying* essentials because production for trade prevails. This often means making purchases at prices we don't think are reasonable, and buying products of insufficient quality or quantity. Sometimes expense precludes us accessing some or even all of our needs, or we have to go into debt to purchase them. These circumstances are intrinsic to relations of private property that characterise capitalism, production for trade, for money.

Trade: Enabling or disabling?

Where a society only offers members use rights to enough land for self-provisioning, exchanges of the products of such land use tend to be minimal and generally based on nonmonetary customary logic. For instance, John F. Henry points out that: 'Tribal society is a non-exchange, non-propertied society that follows the rule of hospitality – all had a right to subsistence that was collectively produced by its members on collectively held means of production.'[19] In contrast, private property is not only the result, but also the premise, of trade. Logically we cannot sell something we do not own.

Thus, the idea of private ownership is a fundamental assumption of trade, of monetary exchange. In other words, the exclusive use right that private property conveys is implicit in the logic of monetary exchange because only by owning property can we have the power to give it away in exchange. Markets arise as the transferral of personal use rights to goods, means of production and services increases. As such, trading automatically disrupts and diminishes collective and individual self-provisioning. Trade *disables* practices of commoning and sharing even as it is touted as *enabling* freedom, free movement and free activities.

Money is social, not natural

Monetary and market-based practices undergird, and highlight, a socially constructed duality between humans and nature. Such dualism is often misconstrued as philosophical and cultural rather than appreciated as a material result of daily activities within capitalism. Capitalist practices assume and embody abstraction from nature, human nature as well as nonhuman nature. Every exchange embraces *people* and *things* as if extracted from their natural environs, Earth, and abstracted within a wholly socially constructed matrix of credits and debts determined by an ideal and material set of rituals referred to generically as 'the market'. As more and more activities and relationships are market-oriented and defined in terms of monetary valuation (prices), the market becomes *the environment par excellence*, submerging Earth, the natural environment and its real values, on which the market is actually based.

Today, exchange value is the most *obvious* and the most *obscure* value. Monetary value is unstable, is nothing in and of itself. Rather, money's worth is mirrored in what it purchases. It is *unreal* value compared with well-defined, visible and functioning social and ecological values. If money seems to represent *social trust* because we use it as our common medium of exchange and unit of account, at the same time monetary exchange essentially heightens distrust and *untrustworthy* behaviour in practices of calculated self-interest.

Exchange value is distinctive and unreal because it abstracts from social and humane worth and the ecological qualities of Earth, all of which are best referred to as 'priceless'. Omnipresent and omnipotent exchange value, so often regarded as social and natural, is really anti-social and unnatural. Money is derided, reviled and despised even as it is revered and coveted. Most significantly, separation from nature today is generated in trade and production for trade.

Free and equal citizens?

Most accounts of capitalism draw sharp distinctions between the purported rationality and efficiency of monetary practices, the innovation and speed of capitalism, and noncapitalist societies which are typecast as irrational, wasteful, unscientific, slow and tradition bound. Yet an anthropological framing indicates that ritualised formulas, such as M→M'→M'', link all individual firms into a holistic market system embracing obdurate material and social practices heavily laden with economic ideologies. Even as our everyday experiences and empirical analyses show up these practices as socially and environmentally irrational and highly destructive, there exists a conceit that trade and production for trade, a market society, is the most effective and superior system known to contemporary humankind.

Trading and production for trade is often presented as a sophisticated and pluralistic mode of free and equal exchange. The apparent freedom of impersonal and impermanent trading relations is contrasted to explicitly unequal exchange as in a serf's offering to their feudal lord, the peasant's tribute or tax to a state, and the slave's servitude with respect to their master. Such perspectives regale capitalism for its 'equal exchange' and 'one-vote one-value' representative democracy. Democracy is often considered intrinsic to capitalism even if the Economist Intelligence Unit's *Democracy Index 2020* classifies a miniscule 8.4 per cent of the world's population living in full democracies, with the rest in flawed democracies (41 per cent), authoritarian regimes (35.6 per cent) or hybrid regimes (between authoritarian and flawed, 15 per cent).[20]

Indeed, production for trade ends up with inequitable societies where those with money have the most power and speak loudest. Meanwhile, due to the severe ecological unsustainability resulting from production for trade, we have a dying planet. The sting in this tail is that this planet is our host, putting paid to any sense of superiority.

Equal exchange

There is a popular notion that money, markets and capitalism feature 'equal exchange'. Yet it is hard to see anything equal about the objects-cum-subjects of monetary exchange except that money itself projects some false appearance of equality. When you go into a shop and exchange, say, $25 that you earned at back-breaking or boring work for a towel, a haircut, a box of fresh vegetables, a second-hand coat or a meal in a café, your money acts both as a unit of account (in the price) and as a means of exchange. What makes these purchases 'equal'? Nothing but their self-same price, their forced comparison via ever so many market-based transactions using a claim, itself a variable and unreliable 'measure', a standard reflecting the very things it is capable of purchasing at any particular time and place.

While most monetary practices are two-sided, indeed two-faced, the notion of equal exchange suggests a false sense of unity as a host of goods and services, work and property, are brought into a temporary equality vis-à-vis one measure, monetary value. I hold a pre-analytic 'bunfight' notion of price in contrast to explanations of price formation via labour time or energy. In other words, money is not a proxy for either the time taken or the energy expended to produce a good or service. Instead, the bunfight perspective stays with the chaotic and seemingly irrational price making and taking we readily observe and experience every day, and accepts some of the clearly observed tendencies of capitalist economies.

For instance, a general dynamic of demand and supply pertains to privilege those with money and particularly those with the most money, both as decision makers over production and in terms of consumptive options. Another complication in the so-called 'balance' in supply and demand signalled to producers from purchases in terms of quantity at a particular price level is increasing credit, which is simultaneously debt. In the example of a house which many householders can only purchase via a mortgage, an acceptable price range is determined by the capacity to become indebted, estimated by both mortgagor and mortgagee.

The significant point to make here is that money offers no promise or potential as a rational form of calculating the benefits and disadvantages of producing on the basis of communal and ecological needs. This point will be better appreciated after reading Chapter 3, where I sketch out some techniques and structures to achieve a postcapitalist alternative. Suffice to say that, once it is acknowledged that money and its associated world of exchange value is not an appropriate context for a just and sustainable future, what money and exchange value might stand for has little relevance to the tasks at hand.

In a real value framing – where actual human and ecological needs are the foci of the reproduction of our species – the notion of equal exchange is unnecessary and absurd. Similarly, the bunfight notion of price or exchange value requires no analytic development. Even if labour time involved in production was the basis of price, and the primary influence on the value of money – or we contrived it to be so – this would not assist in either achieving ecological sustainability or a socially just system of production or distribution. As an aside to those who will become mired here in a discussion of the theory of labour value (Marx's labour theory of value), I warn that details in Marx's critical analysis of capitalism do not point to how things ought to exist in socialism, even if they are far too often read that way. I do not subscribe to that interpretation; I do not even think that was Marx's intent.

In instances where monetary exchange is misconceived as somehow intrinsically grounded, just and fair, the notion of 'equal exchange' remains a keystone. Meanwhile, price making, price taking and decisions over whether to sell or to purchase continue in our everyday lives as ever so many individual personal and external social struggles in which environmental and social considerations are impaled with monetary spears. At a broader scale, the common confounding of social and environmental values with exchange value undergirds the popularity of ideas of 'development' and their confusion with real social and environmental progress and the rationalisation of capitalist forms of production.

Concepts of equal exchange have been interrogated by the more philosophic, critical and analytic of thinkers, as in Marx's interconnected labour theory of value and theory of surplus value and, more recently, in theories of unequal exchange between countries and regions related to labour and ecologically unequal trade.[21] There is no doubt that unfair, indeed 'inequitable', terms of trade riddle the exchange between a capitalist employer and their workers just as they have contorted histories and current dynamics between certain countries and regions, including the deleterious ecological and social dimensions of production for trade and of trade itself. I hold that labour is the socio-political substance and essence of the mass of exchange value, including surplus value, within capitalism in a profoundly similar way to Marx's philosophy, but without recourse to the notion of equal exchange. I neither think that 'equal exchange' is usefully resorted to in Marx's theory nor, and this is the most significant point, is equal exchange a useful concept for creating an appropriate postcapitalist society.

Monetary efficiencies are not efficiencies oriented around the interests of workers or ecosystems. Assumed and argued efficiencies of trade are generally demonstrated via a hall of mirrors wherein money is a veritable agent or mirror of the apparent efficiencies of market processes. By way of an example, in some areas the forest industry argues that it is more efficient to clear-cut native forests, even ecologically rich old-growth forests, than to harvest pine trees grown sustainably in plantations to produce timber. So, it is most efficient to be ecologically destructive because monetary efficiency is paramount. The market price, the monetary value, is all-decisive. Such judgements rely on market-based logic, so apparent efficiencies depend on applying monetary evaluations and calculations in semi-religious ways, such as concluding that life is the will of God and rationalising the will of God in all unfolding circumstances accordingly.

Once we go beyond a narrow monetary definition of efficiency, we find vast discrepancies with efficiencies measured and judged using real values, namely basic human and planetary values, social and environmental values. Cutting old-growth and ordinary native forests has reduced both the ecosystem services provided by such forests – such as purifying water, and the habitat required by animal and plant species that are increasingly becoming extinct – while increasing carbon emissions both directly and indirectly. Forests are sacred to Indigenous peoples, who often found forests almost wholly sufficient sources to fulfil their basic needs; thus, as certain forests have been cleared, various Indigenous peoples have lost their main means of existence. This is a simple example of how absurd market-based logic and decision making is once applied to real situations and according to real social and ecological values.

In short, market rationalisation is less persuasive once we frame discourses to ask: 'Whose efficiency?' 'Whose logic?' Even more productively, an ethnographic approach reveals monetary flows as relations between people in dramatic rituals that make money, assets and the stock exchange appear as *facts*. Such facts, in turn, become forces that control us in further market-based processes impacting on capitalists as well as workers and consumers. No one is really sure what will happen next. The natural world, Earth, is obliterated as we become overwhelmed with socio-political machinations. In this monetary world, not only is there no driver but also no driver's seat. The closest we have to a decision maker is the abstraction of money, which usurps potential participatory democracy whereby we might collectively preside over what we produce, where and how we produce it, and for whom.

ASSETS AND DEBTS:
THE GRAND PRODUCTION-FOR-TRADE RITUAL

In our current conjuncture, many people across the globe living within monetary economies have faced heightened distress and social discipline from austerity measures due to capitalist crises and rising debts. Public and private debts and crises are viewed like clouds, as if capitalism ideally operates without debts or crises. This section outlines how and why debts and crises are endemic to capitalists' ways of operating. Business booms and busts not only arise due to some accident or mismanagement, company malpractice, or government interference but, rather, as a generic characteristic of capitalist economies. This is key to understanding the brutal, anti-social and ecologically nonsensical aspects of producing exchange value, with the effect of lifting the blame ordinarily placed on workers, unemployed and the marginalised who constantly bear the brunt of austerity measures.[22]

Assets as debts

As capitalism grows, assets and associated credits and debts grow. Framed simply in terms of servicing and amortisation, debts are wielded like sticks at citizens in ways akin to demands for tributes in noncapitalist modes. In other words, capitalism is an elaborate ritual that creates social responsibilities as surely as social claims, and private property integrates people into vicious cycles of relations of indebtedness. We maintain exchange value, money and capital as continuously existing *social facts* that are central to these rituals.

Productive assets are, at least nominally, worth – in prices on stock exchanges – a multiple of their income-earning capacity for investors. Such prices or 'values' are largely speculative in nature because they are based on forecasts of future operability and profitability. For example, you decide to purchase shares in a particular company because you expect that they will deliver as much or more by way of an income through dividends vis-à-vis other investment opportunities. But, if the company fails to produce as expected, or if sales are low or not at the forecast prices, then the monetary value of such shares is referred to as 'lost'. In this pro-capitalist framing, the capitalists' *dreams of their ostensible worth* are indeed lost, as highlighted in prices of stocks and shares and GDP. In a pro-worker and environmentalist framing of such losses, *the effort of workers and Earth's materials and energy have been wasted under capitalist management.* But, the latter dimension is regularly submerged, as mainstream discourse focuses, instead, on unrealised income for owners and managers, and stoking capitalism's fires.

Double-entry bookkeeping

At the heart of monetary calculations that drive capitalists' plans, and the accounts that record inputs and outputs of production, is the social fact that money can only be a *substantive store of value* when it exists as capital, as active use values contributing to production. As such, Marx describes the worth of money kept under a bed, a hoard, as akin to treasures or jewellery. But, money as capital is lent to, becomes active within, production. Consequently, banks, banking and capitalist production are based on double-entry accounting, which privileges every asset – private property *par excellence* – as if it needed to be sustained and reproduced just as people and other animals need to sustain and reproduce themselves.

Emerging with merchants' trading activities, double-entry book-keeping has been practised at least since 1300. Like a pair of scales, double-entry bookkeeping registers debts on one side of the balance and credits on the other, in the same unit of account. Such accounting records each owner's business, financial and transactional balance (their status and worth) with the rest of the world, showing their holdings of cash, goods and assets, and their debts and loans to others. Debit and credit columns, which include dates for all transactions, allow for calculating the business owner's equity, and profit or loss over a particular period of time.[23]

In short, double-entry bookkeeping establishes an individual's wealth and makes capital and income distinct, facilitating arrangements involving shares and dividends. Jane Gleeson-White highlights significant effects of this accounting, that has 'provided the means of discarding all information extraneous to decision-making, leaving behind only numbers' and, consequently, the 'cost-benefit thinking that plagues contemporary management, from government and corporations to health care and education'.[24] Similarly, American cultural historian and literary critic Mary Poovey begins her work on how 'numbers have come to epitomize the modern fact' with discussions on credit, credulity and creditability, and goes on to argue that double-entry bookkeeping 'produced a prototype of the modern fact'.[25] Accounting codified the practices, confirmed the legitimacy, 'accuracy', 'virtue' and 'honesty' of traders, displayed in ways reminiscent to 'both the scales of justice and the symmetry of God's world'.[26] Indeed, German sociologists Max Weber and Werner Sombart (who was also an economist), and Austrian political economist Joseph Schumpeter, all highlighted the roles of double-entry bookkeeping in introducing and maintaining capitalist reasoning, culture and material practices.

The general effect or implication of double-entry bookkeeping is the expectation – heightened in neo-liberalism as if a demand – that workers not only work to reproduce themselves but also to materially reproduce capital, the capitalist's power base, and a surplus via expanded reproduction, appearing as profit and growth. This sleight of hand is as essential and significant as the more generally acknowledged exploitation of profitmaking. Double-entry bookkeeping offers a technique for those owning capital to effectively become immortal within and through companies that 'live' in perpetuity yet with limited liability.[27]

Invested in means of production both sourced from Earth (in the form of material and energy) and human effort (waged labour), at the start of the productive cycle, a capitalist spends money (M) on all kinds of natural and human means of production with the sole intention of supervising the production of saleable goods to result in more money (M'). Depending on the duration of production, the cycle of investment and returns might be one month, several months, or extend into years. If there is any hiccup in the capitalist's productive plans, they 'lose' a profit they never actually had, but only expected. Even if profit is rationalised as a reward for commercial *risk-taking*, capitalist ideology demands a profit as the right of investment and refers to unprofitability as *losses*, not simply a result of risk-taking. This too is a sleight of hand.

All assets are considered as if valuable in and of themselves

Double-entry bookkeeping presents investments, costs of inputs, in the expenses column to inform the calculation of asking prices in the expectation of profitable production. Such accounting practices imply, through the imputed values of assets, a *society-wide debt* to realise capitalists' plans to make money via producing goods and services. As such, *money as capital incorporates the claim character of money as an activity intrinsic and definitional of their socio-political ritual*. Assets are only worth what they might ultimately be seen to produce by way of an income to the owner/s. As such, a financial asset is not peculiar to a particular stage of capitalism, as concepts of financial capital, financialisation and financial capitalism infer. Rather, the mentality displayed in this bookkeeping accompanies capitalism from its beginnings, and pertains equally for owner-managers of one-person businesses and globally operating transnational companies with umpteen shareholders and bank loans for liquidity and expansion. As long as the expectations of investors are realised as profits and growth, the system works for them. Left with more money to invest than before, this translates to more societal debt (in the form of growing assets) to fulfil their ambitions.

Of course, as in all human practices, miscalculations, over-optimism, corruption and cronyism account for certain commercial calamities and even crises. However, no improper conduct is necessary for debts to grow in unison with capitalist expansion and intensification. These debts appear as a shadow of private assets. An allied question – that nagged Polish-German Marxian theorist and revolutionary Rosa Luxemburg but was satisfactorily accounted for by Egyptian-French Marxian economist and world-systems analyst Samir Amin – is that even the money to purchase the expanded amount of goods and services that engender monetary profit is lent into society by *banks*.[28] Yes, money is issued as bank loans and, given the system's drive to profit and grow, so does money lent to capitalists grow.

In all these ways, capitalism creates debt just as surely as it creates saleable goods, means of production (assets), infrastructure and services. Capitalist activities will not enable society to clamber out of indebtedness but, rather, capitalism will continue to create mounting debts.

Crises

The perpetual existence of capitalist crises has its source in the fact that any pause, let alone seizure, in the erstwhile unending ritual of production for trade leads to ever so many dominoes falling in credit–debt relations. Numerous tendencies in capitalism predispose the economic system to delays and lacunae in activity. All such crises ultimately involve debts or reductions in the value of capitalists' assets. In every crisis, capitalists are aghast and the logic of their as-if-preordained-right to earn, not only an income from their assets but also a profit on top of that, is assaulted. Thus they strike out at all and sundry, not least of all at workers, the marginalised and the government. Particularly in late stage capitalism – euphemistically referred to as 'neoliberalism' – austerity, wage cuts, retrenchments and so on ensue.

Such crises and debts only – and contradictorily – hide and amplify current conditions of ecological imbalance and social precarity. Inaction on climate change is a symptom and expression of the smooth functioning of capitalism in the same way as it fails to satisfy the needs of people and planet. Thus, it is the 'economy' – read capitalism, assets and capitalist owners and managers – that is to be saved before, and rather than, the planet and people.

EXCHANGE VALUES OF PRIVATE PROPERTY ARE REPRODUCED BY SOCIETY

In the context of a society of people either amenable to, or circumstantially forced to, work for a monetary income within capitalism to satisfy their essential needs, a successful business appears as an asset in and of itself. Similarly, money in exchange and in production appears as a value in and of itself, even if both values are actually created by the reproduction of capitalist socio-political relationships. This is the way exchange value exists, in and of itself, and how money appears as a thing, even if – when all is said and done – money and capital only result from specific relations between people and how they see and interact with the nonhuman world. They are very effective social facts.

In short, due to our socio-economic system, it seems quite normal for owners of assets, who are often shareholders, to speak as if established businesses have an as-of-right exchange value, a *wealth* that the likes of Thomas Piketty measure. On the one hand, this wealth is an effect of the capitalist process and associated prevalence of trade in means of production whereby farmed land, for instance, implicitly gains a market value on account of its productive farming potential. By owning land, the farmer accesses natural materials and services while other components of their productive activity, such as rain, sun and air, are free. The actual prices or costs of environmental inputs cannot reflect or express their ecological value to humans or biomes. Rather exchange value reflects market-based evaluations, for example, the market price or market rental of a farm.

On the other hand, this as-of-right effect on productive assets arises because the production-for-trade ritual produces not only material things but also associated social relations. Yet capitalist discourse is saturated with pride and ceremony around businesses existing to provide critical necessities, even as these businesses expect workers, governments and Earth to continuously contribute on capitalistic terms – for instance, the expectation of a government stimulus or hand-out to kick-start a slowed or grounded capitalist process.

However flagrant, every single cost of production – including advertising, packaging, transporting, storing and marketing – is covered by end sales, reimbursed to capitalists by consumers ideally inclusive of profit. Yet neither workers nor consumers have any direct say in what is produced and how, or where it is produced, but rather have to rummage among what competing capitalists decide to produce and offer on the market at particular asking prices.

Business activities are managed as private property, as assets that are simultaneously a result and basis of production for trade and capitalist reproduction. In contrast to shared access and use, private property offers an exclusive right of use. As such, private property, assets, deprive as well as privilege, instituting and reproducing the inequalities characteristic of capitalism.

In short, private property results in the fragmentation of society's productive capacity held in dispersed and competing private hands. At the pointy end of late stage capitalism, as M multiplies in unending growth ($M \rightarrow M' \rightarrow M''$), umpteen efforts and things are enlisted as private property and income-earning assets. Patents and copyright agreements increase apace, along with platforms to offer erstwhile homely rooms as tourist accommodation (B&Bs), and paying passengers in personal car trips. People stop offering friends a bed or giving them free lifts in their car, instead charging for every conceivable service. Free sharing is commuted into an opportunity to create an income-earning asset. In the process, the room or car becomes 'capital', just as surely as housing has become an asset. In short, the entire complex of capitalist practices reproduces, in more expansive and intensive ways, wholly social categories and ways of relating to other people and dealing with artificial and natural things.

Capitalism is a set of practices creating the form of money as capital, just as money develops from capitalist practices. Living in this ritual, the market economy is feared one moment and regarded as wondrous the next. Accepting the responsibility for working for 'the economy' actually implies that owners of assets deserve a tribute, private property earning an income packaged as a debt that others in society continuously service. We face an unforgiving elite whose singular and collective power based on private ownership of property does not just mean that *they have* but also that *they prevent* others from having what they have.

Earth's limits are people's limits. So, as capitalism's grasp on the world of things and people has expanded and intensified, with power transferred through ownership and control of private property via monetary accounting systems, the opposition between the haves and the have-nots is set to become even more stark. Indeed, we have seen all this play out with the COVID-19 pandemic, which has heightened existing capitalist crises, even if they are temporarily ameliorated by states stimulating capitalist activities.

CONCLUSION

Money is the defining and characteristic ingredient of trade vis-à-vis other forms of exchange. A socio-political interpretation indicates how monetary value, exchange value, has come to dominate our social relations and the overuse of planetary materials and energy. The omnipotence of monetary values is an effect of social practices. The domination of exchange value cannot be underestimated – reflected in contemporary economic ideology and discourses, which rotate on tautologies, such as so-called 'efficiencies of production' with associated notions based on saving money, rather than on social and ecological effectiveness and appropriateness. Money is the measure used to prove that the money system, capitalism, is the best of all possible worlds. It is because it is, and it is great!

The conclusion is clear: we need to do away with money, not simply capital. Unless postcapitalism is money-free, we will fail to establish a world beyond capitalism. If money is the strategic organising principle of capitalism, then no money, no capitalists. Money is not only the form but also the seed of capital. Nonmonetary production and exchange – collective planning, commoning and sharing – undercut capitalists' power absolutely.

But, especially given the complexity of production within the current conjuncture, how might we transcend capitalism? How can we achieve an equitable and fair postcapitalist world that would allow us all to fulfil our basic needs and address ecological unsustainability? Before analysing and discussing strategies appropriate to achieving these ends, let's clarify our vision. The next chapter outlines a plausible and feasible nonmonetary postcapitalist local–global commons.

3
Yenomon: Commoning

Bound to principles of participatory governance, democratic utopians have tended to simply outline characteristic principles, sketches and features of 'utopia' in the sense of an ideal social construct rather than an impossible or fanciful dream. Indeed, nineteenth-century revolutionary Karl Marx devoted most of his works to critical analyses of capitalism. Even the *Communist Manifesto* is more of a call to action than a vision. Similarly strategic analysis and critique characterises the final book written by democratic market-socialist Erik Olin Wright, *How to be an Anti-Capitalist in the 21ˢᵗ Century*. Both writers' argument is that direct people power implies popular determination rather than signing up to a pre-determined vision.[1]

Yet the urgency of our current situation demands end-game clarity. As such, publishers' catalogues are filling up with visions of postcapitalism as utopian speculation, discourse and experimentation has become a necessary and significant form of activism. The necessary wide-ranging debate around our future requires multiple visions as reference points, visions that can be honed as working documents. This is especially so where money-freedom in a money-dominated world is concerned. The imaginaries of many members of contemporary global capitalism are so populated and patterned with monetary values, relations, structures and institutions that to suggest a world without money often results in incredulity. Surely, an ordered, sustainable world without money is impossible?

This chapter aims to outline a plausible and feasible nonmonetary postcapitalist local–global commons. It begins with a value statement and a vision for the sustainability of Earth on which our life depends. I propose an ultimate pattern of settlement based on cell-like 'ecotats' and sketch out the productive and consumptive activities of community-based units of human settlement, discussing households, duties and optimum collective sufficiency. Complex multi-layered exchange networks would exist between settlements, and 'glocal' principles would ground this global social order. The vision draws on select existing technologies and experiments, and is inspired by developments and models that demonstrate that such a proposal is feasible.[2] Relevant practices and principles have arisen in specific places in both the global North and global South, especially with respect to certain Indigenous peoples, as in Chapter 7. Here I draw out ways to integrate such techniques and practices using 'real values', rather than money and 'exchange value'. Yenomon is simply a sketch of some kind of end-point, so that you might get a better sense of my vision.

While the first two chapters of this book argued why a money-free world is necessary and this chapter tries to show that a money-free world is possible, the chapters that follow focus on transformation, identifying fires already lit, and offering strategies for moving from here to there – in short, the means towards such an end. Chapters from hereon take aspects of this future vision to show how well-established anti-capitalist currents within environmental movements, the women's movement and among Indigenous peoples are already grappling with and contributing strategically to establishing such a humane and sustainability-oriented world. So, please suspend disbelief related to imponderables associated with transitions, and read on.

REAL VALUES AND COMMONING

Instead of the old unreal, abstract 'exchange value' and 'money', in Yenomon we perceive and approach the world using 'real values'. Real values go beyond simple utilitarian meanings of a 'use value' to incorporate all those environmental and social qualities and quantities that comprise the needs of both people and planet. Real values are drawn from biological, ecological, social and popular knowledge of our needs, and the needs of our natural environments, and embrace all aspects of how to satisfy, sustain and care for both.

By way of a simple but partial example, from a seedling to its senescence, a tree has ecological needs, including for water, soil and sunlight. A tree also satisfies needs of Earth and people including through transpiration, a significant stage in the holistic water cycle; by sequestering and storing carbon as part of the carbon cycle, and by producing fruit harvested by animals, including humans, who also use pruned branches to make furniture and bark for medicines.

Production and exchange is based on real values; caring and decision making is based on real values. We live for, of and by real values. This is a global as well as a local reality. We live 'glocally' in unique and rich eco-habitats, adapting to them as they adapt to us.

This real value way of conceiving and treating our world would not be possible without dispensing with private property and engaging in commoning. The world of things and beings is now held in common at every scale. We have intricate, humane and ecologically sensible principles for use rights, the rights – which entail responsibilities – to use human and nonhuman nature in ways that perpetuate our and other species' co-existence with Earth. We engage in nurturing, gardening and caring activities, and regenerative tasks to heal Earth and people from the vestiges of the Anthropocene. We are establishing a world firmly oriented on real values.

We live glocally, meaning that we live by universal global principles, processes and practices that guide us in our decision making and activities in local areas, in communities that are as collectively sufficient and as politically autonomous as possible. We have established global notions of needs of people and the planet. The limits to our collective sufficiency are set by our needs, our locality's ecological needs, the potential offered by our environs and our capabilities. Our glocal standards enable us to live healthily and facilitate regeneration, continuously nurturing Earth.

We satisfy certain 'wants' too, as long as they do not prevent the satisfaction of either other people's needs or the planet's ecological needs.

Our communities are settled in, and as needs be re-settle in, eco-habitats. These 'ecotats' are peculiarly appropriate environmental habitats for a human community. They are environs capable of meeting a community's needs. An ecotat has sheltered areas suitable for settlement, accessible water supplies and is designed for food self-provisioning using techniques and practices developed in permaculture and agroecology approaches. The borders of ecotats are somewhat fluid. Our community shares use rights to a lake adjacent to land we use and adjacent to land used by two other neighbouring communities. We harvest fish from this lake not just to feed ourselves but also to preserve some for neighbourhoods beyond the adjacent ones who directly access the lake.

What we need and cannot provide for ourselves locally is provided for through temporary, semi-permanent, or permanent exchange arrangements with other communities and their ecotats. These arrangements take the form of a 'compact' rather than a monetary contract. We try to make such compacts to fulfil our needs with as immediate, as local, communities as we can. We have compacts to give, compacts to take and compacts that involve give-and-take. These compacts allow us access to a surplus elsewhere, whether any surplus to another community's needs has occurred by design or by accident. Compacts focus on needs rather than wants. We have arrangements around wants too, but they neither have the status nor name of a compact. Wants are secondary.

We no longer use fences to define boundaries as in the Anthropocene, when land was privatised. Small fences are used to protect, say, certain plants from certain animals. Where natural yields are bountiful, Yenomon's closely settled communities combine production and exchange with more fluid notions of collective sufficiency between them than in sparsely settled communities that are more profoundly collectively sufficient. So, wherever they are located on Earth, our ecotat-oriented communities have a complex, sophisticated and globally networked connection and responsibility for their immediate locale and Earth more generally.

Let's say my community supports around a hundred people of all ages – a number that seems particularly appropriate for collective decision making, production and sharing. We know and grow with and apart from one another. We exist in a creative play of diverse responses to challenges. We have learned skills around conflict resolution that clarify, modify and settle conflicts in consensual decision-making cultures of embrace. Our community has developed an intricate knowledge of the land to which we have use rights and we share all of this knowledge and help one another in learning and applying skills to manage it. This knowledge and these skills are shared not only between us within our community but also with others who live elsewhere yet need or want to know, and those who visit or stay with us.

Real values are basic to all our discussions and decision making around our use rights, communities, community members and compacts. In short, real values refer to qualities and quantities of social and environmental values. These are qualities for us and for other beings. Everything has benefits and disadvantages, magnificent and dangerous qualities, for people and planetary ecological integrity. We recognise wind, rain, all kinds of plants and animals, geological formations and matter more generally in terms of these real values. Real values are characterised in rounded ways, such as 'wind hardy', 'light sensitive', 'long-lasting', and define properties such as 'mordant' (to facilitate dying), 'absorbent', or 'repellent'.

Our knowledge systems, research and understanding are all formed around such real values. No longer clothed, masked, or torn asunder by privatisation and monetary, financial and market considerations linked to production for trade – we are able to approach our social and environmental needs directly in terms of human and nonhuman effort, the time taken to accomplish tasks using this or that technique, appropriate tools and clever design. We see simplicity and efficiency of human effort and eco-demands as key principles to fulfil our needs and, in a complementary way, Earth's needs.

Our concept of efficiency is holistic. Some means for achieving certain ends might be slower but also less stressful for us or for Earth, so we regard such an approach as efficient. In other words, efficiency is measured by criteria such as effectiveness, appropriateness and conviviality. Conviviality refers to technologies and institutions that are as widely accessible, understandable and manageable as possible, and facilitate cooperative and sharing approaches.

ECOTAT

The 'ecotat' is an ecologically rational human settlement, a landscape that members of a community inhabit, satisfy their needs within and care for. Its size in terms of hectares and human populations is dependent on the carrying capacity of that particular area, which sometimes fluctuates over time. Each community seeks to be as collectively sufficient as possible within its ecotat, but often has substantial compacts and spaces shared with neighbouring communities. Ecotats have grown away from, within and in contrast to the fragmented private property of the Anthropocene where landscapes were shaped and scarred by production for trade and cancers of urban overpopulation. Ecotats in our settling stage of Yenomon show distinctive shifts to ecologically sensible settlement in natural and cultivated landscapes.

Dense settlements occur within rich ecotones, where landscapes can support high populations. But gradients of density ebb and flow across and between regions on the basis of ecological and social rationales. The environmental rationale behind the ecotats is the creation of modest ecological footprints. The most direct and efficient production is conducted as close as is feasible to end-use, end-users and consumers. The satisfaction of all our basic needs is made as local as possible because transporting inputs and outputs amounts to environmental and social waste. We minimise transport as well as travel but enjoy long-stay visitors and visiting.

We have expansive gardens and orchards around buildings where we live, make and store things. We encourage a balance of indigenous plants and productive ones, a balance guided by our needs and Earth's regenerative needs. We have woodlands; water-storage systems; animals that provide, for instance, eggs, milk, feathers and skins; we build soil and use rocks. Much of our gardening, food self-provisioning and design is inspired by permaculture. Our gardens produce vegetables and herbs and our orchard trees bear fruit.

We approach production first and foremost to fulfil basic needs, evaluating techniques in holistic ways based on real values – going beyond the technological foci and fantasies of the Anthropocene. We have simple and sophisticated tools, that we repair and we manufacture some devices. Most ecotats fulfil tasks according to a light form of division of labour within regions of ecotats but all knowledge of tools and techniques is shared and held in common right across the planet. Where manufacture and production of certain needs occur at distant nodes we do work exchanges so we know how those products are made. Consequently, we are informed to make decisions about how these workplaces develop.

My community has a 'tofuary', similar to an early- to mid-twentieth-century milk dairy. We smash beans to produce soy milk and soy skin. We mill some beans to make soy flour and we create soy butter. Some of the material left over contributes to a plant fertiliser and animal feed. The rest we compost. Some soy milk is turned into tofu and fermented to produce tempeh. We also use fermentation techniques to make miso and tamari. Our tofuary produces on demand for neighbouring communities. Each one of those communities arranges with us for some of their members to work in our tofuary, so we share the knowledge and skills to operate the machinery in this soyhut.

All of our ecotats have repair centres because all our devices, clothes and buildings are designed and created to last, and ways of maintaining and prolonging their life are part of our daily lives. There is no such thing as a patent, which disappeared with other assets and private property. We share knowledge but still celebrate those who contribute to developing knowledge and skills. For instance, one of our members who sometimes works in the tofuary worked out a neat new-to-us way to process the beans, which we call 'Will's way'. We share these techniques on the digital commons library where anyone can learn various ways of achieving similar results in a massive archive, where we can ask questions, offer solutions and so on. Yes, we have access to digital devices and a global internetwork, but we share and minimally use such devices and services, given their high embodied material and energy costs.

We have re-inhabited and renovated some buildings that remain from the Anthropocene. We have constructed anew simple dwellings and buildings for collective productive activities. Some people live alone or in couples. Other households are collectives of singles and couples, whose members each have a private space but all share living, dining, kitchen and laundry spaces. We are a community centred in and on community ecotat land and waters to which we have semi-permanent (conditional) use rights. All our buildings and facilities are created in eco-friendly ways, minimising our footprint, encouraging regeneration and healing. While we often use techniques that minimise effort and time we sometimes find great personal and collective value in doing tasks slowly and deliberately as diligent craftspeople tend to do.

We share all our ecological knowledge with one another in the community and beyond. We carefully and respectfully use certain animals in light ways for travel, transport and farming. We are all involved with doing everything in ways that nurture and save Earth. Much of our land and the sources of our water are shared as commons not only with neighbouring communities but also with regional ones. Deliberations around what we do and how we do it involve all these communities in various specific ways. Our community has representatives on numerous regional river, eco-corridor, forest and ridge working groups. The working groups cover distinctive spatial areas. They do not focus on 'water' but, rather, distinctive natural sources – such as our co-governed lake – and consider our water practices in relation to Earth's and our suite of surrounding communities' needs. As such, our substantively autonomous, collectively sufficient community, our ecotat, is not only a primary eco-material unit but also a key eco-political cell within Yenomon.

THE ECO-POLITICAL CELL OF COMMUNITY: CREATION-ON-DEMAND

Our efficient and effective form of production starts with assessing diverse individual and collective needs, and proceeds as creation-on-demand. In my household, there are three adults, one young child and a teenager. With respect to food, we discuss our expected needs for the next year based on the past one. We usually do this – just like everyone else in the community – during the winter months. We're familiar with what grows best and most easily locally, so we concentrate on an achievable household order. We're used to the system and reflect on what we'd like to eat more or less of compared with the previous year.

This year, our teenager expects to be away visiting another community for three months so the food order takes account of their absence. Our toddler has special needs and we estimate the quantities on the basis of their expected growth. We know that our order will go through a check by other community members so what, and how much, we want will be questioned in terms of whether it might be too much, not enough and how we might process any surplus in ways beneficial to the whole community.

Once all the orders have been verified, our community's food working group adds an extra order for the buffer store and takes account of existing compacts with other communities. They always plan to create a bit more than has been ordered, especially in terms of growing more easily stored and nutritious foods. This acts as a surplus which, beyond use in our community, can be made available to other communities as needs be. Some communal cooking activities preserve foods by drying or adding ingredients such as vinegar, sugar and salt for the buffer store. We have a compact to obtain rock salt from a community 95 km away.

We always have surplus quinces, which are nutritious and can be used for various disorders. We have compacts with other communities to deliver them raw or dried, as cordial and conserved as paste and jam.

The total community order is divided into types and amounts of food as dealt with by distinct working groups such as the pome fruits (e.g., apples, pears) group, the green seasonal vegetable group, the tofuary group and the dairy group. Each group assesses the feasibility of meeting the total 'asking' demand in their area, taking into account a range of natural, social and practical matters which will, or might, impact on their production. They might gauge the impact of drier and warmer weather conditions, if expected. They will review what types and amounts of seeds they have available, and assess the most preferable given the draft order. Sometimes this means checking with other communities if we can access extra seeds, seedlings, or reliable substitutes. The working group members estimate work hours required at different stages to report back to the community for assessment and comparison with similar tallies made by other groups. Some of their reflections and responses mean that residents are asked to consider other options and revise their requests.

The real values important for food production include levels and types of nutrition, ecological feasibility and sustainability in terms of land and water, and how much and what type of effort, skills and knowledge is required. After all their research, discussions and revisions, a series of general assemblies hear from each group and certain individuals about the challenges and solutions to the demand side of creation-on-demand. Decisions are made to proceed with everything that looks feasible to fulfil in this community, or another community via a compact already in place or confirmed as feasible. Everyone needs to feel confident the food order is of a sufficient size and achievable given the community's work-loads in non-food areas.

This is a very brief sketch of how the community discusses, nego-tiates and makes decisions regarding the satisfaction of food needs. It indicates the types of processes used in a whole range of areas in our creation-on-demand system. A slightly different process takes place in terms of clothing. The turnover is slower and smaller than with food, even in the case of growing children. We share, lend, borrow and pass on clothing. We still have some left from the Anthropocene! We have great designers of clothes and cloth-makers and menders who tailor already used cloth and clothes. A lot of us like to knit and crochet and sew. We have silkworms, alpaca and sheep from which we gain materials for textiles we weave. We look at what the community needs by way of clothing and volunteer to satisfy certain demands by piecework. Others are scheduled to spend time in workshops, working collectively on making footwear as well as clothing, bedding and a range of goods made out of textiles.

Our general assemblies, working groups, household meetings and everyday chats enable us to make decisions over production and exchange that are especially taxing through the latter half of winter. During the rest of the year, our weekly assemblies hear how production is going: Is it on track? Have any challenges arisen? We share problems with other communities, calling out for quick suggestions by way of solutions – and assisting them where and when we can.

Because we focus on satisfying our basic needs within the regenerative limits of our locale – and somewhat beyond – distribution is decided simultaneously with confirmed orders. The order is fed into our collective agreements on our productive goals and, once achieved, when the goods are ready for collection, those who ordered them are notified and an arrangement made to collect them. Similarly, we find out about surpluses and make pitches to the assembly or delegated working group on using them productively. We have open stores where unwanted things are left and available for anyone to collect; other unwanted things are handed on in more personal ways. A lot of these types of communication are made via the global internetwork.

There are numerous points in our ecotat where potable water can be collected, stored and supplied. Most of us collect water from the buildings we live in and that is our primary supply, via piped water taps inside and outside the walls. Some buildings on a slope near our main river divert water from the river for use in their households and filter grey and black water from their dwellings through evapo-transpiration reedbeds and wetlands before returning it to the same river downstream. We use the water from the lake for vegetation.

Similarly, we have various locally distributed devices for collecting and storing sun and wind energy. These services are regularly maintained and, under commoning schemes we are allocated use rights, which specific working groups check and re-check for appropriateness, efficiency and sufficiency and regularly report on to our general assembly to discuss. Many of these processes are well-established and, due to environmentally friendly approaches and practices, only need monitoring. It doesn't take up much time. Tasks aren't onerous.

You can see, then, that our communities live in much more efficient and democratic ways when it comes to sharing and arranging water, waste and electricity supplies than in the Anthropocene. Then such services were supplied by centralised and controlling state and private agencies in expansive systems using much more in the way of embodied materials and energy, and human effort in management, than our off-grid communally managed and modestly used services do.

In our community, each person contributes an obligatory 35 hours per week to collective production, which includes caring and what used to be referred to as 'housework'. This is an average contribution that has waxed and waned since I have lived here. The amount starts much lower, when we are in our teens, and grows, to the quota for everyone who is more than 15 years old and under 55 years old. Children, as well as adults, often volunteer at various tasks and community-based learning obliges them to grasp, even master, many skills before they start working a formal quota. We can choose what we work on, where and how, within limits established by general assemblies. In return, our basic needs and many wants are met.

Of course, we have several weeks off every year and do not work when we are sick. We do work swaps with other communities. I have spent months at a time at several other communities working on various tasks, such as establishing a regional textile centre. After 55 years of age, the number of hours of the expected quota of work to be done by an individual drops each year. Most of the time I manage to work just three or four days a week. They are heavy days but that leaves me three or four days free of necessary work. Some rostered jobs, such as in the community kitchen, need to be done at a particular time. Other jobs can be done as piecework, just finished by a certain time, as organised by, or with the working group contact point. I do a lot of herb gardening. In fact, I am the main herb gardener. We use herbs a lot, including for food and gardening techniques, for dyeing, medicines and decorations. We dry herbs and store them in cool rooms simply built into sides of slopes, under the Earth.

The reward for our work is the security of having our lifelong basic needs met and the right for continuous input in making decisions on both local production and compacts with other communities. We have personal property and space. I have a large room with a desk and bookcases as well as my bed, wardrobe, chests of drawers and a couch. But private property no longer exists. I love to spend time reading and writing. I am involved with performing groups, mainly assisting with production.

Earth is a multiplicity of commons with clear, efficient and universal principles and terms for commoning. Where I was born – my birth community – is more than 200 kilometres, a dividing mountain range, away from here. I moved with my father as a teen to a community adjacent to my birth community. Later, I found vacancies in two other communities before moving here; this is our toddler's birth community. We can stay now we are here, more or less as long as we like. If we moved, we would need to arrange it with a potential new community and ecotat. We would arrange to visit there, to speak a lot with the residents and to try it out.

FROM COMPACTS TO NETWORKS: OUR GLOCAL INTEGRATION

Collective sufficiency in communities is a sustainability prerogative that simultaneously enhances individuality, personal power and social cohesion. While members of our community gain a modicum of independence within our global world – from our community's collective sufficiency and substantive decision-making autonomy – all community members, and our community as an entity, are simultaneously deeply integrated in regional and global values, relations and activities.

Our commons blend into other commons just as our communities integrate with other communities. We not only share air globally but also share land and water sources that are jointly managed. The spring in the centre of our community is fed from underground water commons. A fractured rock aquifer supplies this spring, so the water comes from a source that supplies other springs in our region. A neighbouring ecotat still accesses some water from bores kept post-Anthropocene because they were deemed useful. Most other bores were decommissioned because they were ecologically exploitative. Where our land rises into a steep range, we share the management of the entire range with numerous other communities who also have use rights to parts of the ridge-scape.

In the Anthropocene, there were regimented 'schools' to create 'workers' and knowledge was privatised, professionalised, packaged and patented. In Yenomon we learn, as they used to say, 'on the job'. We all teach young ones to read and count, to divide and multiply. There is a children's learning working group, which involves parents and people who like and are good at conveying basic skills. The young are taught singly and in groups. They are all expected to learn a series of basic duties and responsibilities. They attend the general assembly unless and until they are too noisy or prone to muck up. Children learn by hanging around us as we work. They learn by observation, and trial, that some work requires privacy and focus. We pride ourselves in developing personal skills of adjustment, flexibility, responsibility and reliability while understanding how our ecotat breathes and reproduces, as an ecological being that includes us.

Our glocal integration is facilitated by shared values. Everyone's basic needs must be met so satisfying wants are secondary activities. Still we engage in lots of wants of free-roaming, celebratory and artistic endeavours. We have a direct responsibility for local community sufficiency. The sufficiency of neighbouring and regional communities is an indirect concern. Where sufficiency is – or is threatened to be – unmet in any community, reasons are examined and open to comment by other communities. Where explained by temporary factors, gifting surpluses is a remedy. Where and when consistent shortfalls occur, we often work on restructuring the community; some members might leave or there is a call-out for others with appropriate skills or knowledge to join the community temporarily – or even permanently – to fulfil essential roles directly and to train community members.

There is no duality between nature, Earth, and human, social, worlds in Yenomon – in contrast to the marked duality in the Anthropocene, which was essentially caused by monetary practices. Instead, we make a concerted effort to meld the sustenance of our human selves with the regeneration of nonhuman nature. This sustainability is a continuous work-in-progress, a struggle commensurate with life itself. In the process, we keep developing knowledge and skills around real values. Every new technique, every new way of doing and creating things reveals new real values, real values of us, real values of Earth.

4
System Change, Not Climate Change

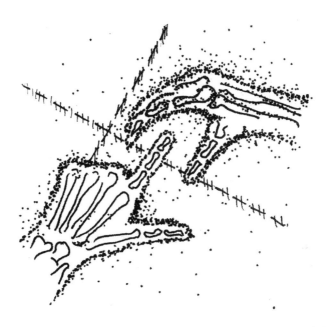

The rallying cry 'System change, not climate change' is clear and direct compared with most other analyses of sources and solutions to climate change. The call acknowledges that carbon emissions are simply the tip of the blade of environmental crises that hold our species to ransom. In contrast, states and industry have tended to narrow their efforts to proliferating market-based strategies to curb emissions in order to quell climate change as if it were the main, even sole, environmental crisis. In fact, rising carbon emissions are simply a symptom of much broader and deeper human exploits of Earth.[1]

Capitalist-inspired solutions to ecological challenges have been delayed and simply extend business-as-usual with green innovations, green technologies and green commodities – commercial solutions that focus on trade, markets and money. Neoliberal states are prominent agents in international associations and negotiations over coordinated action plans determining targets for reducing emissions, and are wary of directly regulating business. Even if environmental advocates call for governments to ban, tax and regulate anti-environmental developments, certain activists and environmental non-government organisations maintain a naïve confidence in supporting market-based approaches, such as trading markets for carbon and water, 'pricing the environment' and integrating costs of externalities. This direction has consistently proved fruitless, with only marginal and minimal success. Promoters fail to acknowledge that monetary values (prices) are reductive and more or less irrelevant to the multitude of incomparable and incommensurable real values involved in satisfying our basic needs within the regenerative limits and needs of Earth.

Other ways of living, based on real social and ecological values, are possible and preferable solutions. Indeed, the call for system change not climate change singles out capitalism as generating and reproducing climate change. Consequently, reducing carbon emissions demands a transition to postcapitalist ways of living. Arguing for system change is a pointed demand spoken with a strong sense of do-it-ourselves and do-it-together agency. In the context of insufficient clarity on visions of postcapitalism and appropriate strategies for achieving such a state, this chapter argues that market-based framings and solutions are redundant – we must go beyond money to achieve oneness with Earth.

CARBON EMISSIONS: THE TIP OF THE ICEBERG

In 2014, palaeontologist Anthony Barnosky pointed out that 'even without human-caused climate change thrown into the mix', human activities such as land clearing, polluting the atmosphere and overfishing were contributing to the sixth mass extinction: 'We've completely plowed, paved, or otherwise transformed 50 per cent of Earth's lands, taking all those places out of play for the species that used to live there.' Barnosky argued that climate change is happening far too fast for most species to adapt and is ubiquitous, meaning there is no place to escape to avoid the heat threatening their physical viability. He referred to an International Union for Conservation of Nature (IUCN) figure of 'well over 20,000 species' under threat of extinction.[2] Proving his point, by mid-2021 the IUCN's list of threatened species had leapt to include more than 37,400 or 28 per cent of those species assessed.[3]

Scientists have driven studies of climate change. As such analyses have grown over the last half-century, many ecologists have argued that slowing down and addressing the current catastrophe is not just about reversing the rise in carbon emissions. It's about the poor state of entire ecosystems and the whole way we live. An unusually megadiverse country, Australia has one of the highest species extinction rates in the world. In the last two centuries, mammal extinctions have been due to a host of factors, including habitat destruction and introduced predators, such as cats and foxes.[4] The ecological state of Australia shows that action needs to go far beyond addressing the mere symptom of global heating through efforts towards 'zero carbon emissions' or 'beyond zero carbon' to broad, deep and holistic ecosystem-based change.[5] To make matters worse, significant scientific facts are being suppressed, especially with successive cuts to funding ecological research and public news services.[6]

By the time Australia experienced its catastrophic 2019–20 summer bushfires, it had already lost two-fifths of its forest cover since white settlement (1788–), at which time around 30 per cent of the continent had been covered by forests.[7] Even as they were fragmented and degraded through clearing, many of these forests remained of international significance into this century. For instance, East Gippsland's forests in Victoria were assessed by English botanist David Bellamy as 'the most diverse range of temperate forest ecosystems on Earth'.[8] They were among the 20 per cent of existing forests burned in the 2019–20 fires, which broke global records for forest devastation. The fires' extent and intensity has been directly linked to anthropogenic climate change.[9]

Plants in complex forest ecosystems absorb and store carbon dioxide emissions – including an estimated one-third of those induced by human activities every year – so any forest degradation contributes to global heating. Moreover, preserving current mature forests and halting deforestation worldwide would double the uptake of carbon from forests.[10] Today, a key environmental challenge for Australians is regenerating the vast tracts of various tropical, sub-tropical, wet and dry temperate ecosystems destroyed and denuded in the massive bushfires.

Furthermore, water over-use and pollution in Australian rivers, lakes, bays and oceans present many challenges. Except for Antarctica, Australia is the driest continent on Earth. Water is always a concern for both urban and rural settlements. Ninety per cent of the coral constituting the iconic Great Barrier Reef on Australia's north-eastern coast was bleached during successive summers from 2017 to 2019. Bleaching has resulted from marine heat waves, ocean acidification due to absorbing rising levels of carbon and nitrogenous fertiliser run-off from farms.[11] All this, and then, in May 2020, a prominent global mining company Rio Tinto destroyed – with relative impunity – Juukan Gorge, a 46,000-year-old registered Aboriginal heritage site, which led an expert to reveal that hundreds of other sites were under threats from mining.[12]

In short, our socio-cultural and political systems suffer debasement just as our land and waters – sources of our food, shelter and clothing – are being eroded and devalued. Even without carbon emissions and global heating, we face massive environmental crises. What is being done to address this situation?

INAPPROPRIATE STRATEGIES: CARBON TRADING AND OFFSETS

Economic activities account for the vast bulk of environmental damage contributing to global heating. Capitalist activities have been too fast and radical for the ecological environments in which they developed. Yet, rather than acknowledge the need for root-and-branch system change, many carbon reduction policies focus instead on commercial market mechanisms, typically involving a carbon price and trading.

Carbon trading

The size of the global carbon market in terms of value was over US\$215 billion, or €194 billion, in 2019. Even though the carbon volume of Europe's carbon market fell during 2019, its value increased by 30 per cent to €169 billion. This increase in the value of the European carbon market was mainly due to strengthening demand and steep rises in allowance prices as the European (Commission's) Green Deal heralded rising targets for cutting carbon emissions during the 2020s.[13]

The European Union (EU) market centres on a climate change policy cap-and-trade Emissions Trading System (ETS), its main emissions reduction policy mechanism covering almost one-half of the EU's greenhouse gas emissions. Breeches of set caps on emissions are remedied by purchasing credits or offsets tied to negative carbon activities, such as tree planting. The Clean Development Mechanism of the United Nations (UN) is the world's main offset programme, with all its projects in the majority world. The dominating EU ETS was established with confidence that trading is the most flexible and cost-effective carbon reduction process, with a 'robust carbon price' facilitating investment in low-carbon technologies. Rules include fines, and allowances are auctioned. Recently, China's ambitious ETS has been mooted to overtake the EU's domination in this market sometime in the future.

Numerous criticisms are made of both compulsory and voluntary carbon trading and offsetting programmes, especially in terms of reducing emissions of commercial and state operations and of individuals' carbon footprints, for example, to assuage guilt over carbon-emitting air-flights. Although permitted, even encouraged, in many compulsory net zero emissions accounts, carbon offsets are suspect instruments. They seem to excuse – and are mistakenly thought to counterbalance – emissions that ought not, and might never, have been made in the first place.

Carbon offsets

Carbon offsets allow a purchaser to invest in an activity deemed to reduce carbon emissions, including promises not to deforest areas, to plant new trees (plantations), or to replace non-renewable with renewable energy sources. In other words, future benefits of carbon emission-reducing activities – that might have happened anyway – are traded as 'goods', for 'bads' of activities producing emissions elsewhere. Such offsets are attractive to the rich who want to pursue carbon-emitting activities regardless of their ecological and, ultimately, social costs. As Umair Irfan points out, 'carbon offset projects have a long history of overpromising and underdelivering, threatening fragile progress on climate change.'[14]

Why might carbon offsets fail to deliver? Offset schemes can become oversubscribed or undersubscribed, or fail like any other business. Planted trees constitute offsets on the basis that their growth will absorb carbon. Yet there are very real risks that such trees will be destroyed in the future, say by pests, disease, floods, or fires – all of which have become more numerous, extensive and intensive with global heating. Indeed, offset schemes have been so beset by, and potentially subject to, such risks that the sector has had to develop elaborate standards, accountability processes and models of best practices. Still, many weaknesses have been exposed in schemes compliant with the UN's expanded Reducing Emissions from Deforestation and Forest Degradation in Developing Countries programme (REDD+), which started in 2005.[15] Consequently, a significant proportion of the purchase price of offsets does not end up directly ameliorating emissions but rather remunerates work on transparency, monitoring and reporting on such carbon sink schemes. Moreover, all these schemes, as well as satisfactory offset prices, are highly reliant on market demand for their continued viability.[16]

When the carbon offset was initially developed as a so-called 'tool' for reducing carbon emissions, detractors immediately framed offsets as institutionalised cheating reminiscent of a bizarre practice of religious orders, known as 'indulgences'. In the Middle Ages, Catholic clergy ('pardoners') would sell on their surplus good works as indulgences to cashed-up sinners without 'the time or inclination to repent for themselves'. Green capitalists follow this pardoner mould, neutralising their carbon-emitting sins by buying carbon offsets. The Rolling Stones, for instance, offset emissions caused by their tour of the United Kingdom in 2003 by funding the planting of 2,800 trees via the entertainment industry's Future Forests company. This transaction alone raised a gamut of questions around the substance of such redemption, calculating carbon debts and credits, transparency, legitimacy, credibility and reliability in accounting for additional tree planting, and trading on effective carbon futures – issues that have beset the subsequent history of carbon trading and such credits. As Kevin Smith of Carbon Trade Watch concluded back in 2007, 'The sale of offset indulgences is a dead-end detour off the path of action required in the face of climate change.'[17]

Yet, we find that low-performing market-oriented schemes have only expanded and intensified.[18] Furthermore, biodiversity offsets exaggerate all the contradictions of carbon offsets. With a biodiversity offset, a developer can clear lands and ecosystems for buildings and infrastructure – that will continue to deplete the environment – by simply buying a one-off 'offset' in another place where, one might argue, the ecosystem might have been preserved anyway.[19] As The Corner House researcher and advocate Larry Lohmann contends, with all such ecosystem service trading:

> Entrepreneurs and landholders are being invited to manufacture biodiversity, wetlands quality or species-equivalent tokens that industrialists or developers can then buy to 'neutralize' the destruction for which they are responsible. None of these 'market environmentalist' initiatives has any potential of being able to resolve or even address the climate crisis, the biodiversity crisis, or any other crisis.[20]

The whole framing of offsets is based on spurious concepts of assets, trading, private property rights and double-entry accounting within which the real values of ecosystems and offsets are reduced to, and obliterated in, an anthropocentric price. While all this fiddling continues, the data on actual emissions reductions and our ecological demise just get worse.

INAPPROPRIATE STRATEGIES: WATER TRADING

Even as ice at both poles melts, releasing organisms that have the potential to cause plagues, water is a key source of concern for cities. Urbanites are already experiencing shortages that the UN warns could impact on 5 billion people or every second person on Earth by 2050. The twentieth century saw the loss of around 65 per cent of the world's wetlands and forests. Significantly, UN Water recommends 'a move towards nature-based solutions that rely more on soil and trees than steel and concrete', and more on traditional and Indigenous peoples' farming and food-provisioning techniques. Yet the World Rainforest Movement points out that 'nature-based solutions' and 'natural climate solutions' signal the extension of corporate activities. Similarly, the recommended use of 'green bonds' and ecosystem service payments indicate business as usual, furthering market mechanisms and detracting from both necessary transformation, and immediate and direct remedies.[21]

The Murray–Darling Basin (MDB), which covers around 14 per cent of the world's driest continent, Australia, offers a case of applying market-based solutions to water scarcity. By the early 2020s the MDB Plan market was worth A$16 billion.

The Murray–Darling Basin

Various governments managing the MDB decided to reduce extraction from it in 2002. Even without human use, this immense basin has had a relatively small and seasonally variable amount of water flowing through its system. Agricultural use, via irrigation, has been the main competitor for water sorely needed to maintain riverine ecosystem health. Vegetation clearing has increased salinity, further threatening the basin's productive and environmental potential. Most significantly, in 2004, the National Water Initiative separated water from land, triggering its commodification.

Rather than directly regulating water use, governmental approaches have been market-oriented, focusing on traded allocations – based on a scientific measure of available water – and permanent water rights, inferring compensation if relinquished. In other words, the MDB water market is capped with changes in water supply and demand – tending to rotate around rainfall and institutional factors such as Commonwealth environmental water recovery – impacting on both prices of water and water trade flows. This economic approach of policymakers has entrenched deep tensions in determining the amount of water made available for producers versus the crucial needs of the MDB's complex ecosystems.[22]

The key decision that production for trade must not be compromised has continuously threatened both the immediate and long-term ecological health of the MDB. By 2020, one in ten Australians lived in this food bowl, which reaches out to five capital cities on its edges and just beyond, with more than 3 million relying on it for drinking water. Around one-third of Australia's food is cultivated or grazed within the MDB's complex riverine systems that struggle to maintain sufficient water for human wants and ecological needs. Production includes rice, 90 per cent of it exported, which demands one in every four litres extracted. Modelling for 2012–19 by the Wentworth Group of Concerned Scientists (2002–) assumed 20 per cent more water than indicated by flows monitored since. While modelling is imperfect, it is acknowledged that real losses and shortfalls ensued. Explanations include water theft, such as floodplain harvesting by irrigators and graziers, who are rarely caught and fined, according to the Environmental Defenders' Office.[23]

Moreover, dry years have caused significant water depletion, with ecological impacts such as fish kills. Previous average temperature records were broken in 2017, 2018 and 2019, every year recording greater than 1.5° more than the annual mean since 1910 and causing losses of basin water into the earth and atmosphere. Research in the state of Victoria indicates that water systems are now failing to bounce back following droughts, and that 'drought could result in a permanent reduction to the water supply.' As such, the MDB case accords with estimates that every degree of global heating diminishes regular cereal crops by around 10 per cent.[24]

So, has a water market, commodification of water, offered solutions? No.

Irrigators are unprepared to give ground in terms of their so-called 'sustainable diversion limits'. Scientists argue for money to improve modelling and to collect more empirical data. Meanwhile, an expert member of the Wentworth Group of Concerned Scientists points out that arguments over less water in the system must focus on deciding between competing use(r)s. Irrigators are on one side of the equation, on the other are wetlands, ecosystem health and Indigenous peoples' cultural sites of significance.[25] Indigenous peoples have to buy water from the market to use for economic gain and have no say in water management. A 2019 royal commission concluded that they 'rightly feel that their interests have been marginalised.' Indeed, Aboriginal academic Brad Moggridge (University of Canberra) has stated that 'all our value sets and all our knowledge clashes with the way water is managed on this continent.'[26] The conflict is clear – real values versus exchange value.

The conflict

Businesses will not give ground, given that they operate in an inflexible economic system where market-based prices, costs and profits prevail. Typical of capitalist state practices, governments are wary of regulating, although banning even just rice production could substantially ease pressures on water use. Earth is exploited further as commercial activities continue to overuse water, emit carbon and pollute soils and water – feeding into vicious cycles of degrading habitats and species extinction. Conservation efforts are limited and time-consuming. In 2021, a study by dozens of scientists named the MDB waterways as just one of 19 collapsing or collapsed ecosystems within Australia and Antarctica that are at risk of complete collapse unless awareness is raised, anticipatory assessments made and action undertaken.[27]

The Australian Bureau of Statistics has used the South Australian section of the basin as a case study for applying the international standard System of Environmental-Economic Accounting for Agriculture, Forestry and Fisheries. That study reveals that environmental accounting intensifies economistic approaches, reducing complex and sophisticated ecosystems to 'natural capital' presented in terms of physical flow accounts, say for crops, and asset accounts for plantations.[28] In economistic accounts, precious biodiversity is either ignored because it is not commercially productive and apparently worthless, or accounted for specifically in terms of its monetary value.

In this case, we see the great conflicts and challenges facing humanity in the 2020s in microcosm. Such challenges are of our own making. In many regions, Earth is straining from human overconsumption and conflicts in understanding the natural environs off which humans live. Many hang onto the old ways of capitalism. Others argue that we must change our practices radically to live in balance with nature. The conflict is between those who frame their reality in economic terms dominated by the market, accounting and monetary value, and those who view the world in terms of real social and environmental values.

INAPPROPRIATE APPROACHES: 'PRICING' THE ENVIRONMENT

Decades ago, certain scholars working in ecological economics decided that imputing a price to ecosystem services, ecological 'assets', or 'natural capital', would demonstrate the massive reliance of capitalism on Earth and its limits and lead to Earth's greater protection. In 1997, a team led by Robert Costanza estimated that each year 'the entire biosphere' provided at least US\$16–54 trillion (10^{12}) – US\$33 trillion on average – worth of gratis ecosystem services, swamping the global gross domestic product.[29]

Indeed, various professionals and practitioners have pointed out that ecosystem services are bound to be degraded specifically because they fall outside of capitalists' accounts. The argument is that the free use of nature and disregard for deleterious environmental impacts arises because such activities are regarded as 'externalities', rather than costs for producers. Ecological values, for instance of forests purifying water supplies, have been made invisible or neglected as the case might be. Free and cheap disposal of wastes has resulted in toxic effects that are expensive to remedy. State-subsidised water and energy services are potentially subject to overuse. The suggested remedy is to integrate such costs of production into markets.

Consequently, a frightening number of environmentalists support businesses incorporating 'green accounting' approaches, using a naïve logic well-expressed by writer Jane Gleeson-White:

> Through the way it values – or does not – the finite resources of our planet, double entry now has the potential to make or break life on earth. We can continue to ignore the free gifts of nature in the accounts of our nations and corporations, and thereby continue to ruin the planet. Or we can begin to account for nature and make it thrive again. If numbers and money are the only language spoken in the global economy, then this is the language we must use.[30]

But, how on earth do you reduce to a price, or prices, the multi-various ecological aspects of, say, ecological services of water and air purification, and carbon absorption, relating to forests? Does one focus on how the forest developed, gratis to us, or on the expected costs of regenerating pure water and other such services in the future? A tree is not equal to another tree, in size, as species, in terms of age. If it is priced as if an asset, how does the price change to reflect all the changes in its ecological state? Who pays that price, how is it paid and how can we ensure it is used appropriately for stewardship of the forest? The practical examples considered above of water and carbon trading are enough to make one very wary.

Nevertheless, the international journal *Ecological Economics* is replete with reports on methodological experiments to measure aspects of nature in terms of artificial prices, such as inferences from existing costs, willingness to pay surveys, and estimates of costs of supporting regeneration and compensation for natural losses. Not just conventional but even many heterodox economists rationalise market practices and prices as constituent elements of allocating scarce resources in order to maximise social welfare. Assuming a highly controversial proposition – that capitalism does result in optimum social outcomes – they reason, why not include Earth's welfare? If this seems totally rational from a market-oriented perspective, how does it seem from the perspective of the multi-various real values of Earth?

Exchange values, use values and real values

Thinkers have been unsettled by the nature of 'price' and exchange value since trade began. In *The Wealth of Nations*, Adam Smith addresses the apparent paradox that a relatively useless diamond has such a high monetary value compared with water, a basic human need.[31] Responses from those rooted in labour or utility theories of values might focus on the essential character and creation of monetary value within production for trade. Another take on the water–diamond paradox is to recognise its source in framing the question in the realm of use values, while the question itself arises in the realm of exchange value, in prices.

The price of a good is formed through trade, multiple transactions, which has naught to do with the good's use value, its qualities or purposes for users, consumers. Instead, prices are subject to dynamics, most obviously of supply and demand, with suppliers compelled to cover more than their costs, and purchasers weighing up their preparedness to pay according to the extent of their need and their capacity in terms of money at hand or available as credit. In the market, everything is interpreted and negotiated in monetary terms, even if the purchaser assesses their needs in their calculations of whether to buy and at what price.

Now, given that trade subordinates the realm of use values to that of exchange value, it would seem to follow that applying market mechanisms would be inappropriate to solve welfare or, indeed, ecological issues. It even reveals the irrationality of the claim made by Robert Costanza's team that valuing ecosystem services 'has become an effective bridge between ecological and economic approaches', that participatory and integrated valuation processes can be usefully applied to address environmental management and crises.[32] Reviews of empirical cases and pure logic point in the opposite direction.

Monetarising precious, indeed 'priceless', ecosystems with all their incomparable and incommensurable elements simultaneously rationalises private property values and market-oriented systems for planning and producing our future. The approach ignores the analytical and practical distinctions between real and monetary values, which have culturally evolved in separate realms even if integrated in everyday life. For instance, as a civil engineer, my father used to remind us not to use water excessively, not because it cost him more money if we did but because 'four men died for every mile of tunnelling that brings you that water.' Not only is there no point in artificially assessing the value of ecosystem services but, in fact, the exercise limits and confuses the entire analysis and discussion of what really matters, and what we need to do in order to make ecological, and social, values matter.

Such confusions around 'price' – as if real values could be reflected or expressed in prices – are compounded by confusions around what 'money' is or might be. In the first few chapters of *Capital I* and elsewhere, Marx pointed out that the monetary and financial economy of capitalism exists as *practices* whether deemed legitimate, simply tolerated, or even actively resisted. Neither economists nor philosophers created the primary structures of the economy, such as the guiding formula of making money, profits and growth, banks, companies and accounting practices. They arose as practices of traders, bankers and industrialists. Economists simply *analyse* practical economies, even if they do so in order to advocate policy and regulatory changes, typically via state regulation and to perpetuate capitalism. Consequently, economists have marginal agency within the capitalist system.

Marx underscores this impotence when criticising proposals for alternative monies, such as ration chits. He argues that their proposers do not sufficiently appreciate the practical power of capitalists, owners of private property and market-based agents, market forces, market-based language, market-oriented logic and market practices. By definition, free trade is more or less uncontrollable exchange using money. Market prices are made in and by markets as collective free-for-all practices. Here, one price often impacts on many other prices. So, the more you set prices for goods and services, the less exchange can be seen in terms of a market.[33] Yet the notion of setting prices, as in a 'fair price', has maintained its grip.

Fair prices

A long-standing quest of social and environmental reformers, as revealed in the work of E.P. Thompson, is to establish 'fair' prices, which assumes that exchanges might readily express individual and collective intents in a *just* way.[34] There are several difficulties in setting any type of 'fair' asking price. Fair for which party or parties, given exchange by its very nature involves at least two parties with differing, even competing, interests? We might set a low price for bread so everyone can access it as a basic food, but that risks unfairly reducing the income of wheat farmers and bakers for their efforts, and risks lowered supplies if they stop producing wheat or bread. A really fair price for their efforts might make bread inaccessible for many people. As a set price, for example, for bread, the purchaser has no say in it: the purchaser either pays the price or goes without. Is that fair?

An even greater challenge is to set a fair price that expresses or delivers justice for both humans and Earth. Wouldn't setting the price of bread to satisfy the interests of the consumer rule out using organically grown wheat or other time-consuming ecologically sound farming, as in fair for Earth? Again, multiple competing interests arise.

Given it is a price set in a unit that is, ultimately, defined by everything else that is being traded, the price is relative even if 'set'. A price set in one period has a different relative meaning at another period – everything in trading is relative. And, because factors such as floods and droughts, pests and fires, all impact on growing the wheat, it will need to be re-set. So when, and how, is it re-set? Who sets and administers the fair price?

If setting a price for one commodity, such as water or carbon, is not straightforward, once the attempt is made to set prices for multiple goods and services, even more difficulties arise. This is mainly due to the fact that many commodities are inputs in various other productive processes. For instance, wood from trees can become pulp for making paper and textiles, or cut for use either to make furniture or build multi-storey dwelling complexes. Such finished products include various other materials and might be made with substitutes for wood. Multiple independently set prices tend to collide, cause gridlocks, disruptions and frustrations within what would then become very much a so-called 'marketplace'. Setting prices is at odds with the rationale and dynamic of markets – as in sellers and purchasers voluntarily and mutually agreeing on particular prices with flow on effects in terms of supply and demand. Centralised control of production is necessary to set numerous prices which, as one might logically anticipate, has always proved an administrative nightmare in practice.

Even at a micro-scale where 'fair trading' has become a marginal niche market for producers of particular commodities – say, tea and coffee – that are relatively simply produced and supplied commodities, such schemes have a range of critics.[35] Given that set prices and a market are at odds with one another, results of many market-oriented reforms almost invariably contradict the intents of the reformers. A final resort in the face of such failures is most often to let 'the market' decide, so we return to where we started.

No attempts to reform trade have resulted in effective and efficient processes for incorporating all associated ecological and social values, real values. The market as an institution has fatal deficiencies, the most significant of which cannot be overcome.

MODIFYING MONEY

Proposals for alternative currencies as a route to novel postcapital-ist orders are discussed later in this book. Here I confine comments to ways in which alternative concepts of money and monetary exchange have attracted analysts keen to better understand and improve on the prevailing system in terms of ecologically sustainable production. Repre-sentative proposals centre on eco-currencies and biophysical accounting indicators such as 'emergy', and highlight the slippery concept of 'equiv-alence' within monetary exchange.

Even among radical critics, there is a remarkable degree of confidence in maintaining money in some form as an apparently useful tool. By way of an example, a mid-2020 Extinction Rebellion newsletter started: 'Money is an ingenious technology that allows for social energy to operate across space and time.'[36] Similarly, Joe Ament calls for an ecological economics theory of money because money as a social institution is 'a foundation of human civilization' and because the oft resorted-to neo-Keynesian approaches to money are inadequate.[37] Moreover, many critics of money, such as Frederick Soddy, winner of the Nobel Prize for Chemistry in 1921, reserve their attacks for its pursuit, as in charging interest to lend money and to make profits.[38]

Ending money as capital

The first question to monetary reformers who would strip money of its capitalist features is to ask exactly how they might limit the operation of money to a simple medium of exchange and unit of account that is never used for gain, as credit, lent, or invested for making a profit. This question is apposite because a couple of thousand years ago Aristotle's argument against making profits shows that money already functioned as an end as well as a means well before capitalism took hold. Indeed, the practice of charging interest seems almost as old as the practice and notion of using money itself.[39]

One might ban the charging of interest but, in practice it would be hard to ban people giving others monetary credit without strings attached, such as requiring a guarantee – as in a mortgage, risking the loss of one's house – or the requirement to work off the debt and becoming slave labour. Banning such guarantees might well limit lending, even if people really wanted and needed to borrow money, which is quite likely while it remains.

Similarly, proposers for a currency such as Silvio Gesell's *Schwundgeld* – the value of which intentionally reduces, say, over three months, and eventually loses its value altogether – need to address a negative tendency to forced spending encouraged by such a mechanism.

In short, abolishing the use of money as a means to gain seems impossible, impractical and even nonsensical. Why have a 'money' that doesn't function like money as we know it? If capitalist practices and 'unequal' exchange are essential characteristics of money, the logical conclusion is to abolish money altogether.

Hornborg's complementary currencies

Human ecology anthropologist Alf Hornborg – an influential scholar within degrowth, ecological economics and environmental justice movements – is among those anti-capitalist social scientists who explore postcapitalism but cannot imagine a society without money. Similar to my arguments, Hornborg confirms an extremely close connection between money and capital, writing that 'capitalism *is* the aggregate logic of general purpose money.'[40] Yet Hornborg comes to a different conclusion. If money drives capitalism, he reasons, why don't we alter money in order to alter capitalism? In other words, he proposes a novel monetary system that he argues will avoid the irrationalities of current money and he envisages 'postcapitalism' as a capitalism without the abhorrent characteristics of capital.

'I cannot believe that it would be feasible to completely abolish money and markets in human societies', Hornborg writes, 'but I believe that money can be redesigned so that its inherent logic would be to increase diversity and sustainability, while reducing social inequalities and vulnerability.'[41] As such, Hornborg's 'postcapitalism' retains wage labour, entrepreneurs, taxes, trade, production for trade and banking. His proposal centres narrowly on replacing the current world monetary system with distinctive complementary currencies issued to national citizens via a basic income. He argues that 'separate spheres of exchange would insulate local sustainability and resilience from the deleterious effects of globalization and financial speculation.'[42]

Even if Hornborg criticises global currencies in contemporary capitalism for perverting efficiencies and exploiting people and Earth, he argues that 'local' complementary currencies would encourage economic re-localisation and result in efficiencies and benefits à la Adam Smith.[43] In short, his analysis of production for trade has it working in reverse ways at different scales.[44] Apparently, it is mainly at a global level that gross exploitation and negative 'ecologically unequal exchange' occur.[45] Hornborg is confident that people will overwhelmingly favour a local currency and economy. Indeed, a devout faith in small and local operations is common among contemporary sustainability advocates. Yet, the entire history of capitalist commerce is replete with determinedly contrary outcomes when localised economies working moderately well for Earth and people are drawn into competition with regional, national and global merchant (retail), industrial, or financial capital.[46]

ECOLOGICALLY UNEQUAL EXCHANGE

In the last half-century, studies and theories of national and international phenomena such as uneven development, underdevelopment and world-system analysis have been extended and challenged by recent elucidations – including by Alf Hornborg – of 'ecologically unequal exchange'. Ecologically unequal exchange is *'an asymmetric net flow of biophysical resources (e.g., embodied materials, energy, land, and labor) that is obscured by the apparent reciprocity of market prices'.*[47] This concept re-defines a long-observed fact that trade, development and growth are unfair, indeed unequal, and benefit rich countries to the disadvantage of poor countries.[48] By comparing what real wealth is lost from the majority to the minority world through trade, the concept and theory of ecologically unequal exchange simply reveals and re-packages a powerful dynamic that embraces labour time, materials and energy. These processes are seen to contribute to a larger and more complex phenomenon of 'ecological debt', including 'climate debt', framed in models of historic rather than simply synchronic time, or as stocks and flows associated with capitalist reproduction.

Ironically, given their intent, theorists in this area of ecologically unequal exchange resort to monetary exercises or methods of simplistic biophysical accounting to argue their case. By way of an example, Jason Hickel and colleagues re-evaluate South–North exchange using Köhler's method of applying World Bank purchasing power parity exchange rates to show that a \$62 trillion (in 2011 US\$) transfer took place to the benefit of the North from 1960 to 2018.[49] Other theorists refer to gigatonnes of raw material equivalents, exajoules of embodied energy, square kilometres of embodied land, and person-year equivalents of embodied labour.[50] Biophysical accounting tends to reduce a variety of incomparable real values to crude singular indicators, as a consequence sharing some of money's major negative characteristics. 'Raw material equivalents' blend all real social and ecological values into one compound mix, just as monetary perspectives reduce the richness of anything and everything to prices.

The real alternative is to work with real values, most easily appreciated at a micro-scale. For instance, North American degrowth activist-scholar Sam Bliss points to the efficacy of nonmonetary decisions made by self-provisioning household members who typically gain, grow, graze, or hunt in the wild for free food and share its consumption. Here, incommensurable use values are the foci of all participants who determine production and exchange based on appropriate quantities of specific real values through co-governance.[51]

The evidence and analyses of inequalities in labour, materials and energy inputs in production for trade presented by theorists of 'unequal exchange' have parallels with calls and arguments for a fair price, a just price and fair trade.[52] All assume equivalence, which seems to imply a concept of objectively rational value, such as labour-time, as the basis of trade. Discussions of equivalence, inequity and incomparability include Marx's framing of monetary exchange as a contradiction between a formal equality hiding an unequal content – appearing in explanations of his labour theory of value and his theory of surplus value.

My key point here is that, while the empirical data is clear and systemic injustice certainly occurs, the detailed theorisation of ecologically unequal exchange as the source of injustice is weak. Specifically, such concepts and studies are diminished to the extent that they fuse and confuse exchange value with use values (or, better, real values). Using a biophysical indicator reduces distinctive and variable, competing and complementary, biophysical contributions to ecosystems and the humans that live within them. Similarly, an 'emergy' unit related to energy fails to reflect or incorporate the multiplicity of different factors associated with various forms of energy, let alone materials.

AN ENERGY STANDARD: EMERGY

In the latter quarter of the twentieth century, Howard T. Odum developed the concept of 'emergy' as a unit for biophysical accounting within production. Odum argued that the energy contributing to production via externalities ignored in market-based prices meant that *an energy standard would be more comprehensive and meaningful than a monetary one*.[53] He regarded energy as the essential dynamic of human and ecosystem life, and studied ways energy worked in opposition to, rather than in concert with, monetary flows and economic accounting. Using his words, emergy constituted an attempt to design a 'real-value' standard for 'useful work' conceived in terms of energy and embracing energy quality, energy cost, embodied energy and energy 'transformity' which, like many indicators, was designed to quantify an embedded quality. Economic historian John Brolin regards Odum's emergy 'the most comprehensive and inclusive estimation tool of ecological unequal exchange'.[54]

Before Odum was born (1924), in the period between 1918 and 1921, the idea of a currency or standard based on energy had been debated by economists and planners within the Soviet state polity.[55] Similarly, precursors and contributors to the North American Technocracy movement of the 1930s wanted to substitute irrational market prices with an energy unit, a scientific measure of constituent work and materials, to facilitate production planned by engineers.[56] Odum had both a planner's perspective and a scientist's passion for order and classification, seeking a society that could reproduce itself within Earth's limits. However, Odum's concept of emergy has been justifiably criticised for its simplification, reductionism, and even irrelevance, especially with respect to distinctions made between energy and matter or materials.[57]

Interest in a unit of energy as a biophysical unit of account has been revived in recent decades. For instance, a 2013 New Economics Foundation (NEF) report by Collins and colleagues reviews a few dozen energy-related monetary and investment instrument schemes with the aim of identifying a unit of account and accounting system that might more adequately 'price nature' than conventional money and accountancy. Before Odum, Frederick Soddy had sought to use the lens of the laws of thermodynamics to inform the design of a money that might more realistically approximate a measure and monitor of our use of nature in production. Such physical scientists were under no illusion that market-based prices did not take nature into account. However, the NEF economists seem to assume that money itself actually evolved to measure and monitor our use of nature.[58]

Collins and colleagues specifically seek a unit of account and associated form of bookkeeping that might mean that economic practices incorporate the laws of thermodynamics and embrace 'non-substitutability', i.e., prevent the compounding of artificial (human-made) capital for natural capital in current forms of accounting.[59] One problem here is that most production entangles both human-made built and machinery assets, and natural assets, such as land, in varying proportions. Moreover, some forms of production, say ecoforestry, use practices that support sustainability while others, such as logging old-growth forest to produce woodchips for paper, do not. As such, the NEF report illustrates the false leads, imponderables and alleyways that riddle alternative currency proposals, literature and practice.

In short, Collins and colleagues want to remedy the deficiencies of conventional money by grounding its value in energy qua nature. They contend that this will revive trust in money and reduce monetary instability and environmental destruction while supporting a transition to renewable energy. Pre-empting aspects of Hornborg's approach, they declare a demand for 'one or more stable reference units of value attached to the planet's natural sustainable resources', and imagine that 'a range of different and complementary schemes at local, national and international levels' might be unified 'via incremental experimentation, innovation, and development of a multiplicity of new energy monies'.[60]

Yet, all such efforts have lacked traction in practice. Ecological economist Kristofer Dittmer's theoretical and empirical study exploring alternative currencies and other monetary reforms to achieve ecological sustainability and social equity finds that, in terms of a strategic degrowth transformation, there is little potential in local currency networks, in, for instance, Venezuela's experiment with communal currencies, or in Green politicians' attraction to 100 per cent reserve banking schemes.[61]

ECOLOGICAL FOOTPRINT ACCOUNTING: THE CURRENCY OF GLOBAL HECTARES

Yet another approach is taken by Mathis Wackernagel and William Rees in their 'ecological footprint', developed in the early 1990s. For application by businesses and governments, this ecological accounting features '*biologically productive surfaces of the Earth* as its currency'. Ecological footprint accounting goes beyond the monetary approach of the aforementioned international standard System of Environmental-Economic Accounting for Agriculture, Forestry and Fisheries, but mimics capitalist double-entry bookkeeping in that the solution to contemporary sustainability challenges is framed in terms of 'ecological capital', assessing biocapacity as income, and human demands on nature as expenditure.[62]

Ecological footprint accounts are constructed from data at national, regional and city scales, and aggregated at a planetary scale determined to be 1.63 'global hectares' per capita in 2016.[63] According to this ledger, in 2019, global human productive use of nature had overshot the biocapacity of Earth by 75 per cent.[64] However, critics point out that ecological footprint methodology is inadequate, with data constituting the footprint incomplete, for example, failing to account for certain degradation of nature.[65] Significantly, in as much as degradation of resources is *underestimated*, they follow a gross domestic product national account-ing approach.[66]

Most significantly, the ecological footprint's co-creators wax lyrical about money, especially as a tool of comparison. 'Complex processes,' it is argued, 'can be summed up in one single number'; this index or 'essence' of erstwhile complex issues offers a useful term with which to negotiate.[67] As such, the ecological footprint perspective has certain par-allels with the origins of money as a tool of management concocted by state officials for goods of tribute, whereby one form of in-kind tribute might substitute for another.[68]

Other points can be made about misrepresenting the ecological foot-print indicator in terms of a 'money'. In reality, it appears much more like a *ration* ticket than money as we know it today, as a means of exchange and abstract claim to future products unbound by any biophysical limits. Still, the ecological footprint is even better conceived of as an in-kind maximum basic income tied to an imaginary property right over an average area of biologically productive land and water available to each person.

This whole discussion – on ways we might re-imagine money – shows how loosely and confusingly the concept can be applied. Economic framings and concepts of the world, nature, and relationships between us clearly prevent, rather than advance, solutions to our ecological crises. Indeed, authors of a 2015 essay analysing the ramifications of calculating and integrating carbon emissions in national accounting systems con-cluded that, even if such efforts were 'presented as a revolutionary way of simplifying things in order to take action', the mere act of 'quantifica-tion makes things much more complicated and raises many questions'.[69]

So, what is the alternative to both money and alternative monies?

AN ECONOMY *IN NATURA*

Contemporary environmental philosopher John O'Neill highlights the contrast between 'science-based' and 'science-sceptical' approaches to evaluating economic processes in production and distribution, as well as singling out for examination the thought of socialist Otto Neurath, a leader of the mid-1920s–mid-1930s intellectual Vienna Circle. In contrast to the approach of a planner, for whom a monetary unit offers a necessary tool of management, the institutionalist Neurath argued for an economy based on use values, 'a non-market "economy in kind", an economy *in natura*'. As such, he was referring to a kind of nonmonetary economy (one version of which is described in Chapter 3 of this volume). According to Neurath, the singular use of any common unit – whether monetary, work hours, or energy related – was inappropriate for decision making in a socialist economy that focused on quality, needs, well-being, social conditions and intergenerational concerns. Socialist values, principles and aims demanded evaluation based on incommensurable, even immeasurable, social and ecological factors. Decision making would need to be responsible, precautionary and holistic, taking account of incomplete knowledge, uncertainty and risks.[70]

O'Neill describes how Austrian-British liberal economist and philosopher Friedrich Hayek derided Neurath's approach on the basis that it seemed impossible to collect and assess so many multiple factors. Moreover, Hayek idealised market prices and the processes involved in their constitution, believing that they reflected the main interests and factors relevant to production and social preferences. This viewpoint is of singular importance because it reflects a widespread, if groundless, faith in the market. Neurath saw Hayek's approach as pseudo-rationalist and defended his own position for avoiding the 'illusion of complete knowledge' that Hayek attributed to the market system.[71]

Indeed, Neurath stood out within early Soviet debates on a moneyless economy due to his almost unique appreciation of the deficiencies of indicators. 'Neurath was clearer and more definite – there was no place for "intermediate calculation" as such in labour or energy,' point out Magnin and Nenovsky. 'Calculation in-kind was the only alternative to monetary calculation.'[72]

O'Neill has resuscitated Neurath's approach within contemporary debates. He states that from the point of view of human well-being, concepts and mechanisms associated with 'natural capital' and 'ecosystem services' reduce and simplify both nature's contribution to production and its complex, all-encompassing, roles in people's lives.[73] O'Neill's discussions underscore the complexity and uniqueness of particular species, ecological relationships, ecosystems and people – all of which become obliterated or contorted within market prices. Market-based processes of exchange and financialisation abstract elements from their integrated context within human and nonhuman relations and their active co-contributions to dynamic human and ecosystem communities. Markets standardise, simplify, ignore, exaggerate and contort real ecological and social values. In short:

Financial markets fail to capture what is at stake in the loss of places, habitats and ecosystems that matter to people and communities. They create perverse forms of dependence of the conservation of environmental goods on environmental damage elsewhere. The treatment of nature as capital is not a solution to the problems of environmental loss. Rather, it is part of the problem.[74]

NATURAL VALUES VERSUS EXCHANGE VALUE

All the components and aspects of ecological systems upon which we depend in order to live offer a host of both well-recognised and invisible or unknown real values. As such, our authentic and optimum position is to be at one with, to work with, nature. Yet, market-oriented approaches embody dualism between people and the rest of nature as an everyday practice. That market societies objectify nature is clear in the definition of economics as a study of allocating scarce resources for the singular purpose of maximising social welfare. Even more clearly, both the practice of trade (monetary exchange) and production for trade are anthropocentric – marginalising values of Earth. Retrofitting such values using market-based mechanisms, such as water and carbon trading, has proved either impossible or unwieldy and inefficient.

Many environmentalists concur with capitalist critiques of the ecosocialist movement based as they are on the call for 'system change not climate change'.[75] In the early 2020s, the real-valuist camp within ecosocialism proper is a tiny, even if distinct and acknowledged, position.[76] Moreover, the position of majority-world post-development ecosocialists – who envisage a transformation to grassroots community-based modes of production networked across a pluriverse globe – is quite consistent with real valuism.[77] Yet the majority ecosocialist position seems to be democratic socialist, with an associated tendency to see money or other reductive indicators as tools of management. Their approach is top-down regulation of a modified market, again unwieldy and inefficient compared with local and direct co-governance for collective sufficiency, with networks for wider governance and nonmonetary exchange as necessary.

The discussion in this chapter – taken up again in Chapter 8 – shows that those exploring and experimenting with quasi-eco-monies and resource accounting readily expose endemic characteristics of units of account to reduce, contort, or neglect the whole panoply of ecological and human values and potential. Given the urgent need to halt and reverse environmental degradation, there is a strong rationale for eschewing monetary and market mechanisms in favour of a totally non-monetary Yenomon-style society built on real values.

Market-based human–nature dualism can be broken down once we appreciate that climate change and many other environmental crises are generated by capitalism, and that we must move beyond it. As such, postcapitalism is appreciated as direct co-governance on the basis of real values incorporating the potential, limits and needs of both humans and Earth.

At this point, we are at one with those who successfully blockaded the site of a planned international airport in France at Notre Dame de Landes Zone à Défendre with the banner: 'We do not defend nature: We are the nature that defends itself.'[78]

5
Women's Liberation:
Equality and Values

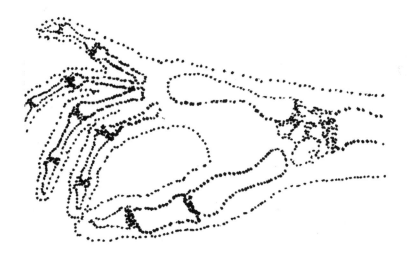

The stance 'We are the nature that defends itself' not only situates the environmental movement as it faces global warming but also resonates within the radical, ecofeminist quarters of women's liberation. Similar to environmental externalities, housework and tasks of care fall outside the ambit of prices and price making for goods and services in the market-oriented accounts of capitalist managers. Even women's integration into paid work over the last half-century has tended to be prejudicial compared with the status, salaries, treatment and conditions of males. Consequently, radical ecofeminists argue for a socio-political revolution that would both overturn exploitation and domination of nature in terms of energy, materials, re-creation and wastes, and embrace women who are essential to the social reproduction of human beings. In contrast, in simply arguing for wage equity, representation in all areas and equal rights, liberal reformist feminists' demands have parallels with market-oriented sustainability advocates: 'If you can't beat them, join them.'

If essentialist ecofeminists regard the connection between women and nature intrinsic, the ecofeminists drawn on here simply observe parallels between capitalist exploitation of nature and women. Significantly, French feminist writer Françoise D'Eaubonne saw the role of the movement that she coined *'ecofeminisme'* as transforming relations between both nature and people, and females and males.[1] Women's often nurturing and experiential approach is both a by-product of performed social roles and more fundamentally human than socially constructed stereotypes of hard, objective masculine approaches. As such, American philosopher and historian of science Carolyn Merchant's constructivist approach upsets notions of objective 'scientific' facts or truths to situate all definitions of nature as malleable and reflecting their authors' understanding of reality. Merchant highlights active, revolutionary ways of conceiving of nature, drawing on recent scientific thinking such as chaos and complexity theories. Challenging a *man*ager's perspective, she concludes that our approach to nature should be one of an appreciative partner and that, in a circumstantial way, our 'real world is both orderly and disorderly, predictable and unpredictable, controllable and uncontrollable, depending on context and situation.'[2]

This chapter engages with select, mainly ecofeminist, work to argue that capitalist market-based practices accentuate and generate socio-political gender dualisms. The discussion reveals that markets marginalise certain activities and that monetary relations function to create social inequalities that disrupt, corrupt and ultimately prohibit humane philosophies, polities and relationships. Exchange value – simply 'value' in political economy – fails to represent or measure real, everyday, humane and ecologically significant values. Instead, our liberation as humans depends on us adopting commoning economies of sufficiency, where all contribute and everyone gains a modest livelihood. For German 'ecommony' advocate and queer feminist Friederike Habermann, this entails moving beyond both markets and money.

'I' AND 'US'

While acknowledging certain radical action and individuals, such as Alexandra Kollantai and Louise Michel, first-wave feminism accompanying capitalist development was characteristically reformist with a liberal focus on equalising women's political and other legal rights with those of men, such as rights to property. In the 1960s and 1970s, at a time of civic unrest focusing on human liberation more generally, second-wave feminism was characterised more by women's *liberation* – drawing on and engaging across classes and cultures of women, thrusting in every direction for women to be free to do anything humanly possible. Theoretical currents delved into radical political economies of women's being in capitalist societies. Indeed, my own critique of money evolved in, and with, the women's liberation movement through horizontal organising in collectives and solidarity, consciousness-raising, exposing and addressing sexualised violence within the fracturing norms of marriage and family. I shared with many other radical women activists the experience of an evolving philosophy of self, of humane being, within this movement.

Following 'personal is the political' agency, and working collectively, we came out as liberationists to men and women alike, if distinctly differently. With men we often wore armours and needed to work hard, with women we used a nurturing approach. The more humane men and women got it: this movement could liberate everyone. I edited a short-lived underground feminist journal in which my singular contribution was to express the argument that we drop gendered language/identities altogether. There were but 'I's and 'you's and 'us'. Even as a cis-het woman, I would prefer to think of myself and others as an 'it'. Through the holistic successes of the women's liberation movement, I became an advocate of grassroots organising for transformational change. One must practice what one preaches; one must test the theory in, not just on, the ground; one must live the thought, the dream, the hell.

After analysing the failures of environmental and women's liberation movements in the mid-1970s, I left paid work as a shit-kicker to enter the already neoliberalising university sector. I continued activism in a program of Latin American studies that enabled me to understand global political economy. I identified more and more with Marxist approaches even if in eclectic, indeed original, ways. In praxis I had all the hallmarks of a nonmarket socialist before I encountered its existence.[3] It took till the late 2010s, substantially through activism in the climate justice and degrowth movements, for me to fully appreciate and integrate both the 'real value' ('no-money') and ecofeminist strands into a solid vision of and strategies for postcapitalism. This personal account is necessary. I do not apologise for saying that this analysis comes from my soul and passions – a weakness only if one believes the brain is an autonomous organ and objectivity a feasible stance.

IS 'WOMEN'S WORK' REALLY 'WORK'?

Many debates within women's liberation revolved around 'work', going well beyond questioning barriers to paid work in the marketplace.[4] A 1969 article by Canadian scientist Margaret Benston highlights this current by arguing that women's housework and care of household members supports capitalist, paid, work.[5] She refers to an earlier classic work, by British psychoanalyst and socialist feminist Juliet Mitchell, that underscores the ways in which women were not only men's personal lackeys but also invisible slaves of the capitalist system.[6] It is a woman's hand that rocks the societal cradle, singularly responsible for social reproduction.[7] In a theoretical sense, this realisation had elements of women becoming a self-conscious 'class' in and of itself. Moreover, political and economic liberation of women became a clearer necessity within, and for, total liberation. Such critiques and ideas of liberation for all contributed to novel perspectives on Marx's works, and of communism in Soviet states that failed to acknowledge that fully human and humane agency required holistic transformation: 'until the last chains fall, freedom will make slaves of us all.'[8]

Benston's article focuses on the unpaid nature of women's home and care work:

> In a society in which money determines value, women are a group who work outside the money economy. Their work is not worth money, is therefore valueless, is therefore not even real work. And women themselves, who do this valueless work, can hardly be expected to be worth as much as men, who work for money. In structural terms, the closest thing to the condition of women is the condition of others who are or were also outside of commodity production, i.e., serfs and peasants.[9]

Her analysis keeps close to monetary aspects, arguing that the site of precapitalist work is the household, variously composed and constituted towards self-provisioning, meaning that productivity is initiated and evaluated on the basis of direct and immediate use values. But all that changes with production for trade, writes Benston. Now, the focus is exchange value with, on the one hand, a substantially male workforce organised in factories and offices and industrialised agriculture with, on the other hand, privatised and non-monetised work in the house, deemed the role of women, mothers, spouses and sisters. Even socialist theory, and social production in the communist experiments of the twentieth century, did not abolish the concept and practice of relegating specific work to women.[10] This is significant because, just as nineteenth-century American economist Francis Walker argued that 'money is what money does', women (and men) *are* what they do.

Arguably, the greatest achievements of the last half-century of the women's movement have relied on its grassroots horizontal organisation, personal-is-the-political agitation and sisterly solidarity. Women's liberation assemblies and advice to one another to 'shoot in all directions' has had a distinctively destabilising effect on society. Women's liberation has meant disputes in kitchens, bathrooms and bedrooms as much as in offices, cultural venues, boardrooms and parliaments. Discussions in the women's movement on social reproduction led in radical politico-economic directions, such as a provocative Wages for Housework current calling for remuneration for all the activities related to social reproduction, and focusing on the economy and capital(ists).[11] If money denoted value, respect and independence, then women deserved direct and explicit monetary recognition.

Wages for Housework?

The New York Wages for Housework Committee – that embraced black and anti-colonial movements – was inspired by the arguments of Mariarosa Dalla Costa 'that, far from being the legacy of a pre-capitalist society, housework has been a fundamental element of capitalist accumulation, being the production of "labour-power" and, as such, the condition for every form of work.'[12] The continuing significance of this line of thought is highlighted by a 2020 Oxfam report where a conservative estimate is made that remunerating all females over 15 years of age for their unpaid care work would cost more than US$10.8 trillion per annum.[13] Indeed, Susan Ferguson indicates that three-quarters of all unpaid care and domestic work on a global level, is performed by women.[14] Just after COVID-19 hit Australia, the effects were unduly felt by women. Women represented more than 80 per cent of the decline in student enrolments in May 2020 compared with May 2019 'likely because of caring responsibilities'. These responsibilities meant that more women were exposed to the pandemic in the course of their work and that they had to work more on unpaid duties at home.[15]

Silvia Federici has called on women to struggle for monetary independence as a strategy for personal autonomy and collective power, to campaign for the right to a job, equal pay for equal work and guaranteed minimum incomes. At the same time, she acknowledges that money is a capitalist tool of 'enslavement', as such recommending an initial strategy of 're-appropriation' in the form of campaigning collectively for free social infrastructure to ease invisible and unpaid 'daily reproduction'.[16] Yet, this avenue has proved bleak.[17] Moreover, most public infrastructure managed by state agencies operates in the context of markets and monetary relations, so the knot at the centre of this wicked problem only really loosens once Federici makes commoning our future, as discussed further below. Meanwhile, a discussion of ecofeminist theory on a subsistence economy, and engagement with notions of 'value', work and economy act as stepping stones to commoning.

THE SUBSISTENCE ECONOMY

By the 1970s, debates of ecofeminists such as the German sociological Bielefeld School were revealing constructive lines of thought in examining and theorising concepts of women and nature, ecology and life.[18] Claudia von Werlhof made an insightful observation on parallels made between nature and women when she wrote: 'The concept of nature is not determined by biology but by economics: it does not distinguish between people and animals but between people and people – and it varies.'[19] Here, workers, material and energy become the same sausage meat known as 'nature'. Equally, every man 'is given a mini-monopoly over a woman'.[20] Woman is nature, exploited, free, taken and humiliated.

Critiquing and embellishing the confounding of 'nature' and 'woman' through a discourse integrating 'ecology' and 'life' has continued within and outside ecofeminist debates. The analysis of Maria Mies in *Patriarchy and Accumulation on a World Scale: Women in the International Division of Labour* iterates hierarchical dualism at every level, from the body and head to what has become known as the majority and minority worlds.[21] In contrast, by asking 'what would a society be like in which women, nature and colonies were not exploited in the name of the accumulation of ever more wealth and money?', Mies concludes that such a society would need to prioritise autonomy, horizontalism and decentralisation.[22] Moreover, women's caring roles mean that they develop intimate knowledge and skills associated with core subsistence tasks essential to fulfil basic needs of humans for food, clothing, shelter, respect, concern, mutual care and support.

As such, the scope of work by Mies and other ecofeminists, including Carolyn Merchant, pre-empted core concerns and principles of the twenty-first-century degrowth and climate justice movements. For instance, Mies would state that 'the aim of all work and human endeavour is not a never-ending expansion of wealth and commodities, but human happiness (as the early socialists had seen it), or the production of life itself.'[23] Mies considers both men and women as beings of nature but she counters TINA (there is no alternative) with SITA (subsistence is the alternative).[24] The parallels with today's food sovereignty, food security, Indigenous and peasant movements are clear. Mies iterates that a simple life of subsistence is necessary because 'our human universe is finite, our body is finite, the earth is finite.'[25]

Growing concerns around unsustainable practices associated with capitalist activities has magnified the importance of this current, who appreciated the organisational prerogatives of fulfilling our basic needs through cooperation, care-fullness and conscious marginalisation of market-based drives associated with paid work and growth economies.[26] The work of the ecofeminist Bielefeld School complements core arguments and philosophies of ecofeminists of the global South, such as Vandana Shiva, and Silvia Federici's discussions of an ecofeminist post-capitalism based on the commons. The Bielefeld School also informs the development of 'ecommony' in the work of Friederike Habermann. But, before discussing commoning and nonmonetary futures, we examine how and why 'value' has been problematically interpreted by key feminists.

TO BE OR NOT TO BE: EXCHANGE VALUE

Ecofeminists have highlighted women's and Earth's unaccounted-for contributions to capitalist (exchange) value. Mies' iceberg economy displays capital and labour atop, such that poking out of the sea, for all to see, are the chief concerns of capitalist manager-owners and economists. Still, holding up the whole and hidden underneath, in the ocean below, is the larger mass of unaccounted-for contributions to value: 'women's unpaid housework, the work of subsistence peasants, the work done under colonized conditions, and nature's production.'[27] Invisible work amounts to the greater part of necessary everyday activities keeping humans alive.

But, what does this insight mean? How might such work be authentically valued given it does not exchange for a price in the capitalist market?

Here, we find ourselves in a similar place to ecological economists who seek to integrate the worth of nature into the reproduction of capitalism. Efforts to acknowledge and remunerate the contributions of housework and care to total production have clear parallels with efforts to integrate nature within capitalist accounting systems (see Chapter 4), and raise similar questions. What price the regenerative activities of forests and oceans? What price the reproductive activities of women? What price nurturing, enhancing and stewarding life? But these questions need to be put into yet another context. What price the work of the underpaid artist or craftsperson?

In the 1970s, I came to such questions not only as a women's liberationist but also as a would-be artist, as a would-be writer, with an acute consciousness that one can create great work that is unacknowledged and unpaid or underpaid despite society benefiting from it, especially after one's death. From the beginning, I had a broader set of questions than women's liberationist ones. I started to wonder whether the unrecognised contributions of nature and housework made the more general character and constitution of monetary values and prices suspect. Did we women really want our social status reduced to, and dependent on, a monetary note or a salary in a world riddled with monetary inequities? Might this tactic for reaching equality mean swapping one form of subservience for another?

Moreover, given the circular and interdependent nature of the value of money, perhaps we could only get paid for housework at the expense of other paid workers in the household? In other words, a small family with two parents who shared their incomes might end up no better – even worse – off as a unit. In other words, I had no illusion that capital(ists) would not pay for our equality. Even if they agreed to pay extra by way of wages for housework, the costs would flow through as raised prices of commodities necessary for our existence.

Nevertheless, the unpaid-for-real-work framing is perfectly legitimate and has great traction in capitalist settings. The quantification of unpaid housework and care, and time-use surveys broken down according to gender, have become regular tasks in the collection of national statistics, as a consequence of a greater consciousness of women's work in mainstream society. They show that, even after reforms to women's status and scope of action, the average woman still spends much more time than the average man doing unpaid work at home for other household members.[28] Associated studies find that even as devices – such as vacuum cleaners, clothes washing machines and dishwashers – have been created to lighten and minimise housework, there is a greater tendency for their use to drive household standards higher, for housework tasks to expand rather than free up time otherwise devoted to housework.

Meanwhile, in late stage capitalism, employers have tended to treat women as an active and reserve supply of labour and to denigrate calls for direct monetary remuneration of work in 'private' homes in favour of subsidies for commercial forms of childcare, aged care and housework. So, the strong tendency in capitalism is for all housework and care tasks to become commodified. Capital continues to colonise, leaving women in their literal 'no-man's land' unless they play the capitalist game, becoming agents of market relations where all work is directly or indirectly linked to production for trade.

VALUING THE UNPAID WORK OF WOMEN AND OTHERS

When Marx refers to economic concepts such as 'value', he refers exclusively to real market-based practices, not ideal norms. In Marx's works analysing capitalist practices, 'value' relates to 'exchange value', 'monetary value', or 'price' in a cascading series of concepts from the most abstract (value) to the most concrete (price). Yet, certain critics, and even sympathisers, mistake Marx's concept of value as his notion of what might hold in an ideal world. As such, in elaborating value, Marx is charged for failing to see that both nature and women's work contribute to the formation of value in the production of commodities.

While authors such as John Bellamy Foster have shown Marx's consciousness of and concerns for nature with respect to capitalist production, much of Marx's economic work marginalises nature. Nature is ignored in as much as the object of his analysis is capitalist practices and relations of production and, for instance, where air and water is free, it is not accounted for as a cost to production.[29] This is not because Marx did not believe that nature, or women, did valuable work, but that ordinary, everyday market practices conspire to denigrate both. The same is true for anyone, man or woman, doing any kind of unpaid work. This point is of utmost significance in coursing through feminist debates that sometimes confuse works by followers or interpreters of Marx or practices of really-existing socialism or communism with his thought and work.

Take, for instance, labourist interpretations of Marx that imbue Mies' conclusion that 'labour for socialists is not only the necessary curse or burden, but also the motor that leads mankind to the transition to the true communist society.'[30] In other words, communism is achieved through technological advance.[31] She labours this point regarding 'Marxist views on technological progress and the communist vision of a true society because these ideas are shared by most socialists, as well as by many feminist socialists'.[32] Yet her interpretation is not readily applicable to certain interpretations of Marx, significantly those such as ecosocialism and Autonomist Marxism, which are streams attractive to current leftist youth, including women.[33]

Autonomist Marxist Silvia Federici intervenes in feminist discourses on Marx in a variety of subtle ways, including addressing the question: 'Why did Marx overlook that part of reproductive work that is most essential to the production of labor power?'[34] While Federici correctly argues that Marx's analysis 'leaves untheorized some of the activities and social relations that are most essential for the production of labour power', I think that patriarchal reasons for his neglect might be as unfounded as environmentalists' conclusions that Marx considered nature insignificant in the constitution of value because he did not value nature.[35] In fact, similar to environmental externalities, housework and tasks of care also fall outside the ambit of prices and price making for goods and services that emanate in the market-oriented accounts of capitalist managers. It was always thus and, given that the constitution of exchange value is the object of Marx's analysis, this neglect exists in the object of his analysis, not in him as the analyst.[36]

Significantly, from Marx's perspective, even if unpaid housework and care constitute vital use values as goods and services, neither constitute commodity production nor a contribution to 'the economy' specifically because they arise within nonmonetary relations. Housework and care are mere use values arising from personal arrangements. Capitalist activities by their very nature take a monetary form; nonmonetary personal relationships or activities are ruled out of court as nonmarket practices. Regarding housework and care, every worker has distinct personal circumstances, which change over time. They might look after themselves or share household and care duties, they might pay people to do housework and childcare, or they might depend on a partner, relative, or friend to gift them such services.

In contrast to housework, labour-power evolves and devolves in certain standard ways under capitalist management of the reproduction of commodities. The capitalist process of spending money to pay for inputs to production/work that produces commodities of greater value than invested ($M\to C\to P[work]\to C'\to M'$) is exclusive. Even so, it exploitatively absorbs ever so many unpaid contributions, such as free air from nature for workers to breathe as they work; workers paying for necessary transport, rest and therapy due to work, and gratuitous unaccounted-for care and energy expended in the office, factory, or field in excess of paid work time. Beyond all this there is so much valuable – for example, cultural and intellectual – work that remains unpaid and without which we would feel bereft. Indeed, Marx's analysis, *his regular unpaid work*, falls into this category. The Marx family more often than not relied on Engels' charity for sustenance. Marx neither defined his own work in labourist terms nor regarded his analytical work a waste of time. He saw it as the most valuable activity he could do contra a brutally unfair, unjust and highly damaging social system.

The very definition of labour power is monetary and nothing outside capitalist accounting is acknowledged in Marxist or non-Marxist mainstream analyses of exchange value. This is the case whether one is a practising capitalist, an economist enthralled with or suspicious of capitalism, or revolutionary thinkers such as Marx. In as much as Marx sees waged labour as the key arena of a monetary contest between labour and capital, he regards it an irrational and unjust relationship and dynamic. Marx did not create or idealise exchange value, or value as such. He examined exchange value as a social fact, a reality of production for trade. Marx despised the notion and practice of creating 'exchange value', capitalism's essential form.

When Marx analyses 'value', the multi-dimensional core of exchange value, he analyses the engine of capitalist development. He does not like this value, he does not defend it. Marx exposes this value as absurd. He calls us to revolt against such value. In a complementary way to Marx's understanding of capital, and its heart 'value', Maria Mies hits the nail on the head when she declares: 'Women should never forget that it is we who produce life, not capital.'[37] This line thrusts in the anti-economic, anti-capitalist direction that we need to take, rather than work towards a deep and broad reform of capitalist exchange value accounting that would ultimately incorporate *every human and nonhuman factor* associated with production by giving it a real or nominal price. Since everything is ultimately connected with everything else, it would be both impossible and a waste of time to monetise all relations. Why not *totally* re-define and substitute value in real, nonmonetary, ways?

Indeed, even if Mies calls for a 'feminist concept of labour' in which work is purposeful and necessary for the worker and their society, she recognises that this is impossible in production for trade. Rather, we require a society based on collective production for direct use, similar to Yenomon (see Chapter 3, this volume) with the significant exception that Mies does not rule out money. Still, writing in the mid-1980s, she concludes that if the developed world's back-to-the-land movement is largely middle class, such 'alternative land freaks' might well be 'the first to realize that one cannot eat money and that food does not grow out of computers'. She binds transformation in such countries with liberating futures for the underdeveloped world, and the liberation of women with men assuming tasks of housework and care.[38]

Indeed, we can fast-forward to a 2015 work to find the practices of majority world women meeting subsistence economy theory. Contra transnational corporatisation of food production, in *Who Really Feeds the World?*, Vandana Shiva argues a way forward that re-locates humans within nature via agroecology, 'the scientific paradigm that covers all ancient, sustainable, and traditional farming systems that were based on ecological systems'. She advocates (re)localisation, nonviolent cooperativism, small-scale farming, biodiversity and maintaining, indeed extending, already women-driven food provisioning 'based on sharing and caring, and on conservation and well-being'.[39] In the penultimate chapter, Shiva refers to her and Mies' 1996 Leipzig Appeal for Food Security in Women's Hands to emphasise the same points, including that 'men must share the necessary work, be it paid or unpaid'.[40] This real solution to valuing women and valuing nature presents a complex challenge in terms of strategy, due to the omnipotence of what Mies and Bennholdt-Thomsen refer to as 'money orientation'.

MONEY ORIENTATION

Writing on urban life and money, Veronika Bennholdt-Thomsen contrasts women's 'subsistence orientation' to the 'money orientation' of capitalism, wherein economic growth absorbs nature's abundance and projects it as if the work of capital.[41] She underscores a point made by many analysts that, without appearing violent, 'money has become the most effective mechanism for destroying subsistence.'[42] Indeed, Mies and Bennholdt-Thomsen identify monetary value as the source of a 'war against subsistence'; capital has denigrated subsistence economies.[43] They wring their hands: 'How did this alienation between people and their work develop to the point that the most lifeless thing of all, money, is seen as the source of life and our own life-producing subsistence work is seen as the source of death?'[44]

Bennholdt-Thomsen refers to all the ways that the capitalist state backs its legal tender in any economic and financial crisis which, by the very nature of the case, prompts a monetary crisis. Think auster-ity measures that cause riots on streets and their fatal repression by the police, even the armies, of self-righteous governments. The centrality of money inspires totalitarianism. She writes that once money symbolises subsistence, 'we are recruited':[45]

Modern humans deprive themselves of their sovereignty and with it their human dignity by daily allowing the laws of the money system to rule their lives. By believing in the equation – Money = Existence = Food = Livelihood – they subordinate their lives to a superior power. The collective fiction that money really has an essential value for survival is only possible if everyone believes that the value of a sum of money is actually the claimed value ... as long as everyone accepts the rule of the superior power which guarantees the equation.[46]

Ethics in monetary exchange

In *The Subsistence Perspective*, Mies and Bennholdt-Thomsen focus on market exchange in 'subsistence markets'. Here, most significantly, they frame price-formation as malleable to the ethics of exchangers, which erects a barrier to taking a no-money route. They argue against econ-omistic analyses of prices to suggest that the *ethics* of price makers and price takers is the real issue. Contra economistic perspectives of market exchange and barter framed as equivalent exchange, and the prevail-ing trend of economists to debunk subsistence markets as irrational, they argue that market exchange within subsistence economies tends to be more ethical. Mies and Bennholdt-Thomsen go further than Karl Polanyi, who framed such subsistence economies as embedded in their socio-political culture, to argue that, in certain contemporary markets, cultures prevail to disrupt and marginalise the calculative and competitive fervour embodied in mainstream economists' ideas of 'homo economicus'.[47]

Referring to a study of trading in the Mexican town Juchitán (Oaxaca), Mies and Bennholdt-Thomsen argue that women within this matrifocal culture tend to cultivate ethical practices by persisting in 'good, fine, nurturing and caring' market practices.[48] They observe subsistence market activities as gendered within a moral solidarity of obligation and fairness whereas the 'supposedly inherent laws of the market belong together with the warlike view of economics and the modern relationship between the sexes'.[49] They regard the idea 'that the market operates according to inherent abstract laws' as a lie upheld to hide self-interested behaviour and ideals, to conclude that the apparently fairer ways in which markets operate in subsistence economies 'should be restored'.[50]

Harking back to a 1992 work of Mies, they call for a new moral economy, and blame 'to a significant degree' Marxist theory for the neglect and tone of discourse regarding what they contend are distinctly different moralities within trade.[51] Significantly, Mies' and Bennholdt-Thomsen's study refers to women mainly involved in exchanging food in a town that effectively banned an American store from operating a branch there. In other words, these women struggled, like workers do in a strike, against the laws of the global market rather than being, as Mies and Bennholdt-Thomsen contend, 'seamlessly integrated into the national and international market'. As such Mies' and Bennholdt-Thomsen's notion that the '[m]arket and subsistence are not contradictory' only really holds once they admit that 'there have been and still are countless different kinds of exchange relationship, both outside the market altogether and in conjunction with the modern market economy'.[52]

It becomes clear in their work that Mies and Bennholdt-Thomsen compound 'exchange' as a universal category with the particular monetary exchange category of 'trade' to imply that both can operate via moral or ethical behaviour. This conflation feeds into a line of argument in their other works which, put simply, is 'Yes to money, no to money-capital'. While, in a 2001 work, Bennholdt-Thomsen judges it 'pure nonsense' to imagine that 'a complex society like ours can't function without money', she finds the real source of the trouble 'in how we deal with money, rather than in money itself'.[53] She iterates a point made in another work with Mies where, in their vision of a subsistence economy, 'Money would be a means of circulation but cease to be a means of accumulation'.[54] Reference is made to economic philosopher Silvio Gesell's theory – redolent of French Proudhonist theories and age-old Christian and Moslem morals around money and its use – to counsel that money used as a means of exchange is not problematic whereas interest must be banned, limited, or regulated.[55] Nevertheless, they criticise alternative local currency schemes in as much as such schemes neglect matters of production, solidarity and women.[56]

This ambivalence continues in a 2011 work even though, by this time, Bennholdt-Thomsen has become more supportive of alternative local currencies where time or an exchange rate with a formal state money is the standard. Furthermore, influenced by Friederike Habermann's reports of schemes that are free of barter and exchange logic (discussed below), she fleetingly concedes that society might institute 'a body of regulations beyond the exchange logic of money'.[57] At the same time, Bennholdt-Thomsen persists with arguments that money as a means of exchange is 'neutral' and that the real problem is money as a commodity, an interest-bearing loan.

Applying her perspective to the future of cities, Bennholdt-Thomsen argues for decentralised self-reliance through self-provisioning, small and personal enterprises, local economies based on the use values of food and housing, with cities bound to their regional hinterlands.[58] Yet, Habermann identifies all such features as incompatible with a monetary economy; 'ultimately subsistence merely means relations of production beyond barter and/or oppressive systems.'[59] Similarly, in Australian ecofeminist Ariel Salleh's 'synergistic economy' – advanced with respect to Indigenous peoples and economies of the majority world – 'a non-monetised society–nature metabolism' flourishes.[60]

Idealist tendencies

In summary, the Bielefeld School is equivocal about ways to deal with money. Frequently, Mies' analyses and strategic concerns are structural. Yet, her focus on the *ethics* of monetary transactors is quite Hegelian (idealist), as if transactors have more room to move and agency than I think often occurs in practice. In an associated way, I find Mies' arguments for a strategic consumer boycott much less convincing than her calls to gain control of production via production for direct use, in order to crowd out capitalism and bring together women of the majority and minority worlds.

Significantly, Mies does acknowledge, indeed even cautions, that consuming for collective use can 'degenerate into the well-known "informal" sector which then, in a dual economy, would only serve the formal sector'. She makes autonomy paramount here, otherwise capitalism (the formal sector) 'would go on as before to produce its destructive high tech and other useless commodities, and the informal sector production would again mainly subsidize wages in the formal sector'.[61] This point relates to the turn taken by the influential Gibson-Graham community economies field, which emerged in the latter half of the 1990s, arguing 'that the dominance of capitalism is more discursive than real, that our imaginaries are colonised by capitalocentric interpretations of economies'.[62] The community economies approach certainly makes a legitimate critique of capitalocentric leftist analyses and approaches. But, is it justifiable to argue that the hegemony of capitalism is 'more discursive than real'?[63]

Is Gibson-Graham's call for collective disidentification – critiquing and disowning the framing that produces victims – a profound enough strategy for holistic transformation? Are economic struggles between subsistence and monetary economies only imaginary? The Bielefeld School of ecofeminists show that this is patently not the case, and even amounts to simple denial. From work around the house for children and spouses through to the world-systems analyses of capital accumulation, and associated trading terms and relations, *there is a monetary system out there which wreaks havoc*. It can fatally interfere with and damage noncapitalist models that attempt to persist alongside it. An awareness of – even focus on – this struggle is not necessarily disabling but, rather, can help us understand our real challenge, and force us to reflect on our own and others' practices, and refine our tactics in combating the profoundly structural forces that we face.

FROM SUBSISTENCE ECONOMY TO CARE ECONOMY

Ecofeminist concepts of care at the micro, household, level have developed into holistic visions of a care economy, care for nature, for Earth as well as people. Ecosystems, eco-communities and all species, including humans, require regeneration and restoration. The relational strength of reproductive and subsistence framings emphasises neighbourhoods, communities and interdependence to create strong parallels, synergies and dynamics with ecosystems. Arguably distinct from other forms of work, carers are peculiarly supportive of the social and material environs in which they act. Carers act from inner motives, tacit experience, and learn skills on the job by reflecting on results of intuitive acts and responses.

A logic of care can be the basis of an economy, especially if framed in terms of a convivial subsistence economy with collective provisioning, craftwork and farming at the fore. As such, Joan Tronto's ethics-of-care approach is bound by its focus on necessities:

> On the most general level we suggest that caring be viewed as a species activity that includes everything we do to maintain, continue and repair our 'world' so that we can live in it as well as possible. That world includes our bodies, ourselves and our environment, all of which we seek to interweave in a complex, life-sustaining web.[64]

Similarly, Hamburg social scientist Gabriele Winker has coined the term 'care revolution' to refer to a cooperative and solidarity approach to living. A strategy for achieving greater gender equality in parental care work is the shorter work week. For instance, a 2010 New Economics Foundation proposal for a 21-hour week, supported by greater wage equality, highlights the potential for more subsistence-oriented consumption and sharing of caring responsibilities in households.[65] In the mid-1990s, socialist feminist Nancy Fraser had suggested a universal care-giver remuneration program for men as well as women to further gender equality of responsibility for caring. Twenty years later, Fraser would observe that the failure to implement such a program in the United States meant, instead, that domestic work was increasingly falling in a segregated way to the heterogeneous class of poorer women.[66]

The approach of care undercuts reformist environmental approaches such as technology-based and market-oriented Green New Deal models, which ignore matters of care and overconsumption.[67] Similarly, Wichterich criticises the UN's iterations of Green New Deals for their 'ecologization of the economy', 'economization of nature', and vain efforts to internalise environmental costs.[68] Such works are imbued with ideas of turning women and peasants into wage workers and entrepreneurs, images of women are naturalised, poverty and vulnerability are conflated, and the stress is on 'agency as resource managers and caretakers of the environment'.[69]

Instead, Wichterich calls for a post-development and degrowth line of sufficiency and subsistence economies that embraces ecofeminist discourses on care and commons.[70] Specifically, she argues for activists 'to challenge market rules and define non-market-based criteria for recognition of care'. Equally, she cautions against voluntary informal work that mimics the devaluation of reproductive work in order to argue, instead, for part-time work so everyone can absorb care into their lives as a non-gendered activity. Moreover, Wichterich calls for a cultural and material concept of 'enough' defined within participatory polities.[71]

Similarly, the Feminisms and Degrowth Alliance (FaDA) calls for a society centred on 'gender justice and the sustainability of life', acknowledging and supporting the full development of 'social and ecological reproduction', and for solidarity economies for diversely constituted households in environmentally sustainable locales. FaDA proposes 'a caring economy that democratizes all dimensions of life, delinks livelihood security from wage-work, equitably revalues both paid and unpaid care work and promotes its gender-just redistribution, for example by the means of a universal basic income and a care income'. This vision is based on outward-looking 'open relocalisation', international solidarity with debt moratoriums and refusal of austerity measures through a specific 'Global Green New Deal'.[72] Although this approach critiques finance, incorporates alternative currencies and refers to nonmarket socialism, there is no explicit or key demand to abolish money.

Yet, as acknowledged in recent work by Gabriele Winker, monetary valuation effectively blocks the satisfaction of social and ecological needs.[73] Care-economy and subsistence-economy approaches are based on social and environmental, not monetary, values. These diverse values are what I refer to as 'real values', as opposed to standardised and unitary monetary values which are encountered in the everyday world simply as prices.

REAL VALUES

Applying the term 'real values', meaning social and ecological values, enables a practical recognition of diverse ecological and humane, including feminist, values. A real values approach rejects monetary values. I see this approach as consistent with ecofeminism, environmentalism, Marx's philosophy and various leftist analyses that critique capitalism and call for a new approach based on real, rather than monetary, values. Despite calls to the contrary, there is no authenticity or merit in applying Marx's insights on value as in capitalism to visions of or strategies for achieving postcapitalism. In as much as 'value' is a useful term in post-capitalist discourse and studies, I constantly refer to 'real values' or 'social and environmental values' and suggest using the term 'real value studies' to refer to explorations of ecologically sustainable nonmonetary production and exchange to fulfil basic needs of people and ecosystems.

From this perspective, 'real value producers' are those who use ecologically sustainable processes to derive and create goods and services with values that centre on satisfying local people's needs. Work is collective and delegated to individuals as a result of collective participatory decision making and volunteering. Within commoning, producers work an obligatory number of hours, or engage in delegated tasks irrespective of the hours involved. They fulfil direct orders of products, orders decided in participatory ways.

'Real value exchange' is direct supply on demand, resulting from participatory decision making regarding the basic needs of identified people. Any surplus is stored, used in a newly decided way, or directed according to need to others outside the producing community. Environmental considerations are accounted for in all decision making. These principles undergird the sketch of Yenomon in Chapter 3, this volume. Postcapitalism based on real value production – collectively decided and oriented around real values of inputs, techniques and outputs – focuses on real values defined in terms of both people and nature. Real value production incorporates all domestic work, indeed any work that contributes to the collective sufficiency of the community – meeting everyone's basic needs and the needs of Earth.

A range of voices, works and streams of thinking – some referred to in this work – can be identified as contributing to this emergent, still to be developed, field. Designating such work as 'real value studies' might encourage more activist scholars to interrogate actual cases of ecologically sustainable nonmonetary production and exchange to fulfil basic needs of people and ecosystems by reflecting on, monitoring and analysing them. Simultaneously, real value scholars might creatively propose, and review proposals for, future production in terms of their social and environmental potential, and identify both convivial techniques of production and essential outputs within particular social and environmental contexts.

Central to such a field are select concepts and works developed by feminists such as Friederike Habermann, a brief discussion of which concludes this chapter.

ECOMMONY AND COMMONS

It is not surprising that certain ecofeminists are marching towards essentially nonmonetary economies to provide the soundest environment
and site of liberation. Among others, Bennholdt-Thomsen points out
that many volunteers in subsistence community gardening initiatives
are women.[74] In her chapter in *Society After Money*, Friederike Habermann points out that, at the start of 2017, around three in every four
people constituting the nonmonetary, barter-free and exchange-free
Tauschlogikfreiheit MOVEment were women.[75] This movement has
organised activities, discussions and communities based on voluntary
contribution and free use – influences that have reverberated through
MOVE UTOPIA, living utopia (utopival, utopikon), a growing number
of locally based communities and alter-globalisation movements. Such
activists create spaces beyond barter and monetary exchange because
they associate barter and monetary exchange with forming a pretence of
holy equivalence.[76] These activists aim for non-alienated, interdependent
social relationships that substitute monetary ideas such as a 'guaranteed
basic income' with concepts such as a 'basic livelihood'. In short, they
view a universal basic income as either a stage or a strategy, rather than a
practice within their ultimate vision of utopia.[77]

The inventor of the word 'ecommony' (a commons economy), Habermann combines an explicit use value and use rights orientation, and an
anti-money logic of care and commoning with voluntary contributions
and subsistence-oriented activities.[78] Habermann refers to subsistence
activities, including both unpaid productive and socially reproductive
work, conducted within a 'logic of care'.[79] Ecommony goes beyond the
state and market with an open, cooperative and diverse approach; substituting private and public property with community governance of use
rights within commons; voluntary contributions to provisioning; and
the sharing of products and creations, such as food and housing. Care
encompasses reproductive and ecological work, with humans as a constructive agent of and with – rather than over – nature.[80]

Women have a tendency to be utopian in distinctive, nurturing, ways.
To the extent that they have had regenerative and restorative responsibilities and experiences, such as caring for young children – rather than
working in self-interested ways for immediate remuneration and grati-
fication – women develop skills of working in other-focused ways, and
are content that their work has the potential to bear fruit sometime in

the future. Feminist economic discourses have emphasised subsistence and care, pregnant with concepts that ultimately require breaking free from production for trade and, consequently, with exchange value, monetary values and prices. Even if most do not advocate abolishing money, ecofeminists essentially (if not consciously) cut lose from the 'logic of exchange' to embrace a logic of care, a logic of commoning, and are imbued with strong notions of agency and autonomy.

The views of Habermann are distinct from the work of Genevieve Vaughan and International Feminists for a Gift Economy.[81] Even if Vaughan recognises that barter 'is only an example of the same logic without money', her writings tend to take the suspect concept of 'equal' exchange on its face value and curiously frame language as 'a virtual verbal gift economy'.[82] Such theories and work on gift economies might inform, but do not represent, a real valuist perspective. In contrast, the gift economy work of Terry Leahy is real valuist.[83] Likewise, Habermann's ecommony is oriented around production with Earth and by all people, both for their common good and for nature's sake, with fair and just distribution on the basis of needs now and for the future of people and Earth.

Finally, in her impressive work on commons and ecofeminist futures, Silvia Federici has stated that 'if commoning has any meaning, it must be the production of ourselves as a common subject.'[84] There is no false unity implied in this 'community'. Anti-capitalist feminist commons are 'declined in the plural ... with the slogan "One No, Many Yeses"'.[85] As such, Federici (and Caffentzis) recognise that political squatting and occupations go far beyond exercising solidarity and mutual support in the present to represent 'seeds of an alternative mode of production in the making' based on commoning.[86] Creating all types of autonomous spaces with cooperative forms of co-governance of shared natural and social wealth, commoning has been present in such remarkable and widespread movements as *horizontalidad* in Argentina (2001–) and the Zapatistas in Mexico (1993–).[87]

Federici argues that many real everyday experiences of women have developed skills and useful knowledge to inform commoning. Women 'as the primary subjects of reproductive work, historically and in our time ... have depended on access to communal natural resources more than men and have been most penalized by their privatization and most committed to their defense'; thus, in various places, they have become conscious and conscientious commoners.[88] Moreover, most of women's invisible housework and care-oriented activities are used immediately (not sold) and exist in spaces and forums distinct from the public, indeed often in counterpoint to, the state.[89] Again. this feminist vision can be viewed as pointing determinedly beyond the market, beyond the state, beyond money.

CONCLUSION

Money-consciousness has taken specific directions in women's liberation, from seeking acknowledgement in terms of money as if it were a legitimate standard of value to challenging 'value', as in political economy and in Karl Marx. Ecofeminists in particular have exposed the market's neglect and distortion of social and environmental values in novel and revelatory ways. By the 1980s, women such as Maria Mies and Veronika Bennholdt-Thomsen were promoting sufficiency, and economies based on subsistence and community, within discourses that have shifted minority-world feminism in profound ways.

The unpaid and invisible nature of caring and reproductive household work is emphasised, even glaringly obvious, in as much as exchange value dominates both relations and status in society. Yet, women, like all of humanity, need to be recognised on their own terms, for their real values, in nonmonetary ways. This is why Habermann heralds an end to monetary values and relationships as core to our future revolutionary agenda, with strategies directed towards co-governing barter-free, exchange-free communities of people who nurture one another and Earth on the basis of real values.

6
Technology and the Real Debt Cycle

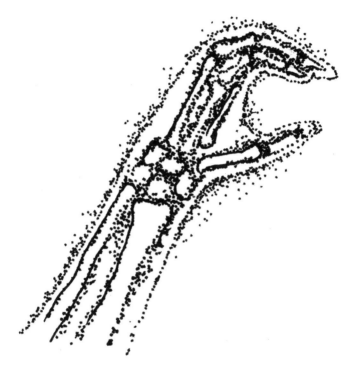

Activists and scholars associated with a variety of social and environmental movements advocate alternative, small and appropriate technologies with multiple social and cultural benefits. Appropriate techniques and technologies include the 'convivial tools' of Ivan Illich, technologies chosen and manageable by most citizens, say adapting traditional craft, transport and farming techniques that Indigenous, permaculture, degrowth, organic, slow and agroecology movements promote. Current challenges indicate a need for simple, direct and slow techniques for living, working and caring for people and Earth to overcome current unsustainability. Yet most alternative ways of living, including alternative technologies, are challenged and marginalised by capitalist forces in political, social, cultural and economic ways – to such an extent that such practices constitute acts of resistance.[1]

Capitalism is touted as characterising freedom, democracy and competition from a base of equality of opportunity. Yet, experience and observation of appropriate technologies and techniques for living and livelihoods show that capitalism is absolutist. If the creation of ideas is a free act, the realisation of inventions requires investors to assess a technology's feasibility in narrow market-oriented terms. Rather than adopt ways to live that are ecologically and socially appropriate, effective and efficient, the bottom line of capitalists' decision making over what is produced is profitability. An example is the electric car, a more environmentally friendly form of transport than petrol-guzzling vehicles. Prototypes emerged in Europe and the United States (US) in the late nineteenth century but it has taken more than a century for electric vehicles to be produced as commodities, by which time cars and vehicular infrastructure have become highly questionable components of a sustainable future.

Clearly, despite extravagant claims to efficiency, the capitalist system often operates inefficiently and ineffectively, if evaluated in holistic qualitative and quantitative ways using environmental and social criteria. Many simple and cheap home remedies and cleaners, such as salt, bicarbonate of soda and vinegar, are not regularly used by householders yet form the basis of widely advertised commercial products, along with environmentally damaging additions that can be risky in terms of human health. In selecting specific recipes, inventions and work processes, wealthy investors display great power. Decision making regarding the kinds of goods and services produced and how they are produced is the privilege of the few for – or, rather at and to – the many. The reign of exchange value, monetary value, rather than real, social and environmental, values is solid.

In movements such as degrowth, activists debate and trial all kinds of devices and techniques to assess the most successful constituents of new futures. Experimenting with so-called 'alternative' currencies, placing moratoriums on onerous debts, or engaging in nonmonetary production and exchange, activists engage in solidarity with communities of the like-minded.[2] They use bikes and walk, avoiding use of vehicles even if electric. They live in shared households and modest dwellings. Alternative lifestyles are multifaceted in the range of 'appropriate' socially and environmentally beneficial techniques and technologies adopted.

To the extent that alternative technologies are embedded in holistic approaches, they point in prefigurative ways beyond capitalism and its growth culture.[3]

In contrast, ever more sophisticated technological advances have become a key frontier of capitalist expansion. Capitalists rely on specific types of technological advance to preserve asset formation and dominate production over and against workers as well as competitors. Hi-tech developments enhance capitalists' assets, power, mystique and control. Examining the essential concept of 'asset' – money as a store of value, and owning and managing means of production as the only way of quasi-permanently 'saving' money – this chapter shows how mainstream technological advances are moulded by capitalist forces, extending and complicating their power in anti-social and anti-environmental ways.[4]

Moreover, this chapter frames key dynamics of capitalist societies as a type of 'gift economy'. Rather than follow the norm of contrasting the so-called 'equal exchange' of capitalist economies to unequal gift exchanges in nonmarket societies, I show how ritual obligations are rationalised culturally, politically and ideologically within capitalism to create a 'real debt cycle', which reproduces inequalities. Lending money with the reward of interest is capital in embryo, forming a bridge to capital as a consolidated societal mode. Assets are the materialisation and pulsing heart of the exchange-value concept within capitalism. Profit is a form of tribute, and management by capitalist forces is a dominating power. Assets signify a quasi-debt on all of society.

This interpretation of capitalist practices accords with degrowth activists' calls for us to 'decolonise our imaginaries' and think of ourselves in novel ways. Simultaneously, understanding the multi-dimensional unequal exchange cycle between workers and owners and managers of capital undercuts arguments that liberating futures, such as degrowth, could be achieved just by reforming money, or by community control of financial institutions.[5] Still, discussion of alternative monies, including cryptocurrencies, is held over till Chapter 8.

Instead, this chapter sets technologies in the contexts of money, double-entry bookkeeping and the financial sector treated as elements of a superstructure revolving on the base of material capitalist relationships of everyday life: the corporate mind of the incorporated body of society; the ideal that prompts, drives and reflects the practice. Consequently, we cannot achieve either a postgrowth state or postcapitalism without dispensing with monetary and financial spheres, and the ideology of 'equal exchange' that developed to advance capitalism.

CAPITALIST TECHNOLOGY

After an international sojourn observing the digital tidal wave, San Francisco activist-writer and experimental sound artist Bob Ostertag reports that 'Technology is spreading across the world far faster and farther than ever.'[6] He interrogates and comments on the human–technology nexus in societies bombarded by novel commodities – specifically, digital innovations. Such technologies one-sidedly exploit and pollute Earth and workers in their production, distribution, consumption and the waste they generate. Think the ecologically devastating ubiquity of plastic, the damaging mining of Earth and unhealthy pollution caused by high-tech cars, transport infrastructure and traffic. Think nerdy elites whose bizarre inventions drive late stage capitalism, exaggerating inequities and determining our futures. Think technological conversion, immersion and alienation, rites of passage which Ostertag argues make us relate more and more with machines rather than with humans. Think how Earth and humanity is implicated, damaged, deranged and lost in all of this.

'The last people to remember life before computers are alive today.' I am one of those people, so I smile when I read Ostertag's advice 'to listen closely to what they have to say, before they disappear'.[7] As someone who vividly remembers a pre-digital age, I frame digital developments along the lines of children's tales by Enid Blyton, a popular author in the 1950s, specifically her series based on a massive Magic Faraway Tree. Up the tree a ladder reaches into the clouds. Atop the ladder one reaches a 'magical' land – one of many lands offering delightful and disastrous experiences, and mimicked today by surprising and uncontrollable assaults of new technologies such as computers, audio-visual devices and smart phones. Using each device and app requires mandatory protocol, learned skills and particular logics with subtle and invisible socio-political and economic ramifications. Blyton's fictional worlds are capable of carrying her characters right away, at which point they make haste to exit for fear of being caught there forever. In contrast, we are prisoners of capitalism's no-exit policy. Experiences of standard technology are rarely voluntary because in everyday life government agencies, employers, and even friends and family force acquisition and engagement with the latest communication technologies.

Technics

The American historian and humanist philosopher Lewis Mumford understood technology through the lens of 'technics', assessing tools-cum-machines in terms of their adoption, invention and use within political, social and cultural contexts. In analysing urbanism and technology, Mumford points to the influence of the clock in the pre-industrial period of the second millennium. The mechanical clock, he observed, was an invention of religious orders in the Middle Ages, only to become a fundamentally significant machine bearing the Industrial Revolution on its back, because the clock projected linear abstract time in space.[8] In Ostertag's words, 'Abstract time became the new medium of existence.'[9] The clock presents a purely quantitative sense of time separate from the qualities of everything it measures, any second equal to any other second – rather like a row of dollar notes.

Mumford makes acute associations between developments in physical sciences, and the rise of monetary social relations and skills in mathematics, literacy and accounting – all dividing and ordering space by linear time and focusing on magnitude as if a measure of change. All this 'in the immediate interests of the new capitalism, with its abstract love of money and power'. In concert, qualitative analytic skills associated with the social sciences today were torn asunder from 'hard' sciences. A socio-cultural enclosure takes place as certain and as profound as physical enclosures marking the death knell of commons and the birth of private property in nature: 'The abstractions of money, spatial perspective, and mechanical time provided the enclosing frame of the new life.'[10]

The city, evolving from what was originally a sacred location for humans to gather and commune with the gods, becomes the artifice in which a contrived abstraction from nature finds space to flourish. Unchallenged by the uneven, variable and numerous conflictual and circular times found in nature, capitalist time is easily impressed on highly artificial urban environments. Cities and capitalist time arise as spatial dimensions that facilitate the operation and duplication of monetary relations.[11] The time beat out by clocks, watches and digital timekeepers become omnipotent, relegating the natural cycles of sun, moon and seasons to inconveniences, to astronomy and astrology. The anthropogenic dynamics of the market alienate us from our genuine source of life in Earth and establish a deep form of human–nature dualism. We become entrenched in an integrated overlay of exchange value, private property and linear time, a capitalist world of money, interest and profit, where technologies are frequently framed and legitimated as 'labour-saving' or 'time-saving'.

Concepts of labour-saving and time-saving are rationalised using narrow top-down perspectives that focus on paying workers. Many novel technologies make production more 'economic', claim capitalists, even as workers find that new technologies neither save them time in paid work nor enable them to more easily and quickly satisfy their basic needs. In fact, such technologies are 'disruptive' for owners, managers and workers. There is no reduction, rather an increase, in the use and abuse of nature.

By way of an example, traditional forms of taking wood from forests used axes, massive saws and mobile mills, and incorporated tree and land care. In contrast, the forest industry today clear-fells and burns vast areas with few concerns regarding their ecological impact. As the Global Forest Coalition reported in late 2020, 'Indigenous Peoples and communities with primarily nonmonetary economies tend to take very good care of their forests, while the record in monetary economies tends to be a lot less positive'.[12] There is no evidence, in terms of real values, for vast generalisations about capitalism's social or ecological efficiencies.

Instead, capital abounds as physical structures of monumental proportions, material commodities, and waste – leaving destruction in its wake as we overflow with ever more sophisticated means of production, making other forms of production obsolete and useless. Financialisation attends this capitalist market mayhem. *While often referred to as labour-saving, capitalist technologies are better referred to as capital-saving or asset-making.* In a debt-ridden world, technological advances offer a strong driver and the most significant global accumulation today, a social fact that requires careful unpacking.

TECHNOLOGIES, ASSETS AND FIXED CAPITAL

If treasures, luxurious consumption and extravagant buildings are traditional ways that religious authorities and royalty displayed their riches, influence and power, capitalists flaunt wealth and public power through monetary signifiers of a self-expanding frontier of objects and subjects under the order of capital and the market. On 7 January 2021, the CNBC television channel announced that Tesla CEO Elon R. Musk was now the world's richest individual, worth more than US$185 billion – based on an increase in the share price of Tesla, a global electric vehicle and clean energy company.[13] Just four days later, Bloomberg Billionaires Index ranked Musk the top dog with US$209 billion, one of the four – out of the top five richest people – who became rich through the technology sector.[14]

Contemporary power and influence is often expressed like this as financial wealth, percentage shares of companies that can live for centuries as an infinitely durable treasure while their owners are doomed to die much more quickly. Marx refers to such paper wealth as 'fictitious capital', distinguishing such negotiable financial *claims to* real materialised and operating capital from the material 'real capital' itself. This distinction is significant for most analysts because the financial market and fluctuating prices of financial claims create a sense of autonomy from the real capital assets on which shares rely for their income stream.

An asset is frequently perceived as capital in and of itself, as in measuring the rich above. Yet an asset's income-earning capacity is actually based on the exploitative relationship between capitalist owners and managers and workers who are simultaneously consumers. The potential of any asset, be it land or a form of technology, cannot be realised without workers' effort and the sale of the products of their effort. Yet the capitalists' ideal seems to be fully automated production, as if their treasure might even exclude active workers. Yet, as Marx so aptly names it, all 'real capital', every machine, represents 'dead labour'. Capitalists' means of production, such as technology, has been produced by work(ers) in the past.[15]

As such, workers' alienation from their product heightens the collective effect of what I refer to as technological 'othering'. Capitalist technology appears to denounce all 'others', from workers and consumers to wild or raw Earth, magnifying their position as capitalist assets while trivialising alternative technologies.

The 'others': Workers, consumers, Earth and alternative technologies

Capitalist technologies are techniques of capitalist production that integrate people, raw nature, and artificial materials and environments into a productive and reproductive system. Today, the spectacle of capital bursts forth in gargantuan forms of industrial construction and urban infrastructure hungry for mined Earth at a macro-scale.

Conversely, workers and consumers experience a two-way assault of sophisticated digital technologies in remarkable miniature, made for medical purposes, as educational tools, for everyday communication, commercial and financial calculations and records. As Uruguayan writer Eduardo Galeano points out, capitalism is sold as freedom but experienced as control: 'We have become servants of our machines. We are the machines of our machines. Without a doubt, the new tools of communication can be very useful if they are in our service – not the opposite. Cars drive us. Computers program us. Supermarkets buy us.'[16]

We are 'the other'.

The technology of capitalists tends to overwhelm this 'other' of workers-cum-consumers. We face technology as sophisticated and expensive; giving form and functions to highly managed work and home environments, with private property restricting access to secret technological know-how, data and operations relating to both production and consumption. Patents make property out of inventions and discoveries, not only out of technological minutiae but also from seeds of Earth and human DNA. Copyright tangles umpteen printed words and images, and appliances are not amenable to do-it-yourself repair. Firms create brand names and symbols, patents for technologies, and productive techniques that no one else can use, or not without paying for it.

Then there is the 'other' of nature reified in opposition to the artificiality of built environments full of capitalist monuments within tamed, owned and managed nature. The city is a stud in a tribute-paying hinterland. The idea of 'natural capital' is as perverted and obscure as other concepts of financially packaging nature.[17] Capitalism evolves human–nature dualisms in abundance and in pernicious contradictions. Capitalist private property is continuously re-valued by the market and, according to the extent of its contribution to capitalist activities, either treasured or neglected and deemed just 'nature' again.

Collective sufficiency, self-provisioning and alternative ways of producing become an 'other' in close opposition and resistance to capitalist practices. Appropriate technologies designed to fulfil people's needs of existence while relying lightly on Earth are at odds with the performance, pace and money-orientation of capitalist technology. Washing dishes by hand is laughed at as an oddity. Why not use a dishwashing machine? Simple homes and productive gardens are not conceived of as an asset as readily as spacious apartments. The SUV crowd see the bicycle as unsafe, unreliable, slow, a poor person's choice. Tree plantations monitored by drones and accountants stand in stark contrast to community-based forestry practised using traditional, appropriate techniques with subtle knowledge from work on the ground.

In contrast to such alternative technologies and ways of living, most capitalist technology arises as 'fixed capital', owned by capitalists as private property solely useful for capitalistic activities under regulations and disciplines defined by linear time and money. Marx made acute observations of political, cultural, even sensual, as well as financial, aspects of the roles of fixed capital – that is, non-labour means of production, such as the technologies, equipment, devices and machinery of production. That such insights made more than 150 years ago are applicable today indicates their primacy within capitalism.

Marx on capitalist technology

Marx elaborates that the worker is 'subsumed under the total process of the machinery itself … which confronts his individual, insignificant doings as a mighty organism'.[18] Technologies become quasi-authorities over workers as they toil in particular ways to accord with the machine's demands, at the machine's pace. Indeed, workers cannot work without the massive factory, computerised office, or mine in which they expend their various efforts. They experience an overwhelming, distorting and isolating 'helplessness', confronted, instead, by 'the communality represented by and concentrated in capital'.[19] Rather than view the technologies they work with as 'mediated and determined by the simultaneous existence of the labour of others', everything seems to amount to an 'advance which capital makes'.[20]

As Earth is held under the principle of production for trade, and workers are continuously divorced from their means of production, companies are spoken about as 'producers' of rare earths, of wood, of coal or gas. Indeed, agricultural land, forests and mines, through to the natural cycles of water and carbon, are integrated into the amorphous and all-powerful market under the discipline of capital. In all its aspects, raw and altered Earth tends either to be obliterated, irrelevant and worthless, or evaluated primarily as exchange value within capitalism. Marx emphasises this 'transformation of the production process from the simple labour process into a scientific process, which subjugates the forces of nature and compels them to work.'[21]

Beyond impacts on Earth, the physical experience of working with machinery amplifies the power of capitalist owners and managers who decide what is produced and how it is produced. The vehicle driver seems like an ant in the context of the steel mill or open-cast mine in which they work. They might work eight to ten hours a day five days per week, but the machines seem to work 24/7. In short, 'the value objectified in machinery appears as a presupposition against which the value creating power of the individual labour capacity is an infinitesimal, vanishing magnitude.'[22]

Most significantly, 'the greater the scale on which fixed capital develops', writes Marx, 'the more does the continuity of the production process or the constant flow of reproduction become an externally compelling condition for the mode of production founded on capital.'[23] This movement from simple tools to ever more sophisticated capitalist technologies:

> is not an accidental moment of capital, but is rather the historical reshaping of the traditional, inherited means of labour into a form adequate to capital … the general productive forces of the social brain, is thus absorbed into capital, as opposed to labour, and hence appears as an attribute of capital, and more specifically of fixed capital, in so far as it enters into the production process as a means of production proper.[24]

As such, Marx's analysis emphasises the multiple peculiar characteristics of capitalist techniques of production.

A final key point drawn from Marx relates to those aspects of fixed capital that endure over comparatively long periods, even as they continue to contribute to production, and wear out. The semi-permanent form of fixed capital appears to develop as if treasure with added benefits for capitalists. 'The productive force of society', writes Marx, 'is measured in *fixed capital*, exists there in its objective form; and, inversely, the productive force of capital grows with this general progress, which capital appropriates free of charge.'[25]

What does Marx mean here by 'free of charge'? Given that *numbers of workers with various skills and knowledge* made these techniques of production, Marx points out that it is simply ludicrous that capitalism is projected as the font and province of the most economic and wondrous technologies. It is doubly ludicrous because consumers pay for all the technological components and aspects of every product of business – and more, in profits – for the future expansion of capital. Of course, producers of machinery sell such means of production to producers of consumption commodities, but *the costs* of these technologies and ever more exotic materials of production *are always passed on to consumers*. Moreover, a significant proportion of profit is used to expand production by purchasing new amounts of, and qualitatively new, technology. So capitalist reproduction effectively means re-making all the used means of production – materials and techniques, technologies, equipment, devices and machinery – along with an expanded portion of similar, and novel, means of production. Nothing comes gratis from capitalists to worker-consumer citizens. Quite the opposite.

In late stage capitalism, we are at the butt end of this ever-powerful, defining and experiential embedding of capital and private property on and in our existence. Indeed, the whole productive and reproductive apparatus of capitalism functions to give money invested in assets that resulted from past work the illusion of having a permanent value that is, however, only fulfilled by workers in the present. As outlined in Chapter 2 'Assets and debts: The grand production-for-trade ritual', capitalism is structured so that assets are quasi-treasure, a store of value, the whole system of double-account bookkeeping recording how owners of assets gain profits as a composite tribute from worker-consumers, with private property earning an income packaged as a veritable debt that others continuously service. Private property is not simply a theatrical stage within which capitalist dramas play out, but materially represents owners' and managers' power increasing over other people and Earth. Clearly, with the capitalist impetus for growth, these debt–credit relations must intensify and expand.

Technologies as assets

In effect, capitalist technologies are better referred to as 'capital-saving', rather than 'labour-saving'. Beyond the expansion of capitalist ownership of lands and built environments, technologies are a key frontier for capital formation. Investment in new technologies takes place as long as such techniques promise to shorten the time of production of standard commodities, releasing 'saved' capital for further investments, or to enable greater output or new production of novel commodities. Technologies progress capital formation – from a Marxist perspective counteracting the tendency, in Marx's theory, for the rate of profit to fall.[26]

New technologies tend to make certain other market-based enterprises and workers obsolete, increasing environmental and social waste. But total capital – as a material, ideological and practical fact – continues to grow in and as fixed capital of a durable kind. Here capital's magic wand simultaneously creates new consumer wants, all the while failing to economise on satisfying mere needs. The monetary aspect of this self-expanding reproduction of capitalism is significant – financialisation and multiplication of the shadow of existing capital in 'debt' acts as a carrot and a stick to growth. Consequently, preliminary to a novel explanation of the role of sophisticated technology in economic growth and asset formation, we need to discuss financialisation – that is, money capital.

MONEY CAPITAL

In general, the word 'debt' refers to any obligation. Today, debt often refers to monetary debt. Debt is intrinsic to the concept and practice of using money. At a societal level, money bears two sides: as a socialised debt, and as a socialised credit. If we receive money, we hold on to it fully expecting to use it in the marketplace, its sole use being a claim to marketed goods and services. As such, money exists for us as a credit in our relation to society – in society's dimension as a marketplace – a claim to future commodities that might be used for consumption or production. Yet, lending and borrowing interest-bearing money for a set period is usually what we mean when we refer to 'credit' and 'debt' respectively.

The investment – financial capital – pre-empts production

The archetypal form of private property within capitalism is a person holding money excess to their everyday needs who 'saves' it by investing in financial assets to function as money earning money: $M{\rightarrow}M'$. In a social sense, this money is simply lent by an individual in the role of rentier to the productive process to earn a reward. Purely a loan to a producer for the gain of a pre-determined interest, default is the only risk. However, unless partly or even entirely lost if the business fails, investments – as in owning a business, or having stocks and shares in it – reap profits of indeterminate proportions. Ideally, profits are reinvested, propelling growth for the individual firm, the particular sector in which it operates, and capital in general. Such re-investment means that financial assets and the income derived from them expand.

As capitalism grows, financial assets must increase and speculation associated with their trade continues by the very nature of the case. Investments in means of production appear in capitalists' records as if debits to be written off, as a company realises income from production. If an owner directly invests in the firm they manage, their investment appears as a debt of the firm to the owner in their role as a rentier, who is as separate in this role as they might be if they were another party. Consequently, the financial sphere is not an add-on to real capitalist activity. In the case of the owner-manager of a single-person enterprise, the financial element is invisible, reduced to its most simple compound form. Once company ownership is separated, as in a range of partners or shareholders, this is not so much a new stage of capital(ism) but, rather, simply an explicit 'coming out' of rentiers and their financial capital.

Owners treat an asset like a *quasi-social credit* that capitalism *is expected to honour*. By implication, capitalism is a debt society par excellence. Much political discourse rotates around the needs of business to make such assets sound, to operate effectively and profitably. States regard businesses as if they have intrinsic value, and are alert and responsive to business people's claims of stress. Moreover, contemporary late stage capitalist states support commercial activities and engage in such, including double-entry bookkeeping, as an overt operational imperative.

Debts and credits: Investments and returns

Money is the symbol, the 'carrot'. Money is offered in exchange for work, an income that workers use to buy their means of existence, and investments of money are made in the expectation of a smooth reproduction and expansion of capital. Investments typically come via bankers or other financiers with faith in particular capitalists. Capital assets (such as factories, equipment and stocks) appear to epitomise the function of money as a store of value. Still, unless workers are engaged to create products and provide services, means of production cannot make profits so that associated equipment, Earth and workplaces lose, sometimes entirely, their monetary value. The value of money and 'productive assets' are nought without workers who create and recreate that value. No work, no capital.

As circuit theorists suggest, the expanded reproduction of capital always requires money lent or invested *in anticipation of profit*.[27] This increase is actually made available to capitalists before they start the great cycle of production and exchange. Bankers, supported by state bureaucrats who regulate this process, conduct a priestly role ordaining certain capitalists with loans to pre-empt, even force, growth. Every credit is a debt, presenting a similar credit–debt conundrum, as in holding money as coin. This circumstance explains many poorly understood aspects of capitalist crises of the kind experienced in, and since, the Great Financial Crisis of 2007–08 and, more recently, related to the economic impacts of COVID-19.[28]

Any slowdown or seizing-up of business activities frustrates a whole series of debt–credit relations arranged on the basis of the smooth running of capitalism. Much money 'lost' in such episodes is simply a case of the *expected* worth of assets not being realised, either in time – to repay associated debts – or even at all. It is a loss of dreams. Looking at this in terms of real values – social and ecological values related to people and Earth – unless based on some kind of natural calamity, the monetary crisis is purely economic, purely based on relationships, a game gone bad.

In fact, capitalist exchange is a dynamic cycle of workers and capitalists facing one another in a vast exchange process, pressing their distinctive services on one another in apparently generous and simultaneously self-interested ways. This is so ordinary in terms of everyday experience that its extraordinariness escapes us. Reality is a counter-fact subsumed in the conceit that capitalism is uniquely efficient and effective, epitomised by free and 'equal' exchange, where everyone seemingly meets one another in the marketplace on an equal basis using a universal equivalent. The effect is to make the entire practice of capitalist economies and theories of economists appear rather scientific and mathematical. But are they?

OBLIGATIONS AND EXPECTATIONS BEYOND 'EQUAL EXCHANGE'

Throughout this work I speak of monetary exchange and nonmonetary exchange as distinctive forms of exchange. Yet numbers of theorists and practitioners reduce monetary exchange to 'exchange'. For instance, the nonmarket socialist position of the World Socialist Movement frames a no-money position as no-exchange, which seems similar to the 'barter-free' and 'exchange-free' position of German no-money communities.[29] Across the board, concepts of 'exchange', including barter, convey a sense of substitution, inferring equivalence. Indeed, David Graeber makes equivalence implicit to monetary exchange, introducing 'mutuality' as an alternate, appropriate, framing and keyword for communism.[30]

Different concepts of equal and unequal exchange have developed following the ideas of distinct theorists, disciplines and stages of capitalism. I challenge the concept of 'equal exchange' at base, arguing that commodities appear equal in the moment of exchange, but this transient state is readily projected on the entire process of exchange and exchangers. I see 'equal exchange' very much as a pre-analytic notion, a *fallacious inference* arising from trade, specifically from monetary exchange.

For most, equivalence exists at the abstract level of (exchange) value, as for Marx in relation to abstract labour or socially necessary labour-time. A labour theory of value is attractive in philosophical and qualitative terms because workers and their work do propel capitalism. Still, there are numerous challenges to workerist notions of value, including those of feminists raised in Chapter 5. If the whole question of a rationale for 'value' at the basis of exchange is controversial, it is also *irrelevant* to anyone who recognises that postcapitalism means transforming ourselves, our values and principles, beyond monetary value. 'When labor time ceases to be the measure of work and work the measure of wealth,' Kristin Ross states, 'then wealth will no longer be measurable in terms of exchange value.'[31] In other words, we move beyond a free-wheeling universal equivalent to co-governed activities rotating, instead, on real values.

At the same time 'equal exchange', and by implication exchange value, can be framed as aspects of capitalism within which monetary exchanges are read as 'total prestations' – a term used by Marcel Mauss for *obligatory acts within an holistic societal paradigm*. As such, capitalism is infused with strongly cultural and quasi-religious indebtedness.

Gift economies and the real debt cycle

In the last half-century, various ethnographers have made increasingly more subtle and sensitive appraisals of noncapitalist economies and societies, understood in their own cultural terms, challenging heroic modernist interpretations and contributing to diverse postmodern appreciations of noncapitalist relations of production and exchange. In contrast, economic sociologists have tended to approach this field more like interior designers than architects, taking money and monetary flows as quasi-natural facts that simply need to be described in ways familiar to them rather than fundamentally challenged using novel perspectives.[32] Much discourse in such areas refers to the early twentieth-century work of French sociologist Marcel Mauss, who raised the act of exchange to a significant social institution, particularly in his theorisation of gift economies.[33]

My point is that starkly contrasting characterisations of capitalist and noncapitalist societies, found as much in the field of economic anthropology as elsewhere, miss important *comparisons* that might be made. After all, capitalism is *production for trade*, for exchange. Setting aside political and sociological currents that develop contemporary and futuristic concepts of gift economies in a utopian vein, I narrow this discussion of gift economies to discourse emerging in reference to Mauss's work *The Gift*. Significantly, I claim that capitalism could be framed as a system of ritualised gift-giving, following Mauss's framework for understanding exchange and reproduction in noncapitalist societies.[34] This approach supports the perception that *debt* is not only omnipotent in capitalism, but also experienced as if in a hall of mirrors existing in multiple forms and at various scales.

Mauss argues that a common pattern emerges in the complex social principles whereby 'gifts' (objects and services) are exchanged in non-market societies. Rather than selfless generosity graciously accepted, the gift is an instrument of social power implying obligations to the extent of burdens. Mauss observes that across all types of societies based on gift economies there are strong socio-cultural expectations *to give, to accept or receive, and to repay or reciprocate*. This veritable cycle of gifting processes is neither random nor impulsive but operates as a deep rhythmic pattern reproducing relationships with both economic and cultural implications and ramifications. As such, Mauss develops the concept of *total prestations*, cycles of economic and non-economic rituals practiced by groups engaged in 'ceremonial exchange', such as the Trobriand Islander kula ring and North American Indian potlatch. Here, the competitive struggle to be the most generous giver perversely expanded exchange to the extent that the damaging effects of superfluity required the intervention and incorporation of either ritual destruction or practices of social levelling.

In stark contrast to such gift exchange, argued Mauss, the exchange of commodities using money is comprised of voluntary exchangers and equivalent exchange. In this perspective, commodity-based exchange is neither obligatory nor culturally embedded. Commodities are transitorily networked in a meta-system of monetary logic seen as a one-dimensional matrix akin to a flat earth, where, ultimately, all the pluses of sales cancel out the minuses of purchases to leave naught. In short, it seems that commodities are produced in rational, techno-scientific, mechanistic, material ways enacted in the mathematical balance of a simplistic notion of supply and demand.

'The reciprocal obligation in gift exchange, the spirit of the gift, the opposition between gifts and commodities and the relationship between the person and things are the four themes in Mauss's work,' points out social anthropologist Yunxiang Yan, adding that 'it is not an exaggeration to say that economic anthropology itself as a distinct sub-field, has emerged from a long series of debates regarding the nature of the gift in various societies.'[35] It is not surprising, then, that Mauss has become an easy reference point for scholars from many disciplines, his approach subtly incorporating many of the biases and arrogance of 'us' in capitalism feeling different from the multitude of noncapitalist 'them'.

Given that mainstream economics is not often framed as a religion and money as a quasi-god, it's no surprise that few explore *similarities* between ways that gift exchange and commodity exchange are practiced. Here I use Karl Marx's formulas and big-picture schemas of capitalism in ways he did not intend, i.e. to demonstrate obligatory exchanges between workers and capitalists, in order to undermine the apparent theoretical distinctions developed by Mauss.

Specifically, I draw creatively on analytical insights and key schemas that Marx devised following the French Physiocrats' understanding of economic reproduction, to reveal in the 'real debt cycle' similarities between 'us' via commodities and 'them' via gifts.[36] My explanation undermines the presumption that capitalism is a rational and transparent system corresponding to human needs and human nature. 'It is not enough to say that capitalism is a constructed system,' insists well-known American sociologist Fred Block. 'The task is to illuminate how it is constructed: to see how a diverse and often contradictory set of practices are welded together to produce something that has the appearance of a natural and unified entity.'[37]

Give, accept, repay

Mauss's framework of obligations to give, accept, or receive, and repay or reciprocate might be gleaned from, on the one hand, regular capitalist practices of investing money in the expectation of getting back more money, in order to invest again and to invest even more. Meanwhile, on the other hand, workers offer their services (work) in order to receive money (wages) to purchase means of existence, and expect to offer more, and more productive, services (work) continuously. Growth in our economic religion means more money for both capital and labour, which flows on to dependents – with marginalised others catered for by social welfare or charity, or going without altogether. There even appears a boom–bust cycle with generous investments followed by ritual mayhem and purification through crises – crises which always appear as monetary and financial crises despite associated underlying causes.

There are strong socio-material pressures for capitalists to invest in production and for workers to keep working. Both are expected to reproduce these relations with one another by producing more and more, a social dynamic that has seen capitalism intensify and expand significantly throughout the nineteenth and twentieth centuries, driving imperialism and neo-colonialism. Any cursory review of sentiments in political and economic discourse today confirms the operation of these critical pressures within capitalist economic systems. In short, contra the assumptions and contrasts made by the likes of Karl Polanyi, capitalism is an embedded economy with holistic gift-exchange-like socio-political obligations.[38]

Still, the familiar approach to commodity exchange classifies it as voluntary, materialist, individualistic and equal exchange. Using money in transactions inclines us to think of a continuous cycle of discrete, free, voluntary and equivalent exchanges. Transactors ritually identify as individuals facing society with money to access a market full of possible goods and services to buy. Fundamentally, to use Mauss's terms, the 'form and reason for exchange' in capitalist societies is money and monetary growth, so citizenship might well be described in relation to this ritual. In short, capitalist economies can be viewed with the spectacles that Mauss developed for understanding 'archaic' societies, where erstwhile fictions are social facts that people obey in similar ways to traffic laws and traffic lights.

In contrast to Polanyi's claims that capitalism is disembedded, we need to acknowledge the disastrous ways in which *exchange value is well and truly embedded*, socially, politically and environmentally.[39] Significantly, through ownership and management of private property, capitalists appear as the very sources of our basic needs. Bountiful raw and developed nature is owned by capitalists as if it were them. *They are our sources of food, clothes and houses.* Yet workers as a totality actually create all these products for consumption, and all the means of production which constitute the means for owner-managers to maintain and expand their power. In effect, as a composite, workers make tributes that become assets – that is, capital. As a corollary to growth, such tributes grow, enmeshing us more and more in capitalism, which faces us as a hungry debt collector.

A different frame of reference, capitalist book-keeping, clarifies this line of argument.

DOUBLE- AND TRIPLE-ENTRY BOOKKEEPING: PAST, PRESENT AND FUTURE

Mary Poovey's impressive *History of the Modern Fact* tracks the spread of originally simple mercantile practices into whole-of-society obligations and rationalities to identify double-entry bookkeeping as the 'prototype of the modern fact'.[40] As introduced in Chapter 2, this volume, the complex networked and ritualised business activities that focus on managing workers to produce commodities sold on the market are streamlined in the double-entry bookkeeping of firms. Double-entry bookkeeping renders all the trials, tribulations and drama of trade and production into a simple, formal and ordered two-dimensional spreadsheet.[41]

Significantly, Poovey argues that the initial development of capitalist double-entry bookkeeping made credible the *use of merchants' bills of exchange as veritable money or credit* – a 'bill of exchange' being a commercial, written promise to pay a specific amount to an individual (or bearer) on a particular date (or on demand).[42] The proliferation of such processes still contributes to financialisation in late stage capitalism. As Poovey notes, the quasi-scientific scalar nature of double-entry bookkeeping, realising a fictional balance, developed greater symbolism as a guide for evaluating the worth of a kingdom or nation.[43]

The layout in two columns of debit and credit, outgoings and income, appears two-dimensional, yet a company's annual double-entry accounting system embraces three dimensions of past, present and future workplace activities. This means that *over the long term, the asset is treated as a responsibility that workers and consumers perpetually reproduce, ensuring incomes to the owners of capital.* This is a fact-cum-fiction for capitalists and their states, and troubles workers interminably. As such, this three-dimensional accounting for past, current and future work might be more accurately referred to as 'triple-entry accounting' rather than double-entry bookkeeping. Why so?

In *Capital II*, Marx shows the composite effect of capital outlays, capitalist production, worker consumption and profit in one cycle using an algebraic form, $M \rightarrow C \rightarrow P \rightarrow C' \rightarrow M'$. Here P is comprised of *present labour* and Earth's materials plus a proportionate replacement of machinery (means of production). Clearly, means of production were created before use in production, Marx referring to such as '*past labour*', even 'dead labour'. With the sale of products made in the current cycle (C'), the capitalist gains not just M but M', with that surplus value or profit (') potentially available to pay for *future labour* and means of production in the next cycle.[44] In short, whenever we make a purchase, we pay for current work in the wages component, for past work in the means of production component, and for what will be future work in the profit component.

While Marx makes much of the past, present, future black box created by capitalist production for trade, his *Capital II* schemas and circuits follow double-entry bookkeeping practices that marginalise fixed capital not ceded to the immediate process of production but nonetheless impossible to conduct without it. In other words, say a printer is bought and expected to last ten years, then the accountant incorporates 10 per cent of its costs each year as a direct cost of production. Still, as long as it is in use, the printer remains an asset in the form of use value and can feature as a relevant cost/asset in financial accounts.

Meanwhile, workers recreate money writ large as 'CAPITAL' with commodities required to fulfil their basic needs and owner-managers' lifestyle wants and the future expansion of wealth and power. Indeed, when we purchase goods and services for consumption or production, we pay for a plethora of gratuitous costs of production, including advertising, marketing, packaging and retailing; often seemingly exorbitant incomes received by managers and owner-managers; and a margin for profit. This profit is considered a reward to the investors who 'risk' their savings by investing in productive activities. The apparent risk is a joke given there can be no real saving unless money is invested in capitalist activities. If held as cash or under the bed, as jewellery or treasures, it does little and is even likely to be 'eaten away' by the type of inflation and negative interest rates that characterise late stage capitalism.

In reality, this continuous cycle of recreating, enclosing and appropriating private property, performed via increased reinvestment, is the moving membrane of capitalism worldwide. As such, capitalist practices and accounting principles combine in such a way that the capitalist asset-owning elite not only oversee the production but also the *reproduction* of capitalism. Capitalists maintain power over what most other people do, without which we might be liberated to collectively, democratically and freely, produce directly for ourselves. If we step back from this scene of market activity, we observe that people with more income than they spend on present needs and wants can only have genuine and meaningful savings if they invest in this complex social game to earn them a perpetual future income.[45]

Read this way, capitalist accounting is a social script and record of *the capitalist game we play*. That savings, investments, represent any monetary value at all relies on the productivity and potential of both the business activity to which they directly relate and to the health of the whole market. Owner-managers cannot do what they like with what they own, because the rules of the game centre on an abstract principle of M→M'. This is the bull's eye of the challenge of sustainability today. Private property is a creature of capitalism, and the abstract and social dynamics of capitalism, such as the imperative of growth, fly in the face of key principles of material sustainability – limits, use values, real values, natural efficiencies, ecological integrity and balance.

As such, one banner for change is 'STOP PLAYING AND FOCUS ON REAL VALUES'.

APPROPRIATE TECHNOLOGIES

It is not surprising that complex technologies with mystifying, secretive and indomitable characteristics arise within capitalist dynamics of growing money and power that rely on exploiting Earth and workers. This is a socio-political game that does not economise on either labour or Earth in terms of real values. Quite the opposite. The game's captivating cultural dynamics insist on bigger, better, faster, more complex and mystifying technologies that contribute to the expansion and intensification of capital, in material terms overproducing for overconsumption by many in the minority world while leaving whole households, communities and regions without their essential needs being met in the majority world.

Many who distrust appropriate technologies and techniques – wherein quality, equity, inclusion, safety, simplicity, sociality, and ecosystem health and balance remain uppermost – often refer to the apparent efficiency of household appliances. To pick up on an earlier example, let's take water- and labour-saving attributed to machine dishwashers compared to handwashing dishes. Almost all key studies which conclude that dishwashing machines save water and labour-time have failed to take embodied energy and householders' awareness into account. A full life-cycle assessment finds hand dishwashing produces fewer carbon emissions. If conducted in highly consciously water-saving communities, say in regional Australia, where water is scarce and householders typically wash in small containers using a range of water-saving techniques, the water-saving of handwashing is impressive.[46]

In fact, using appropriate technologies and techniques might take more time but many comparisons fail to include the extent to which appliances embody Earth's materials and energy and labour time in their production and distribution, use and waste.[47] Moreover, degrowth and other environmental movements advocating modest ways of living and practices save through radically lower consumption. The design, development and use of appropriate technologies and techniques for a light footprint are all oriented around real social, human and ecological values. Interestingly, only certain postcapitalist imaginaries incorporate such real value perspectives.

'Postcapitalist' abundance

'Cockaigne' (aka Cockayne) flowered in medieval myths as an imaginary world wherein abundance is achieved more or less without effort. Beyond personal release from the effort associated with being a worker, slave or serf, Cockaigne is an impossible world of human freedom from earthly responsibilities of self-support. Today, those enamoured of seemingly liberating aspects of digital technologies, envision postcapitalism in terms of widespread use of sophisticated technologies that are meant to economise, mainly, on human effort. As such, techno-futurist journalist Aaron Bastani writes that 'the foundations are cohering for a society beyond both scarcity and work', in short, a 'fully automated luxury communism'.[48]

Yet, none of this can happen within the finite resources of Earth. It has been estimated that, as soon as 2030, the residential electricity requirements of digital appliances will be almost half of global electricity consumption and, even if sourced from renewables, the production of devices and toxic e-wastes will become substantial environmental challenges.[49] Bastani's answer is to 'mine the sky instead.'[50] In this rendition of so-called 'postcapitalism', humans colonise the universe! Bastani argues that massive environmental challenges associated with food can be solved with synthetic products substituting for meat, eggs, milk and wine.[51]

In a similar vein, academics Nick Srnicek (digital economics) and Alex Williams (digital media) advocate that 'the contemporary left should reclaim modernity, build a populist and hegemonic force, and mobilise towards a post-work future', in other words, 'construct a new future-oriented politics capable of challenging capitalism at the largest scales.'[52] Srnicek and Williams see such a future in thoroughly technological contours, 'the ultimate trajectory of universal emancipation … overcoming physical, biological, political and economic constraints'.[53]

Yet designer and developer of networked digital information technologies and information architect Adam Greenfield is just one of various analysts who throw up roadblocks and caution that such utopian visions make many unrealistic assumptions and can become dystopian.[54] For instance, Srnicek and Williams initially argue that automation can allow time for difficult-to-automate tasks such as caring. Yet, they end up arguing for fully automated households, health and care work – even arguing for robots to conduct 'some of the highly personal and embarrassing care work' and floating that 'synthetic forms of biological reproduction' could enhance gender equality.[55]

Technological liberation, or liberation from technology?

So, what might the other half of the world make of the visions of Srnicek and Williams? Decades ago, ecofeminist Maria Mies argued that a shorter working week delivered by automation would not amount to liberation. In contrast to more free time, Mies prefers that concept of time experienced by women as carers and housewives, which is closer to the circular time characteristic of most noncapitalist activities and societies and to the no time and seasonal time of raw or wild nature. A woman multi-tasks, reminds Mies, and their work ebbs and flows, responding to necessity, such as 'demand feeding' babies. It is never ending, never quite work nor leisure but, rather, something beyond. As such, Mies has argued that emancipation is not dependent on some kind of economy of time as Marx and other liberationists imagine.[56]

Moreover, Mies regards bodies as sensuous and vulnerable to violation by technological demands. Workers are demeaned by paid work, capitalist technologies and capitalist disciplines of time and money. Like Marx, Mies elaborates how the machine intervenes between nature and humans, contorting, alienating, even falsifying nature in terms of human experience.[57] She calls for a radical redefinition of labour towards 'a change of work, of work organization, of the sexual division of labour, of the products, of the relation between work and non-work, of the division between manual and mental work, of the relation between human beings and nature'.[58]

As certain so-called 'postcapitalist' and most ecomodernist technological dystopias envisage robot carers and companions, radical autonomist feminist Silvia Federici points out that women's un- and under-remunerated reproductive work has been disproportionately impacted in late stage capitalism. Neoliberal cuts to welfare and services, and a rapacious market 'at the mercy of companies whose only interest is the money they can make out of the needs we have and those they can create' contrive to warp concepts of humanity and care – in ways exemplified by technological futures.[59] Her main point is that 'we cannot robotize care except at a terrible cost for the people involved.'[60]

Women have become the brunt of a host of reproductive technologies, just as workplace machinery has been touted as a way to make up for their apparent lack of strength and energy. Queer feminist Friederike Habermann refers to the contraceptive pill, so often flaunted as a technofix, a driver of women's emancipation but perhaps, instead, it has amounted to a final assault? Marginalising alternative forms of contraception, 'all strivings toward emancipation become insignificant in comparison to the invention of the contraceptive pill.' So, Habermann asks, 'women are only emancipated if they take hormones?'[61] Indeed, early on, 'the pill' became as much, perhaps even more, a way to make *men* feel freer, a real issue with which women had to grapple. Moreover, taking contraceptive pills has produced notorious side-effects. The second wave was not so much enabled by the pill as it was the result of women's outrage. To reduce women's liberation to the invention of the pill is like attributing the rise of capitalism to the steam engine. Instead, social and economic revolutions are driven by real people.

Such real people often interpret and experience technology in distinctly anti-capitalist ways. 'The invisible privilege of your technocratic, one-sided peacefulness is an act of violence,' writes Australian Indigenous scholar Tyson Yunkaporta. 'Your peace-medallion bling is sparkling with blood diamonds. You carry pillaged metals in your phone from devastated African lands and communities.'[62] Despite, even due to, capitalist technological pillages of humans and Earth, there is an alternative politics, which forms the living and beating substrate of a postcapitalist movement that is not new but, instead, builds on hundreds of years of resistance.

Contemplating current ecosocialist struggles in the context of reflections on the Paris Commune as 'a laboratory of political invention,' Kristin Ross focuses on work by William Morris, Elisée Reclus and Peter Kropotkin. She presents a vision of emancipation based on commons, 'collective ownership of the land' and of regional collective sufficiency upholding political autonomy.[63] Nature, writes Ross, 'would then be not just a productive force or stockpile of resources but valued as an end in itself.'[64] Wealth would not rely on technologies but rather techniques of living in a relationship with nature that was creative and celebratory.

What Ross terms 'communal luxury' is akin to the degrowth movement's concept of 'frugal abundance', in which appropriate technologies and practices flourish. 'Appropriate' technologies are often, but not always, simple technologies. In the sketch of Yenomon in Chapter 3, there is infrastructure for a global internetwork, digital commons, but it is used modestly, minimally. Similarly, sophisticated infrastructure exists to capture and store wind and solar energies. A future built on nonmonetary production and exchange enables everyone to have a say and participate in deciding which technologies are developed and used for the common good, all the while being restrained by the implications and ramifications for Earth.

CONCLUSION

The triumph of production for trade, of exchange values over real values, is at the heart of most conundrums associated with achieving environmental sustainability. In capitalism, various technologies perform multiple obvious, and difficult to discern, roles. A holistic perspective highlights the roles of sophisticated technologies in the advance of capital, as a frontier for absorbing the growth in money capital in search of investment opportunities. As debts mount in capitalism, it is clear that this is a function of the formation of capitalist assets and the shadow of a 'real debt cycle' between workers and capitalists.

If certain postcapitalist imaginaries are studded with sophisticated technologies purportedly as a means of liberation, others argue for appropriate technologies – simple or sophisticated, but always convivial, tools attractive for their compatibility with horizontal decision making and light impacts on Earth. Appropriate technologies struggle against the mystique and ideology of the apparent efficiency of sophisticated technologies, which are peculiarly suited to expand capitalism rather than to satisfy basic needs. Just as significantly, ritualised monetary practices of the real debt cycle pattern activities of production and exchange that exploit Earth's ecosystems. Thus, nature–human dualism remains despite other genuine intents and efforts to make our daily living at one with Earth.

In short, moving beyond money is a necessary, even if not sufficient, condition to enable us to use technologies and techniques of production that are appropriate for addressing inequities and unsustainability and, in the process, to transcend nature–human dualism.

7
Indigenous Peoples, Real Values and the Community Mode of Production

Indigenous peoples have constantly struggled against and alongside capitalism to maintain their substantive rights to practice traditional and appropriate collective provisioning. Historically and currently, exchange value paradigms and practices challenge, smother and isolate nonmonetary practices and modes of production based on ecological and social values.[1] In response, Uruguayan writer of both fiction and non-fiction, Eduardo Galeano, has called for a 'community-based mode of production' highlighting real, social and ecological values to be strengthened and expanded inclusive of diverse cultures and practices.[2] By extension, a successful postcapitalist movement will not simply embrace and partner Indigenous peoples' cultures and economies but will be informed and driven by them in key strategic and structural ways.

Holistic and politically savvy communal economies with practical traction have evolved from the activities of movements such as Kurdish liberationists, guiding and guided by the works of Abdullah Öcalan, and by Zapatistas in Mexico. Both movements have strong international networks. To varying extents, they challenge capitalist states and markets enforcing production for trade and the rule of money. Strengthening autonomy and community-based production and exchange on the basis of need and respect for Earth's limits demands a focus on real values. By implication, not only formal currencies and financial structures but also 'alternative' currencies and community banks are weak and distracting transitionary processes to postcapitalism – as taken up in Chapter 8. Meanwhile, this chapter argues that a community mode of production based on substantive direct democracy and decision making focusing on real, social and ecological values is most appropriate for postcapitalist futures.

AUSTRALIA

I live in a settler society on desecrated land, land stolen from the 'most ancient continuous civilisation on Earth'.[3] Since the late eighteenth century, their experiences of an invasion of practitioners of capitalism show the violence of trade and production for trade on Indigenous forms of living that have been so much more at one with nature and cognisant of real values.

Specifically, I live on land of the Dja Dja Wurrung (also known as Jaara) people. There were hundreds of distinct communities of Aboriginal and Torres Strait Islander peoples when the British claimed the continent and its adjacent waters. The length and breadth of the Indigenous peoples' occupancy and their diverse, subtle and ecologically appropriate forms of collective provisioning are testimony to culturally attuned and sophisticated inhabitation of their lands and waters. Their standard of living in terms of basic necessities has been judged as good as, or better than, the average in Europe in 1800.[4] As Gammage has shown, 'Aboriginal people spent far less time and effort than Europeans in securing food and shelter.'[5] They exemplified American cultural anthropologist Marshall Sahlins' 'original affluent society', his 'Zen road to affluence', where 'human material wants are finite and few, and technical means unchanging but on the whole adequate.'[6]

None of this was appreciated by the invaders, whose eyes were firmly focused on trade. In what the National Museum of Australia terms a 'damning assessment', the British claimant Lieutenant James Cook (captain of HMB *Endeavour*) wrote in his journal in 1770 that 'the Country itself so far as we know doth not produce any one thing that can become an Article in trade to invite Europeans to fix a settlement upon it.' So, the British made use of it as a penal colony.[7] Sealing and whaling provided initial exports. Later, free settlers used the land for grazing to produce wool and crops such as wheat to export. In the mid-nineteenth century, there were remarkable discoveries of gold, and mining other minerals would become significant exports, as Australia acted as a niche frontier economy for British and European investment and trade.

Meanwhile, Indigenous peoples' lands and waters were occupied and many lost their lives. They were subjected to hundreds of massacres and continuous and various forms of persecution by settlers.[8] There is still an extremely high incidence of over-incarceration of Aboriginal and Torres Strait Islander people who, in 2018, made up one in every four imprisoned adults, even though they represent just one in every fifty Australians. More than one in every two youths in Australian prisons in 2018 identified as Aboriginal and Torres Strait Islander people.[9] Similarly, greater levels of poverty, suicide, unemployment and low income are found in Indigenous compared with non-Indigenous peoples, especially for Aboriginal and Torres Strait Islander peoples living in more remote areas.[10] As a consequence, the average life expectancy at birth of Aboriginal and Torres Strait Islander peoples is markedly lower than for non-Indigenous Australians.

Not all Aboriginal and Torres Strait Islander peoples had the right to vote in both federal and state elections until 1965. Even then, to enrol and vote was not compulsory – as it was for non-Indigenous Australians – until 1984. Moreover, it took a referendum in 1967 for all Aboriginal and Torres Strait Islander peoples to be included in the Australian census. Prior to that time, an estimated separate count was made by the so-called 'native welfare authorities'. In 1971, the first Aboriginal and Torres Strait Islander person was appointed to the Federal Parliament. Yet an Indigenous Australian did not sit in the Federal Cabinet till 2019 – as the first Minister of Indigenous Australians. Today, there is still knowledge of around 250 Aboriginal and Torres Strait Islander languages, but fewer than one in two are spoken and nine out of ten such languages are endangered.[11]

These indicators of the inequity and prejudice that Aboriginal and Torres Strait Islander peoples have endured are framed in terms of assimilation. What about acceptance on their terms? What about non-Indigenous Australians assimilating with Indigenous modes of operating, of thinking, of living? If, as in Indigenous perceptions, 'rocks are sentient and contain spirit',[12] what of capitalist mining, industrial agriculture, industry and commerce? We are poles apart.

In mid-2020, the Anglo-Australian mining conglomerate Rio Tinto exploded, for iron ore, the sacred Juukan Gorge caves – that had been occupied by Indigenous Australians for at least 46,000 years, including throughout the last Ice Age. Despite outrage around Australia and from the rest of the world, Rio Tinto's iron ore chief executive would state that 'we haven't apologised for the event itself, per se, but apologised for the distress the event caused.' His careful wording pointed to the fact that the activity had legality via ministerial consent in 2013.[13]

The 1972 Western Australian Aboriginal Heritage Act is meant to protect sacred and culturally significant sites from such destruction and lists such sites in a register. But, writing in mid-2021, landholders could still apply to destroy Aboriginal heritage without any right of reply, let alone appeal, by traditional owners. Indeed, the non-Indigenous Minister for Aboriginal Affairs consented to all 18 mining company applications in the decade prior to the explosion of Juukan Gorge caves.[14] Continued threats of damage to, and obliteration of, Indigenous sites with numerous and various cultural values continues as 'destruction by a thousand cuts'.[15] As such, 'Juukan Gorge represents the pinnacle of the colonial mining project,' concludes Australian historian and commentator Clare Wright. 'It fulfils the Four-F rating that is at the heart of Australia's relationship to land: Find it. Fuck it. Flog it. Forget it.'[16]

In stark contrast, Indigenous Australians care for country because 'protecting what made us' is 'how to protect who we are'.[17] To see the deep parallels with scientific rationality of Indigenous peoples' practices and sacred perspectives of Earth and humanity, one only needs to read a book such as *The Sacred Balance* by geneticist, science journalist and environmental David Suzuki, with Amanda McConnell. We are air, water and soil. We use fire and need one another to survive.[18] Yet, 'the environmental equation that we have yet to master' points out James Cowan, is 'how to give back to the earth as much as we receive'.[19]

Even if unemployment figures for Indigenous Australians are relatively high, 'jobs are not what we want', argues Indigenous writer, artist, educator, and wood carver Tyson Yunkaporta. 'We want shelter, food, strong relationships, a liveable habitat, stimulating learning activity and time to perform valued tasks in which we excel.' He is just one of those who point out that, before being invaded and marginalised, they only worked 'a few hours' daily to fulfil their basic needs, spending surplus time enriching their relationships and communities with cultural activities. Culture is 'being like our place' for Indigenous peoples. Now, he concludes 'the land is only a pale shadow of the abundance that once was.'[20]

EDUARDO GALEANO

Uruguayan Eduardo Galeano was a prolific writer most celebrated for his creative non-fiction work *Open Veins of Latin America: Five Centuries of the Pillage of a Continent*.[21] In *Open Veins*, Galeano traces a rapacious history of dispossession as capital's soldiers and managers fractured the continent into territories and nations, and named the whole 'Latin America', an exotic trading playground in which Indigenous peoples almost always lost. They lost soil and minerals, they lost their cultures and virginity, they lost their languages, forms of governance and Indigenous sensibilities – all for the global accumulation of capital centralised in Europe and North America. Galeano details a half-millennium-long history with ethnographic and journalistic flair, embroidering narratives where money drives the plot.

Cyclic seasonal and natural rhythms of Indigenous cultures are challenged by the linear workday clock time of offices, machinery and stock exchanges. The perpetual abstract growth of money as capital concretely means expansive exploitation of landscapes and human energy. Revealing Latin American experiences dominated by and in conflict with capitalism, Galeano's rallying cry centred on the omnipotent force of money. Only prices are free, he wrote, and 'the freer the businesses, the more imprisoned are the people.'[22] But he offered closure: 'We say no to the praise of money and of death. We say no to a system that assigns prices to people and things ... By saying no to the freedom of money, we are saying yes to the freedom of the people.'[23]

Galeano's attacks on the market and his vision of a 'community-based mode of production' point to a form of socialism centred on real values, participatory governance and direct democracy.[24] Consequently, he is much closer to the Marx who railed against Proudhon and the Owenists for imagining that they could deliver justice by tweaking money, than he is to the statist socialisms of Castro's Cuba and Mao's China. Indeed, Galeano criticised Soviet communism: '[S]ocialism is not dead because it hasn't been born. It's something I hope that humanity may perhaps find.'[25]

In his *Upside Down: A Primer for the Looking-Glass World*, the world of exchange values is thrown into stark relief by the everyday search to fulfil basic needs and the struggle to maintain an Indigenous reverence for nature.[26] While mocking exchange values and monetary capitalist structures that contort social and environmental values, Galeano's analysis strips all our worlds back to the essentials of real values. Galeano continually points to the absurdity and vacuity of excessive consumption to reveal qualitative and experiential realities. His socialist vision requires re-growing the human and humane, the natural and ecological, a world of synergies with Indigenous, diverse and mega-natural relationships and values.

Many of Galeano's books comprise short-short stories that cascade into collages of meanings, communities and neighbourhoods of being. These short-short stories are cells with internal and external dynamics, in and for themselves – contributing to the whole just as leaves, fruit, bark and roots constitute a tree. He shows the absurdity of private property in Indian perspectives: 'The land has an owner?' yet 'We are its children ... it nurtures us ... It looks after us ... How is it to be sold? How bought?'[27] So Galeano calls for the restitution of local sustainability in a timeless and time-full approach: 'It's out of hope, not nostalgia, that we must recover a community-based mode of production and way of life, founded not on greed but on solidarity, age-old freedoms and identity between human beings and nature.'[28]

His space is glocal, reading the present as both an embodiment of the past and prescient of the future. The standardisation of human *being* that is characteristic of globalisation is indomitable because it unifies space and time in 'a sort of massacre of our capacity to be diverse, to have so many different ways to live life, celebrate, eat, dance, dream, drink, think, and feel'.[29] These insights support visions and strategies of a community mode of production that embodies diversity, security and plenty in a space full of spaces and a time full of times.

In short, Galeano seamlessly blends the people-and-planet caring approach central to postcapitalism in a language and images of a nurturing and abundant community mode of production imbued with Indigenous perspectives and ways of living. He binds tragedies of majority and minority worlds together by assessing both deplorable, even if for opposing reasons. He attacks disabling hierarchical cultures stuck in economism, and the simultaneous production of overconsumption and underconsumption.

Galeano's passion and politics work in postcapitalist directions distinct from political economy and traditional left politics. He points to a cultural process of *becoming* postcapitalist, through practices that revalue social relationships and Earth in terms of qualitative minimal-ism and efficacy. Galeano shows that another mode of production exists today – even if in tatters, even if as a shadow, even if in hope – in this space, in this time, in embryo.

ZAPATISTAS: GOVERNING BY 'OBEYING'

Emiliano Zapata emerged as a leader of the agrarian movement that was key to various practical and ideological aspects of the Mexican Revolu-tion of the early twentieth century. With the rallying call 'land and liberty', large estates (*haciendas*) were re-appropriated by peasants for collective self-provisioning alongside local councils for co-governance. Although assassinated in 1919, the grassroots character of the aims of Zapatismo were revived in the agrarian reforms of President Lázaro Cárdenas (1934–40) that redistributed expropriated haciendas for collective land tenure and institutionalised *ejidos*. *Ejidos* are tracts of land operated via communal (and individual) use rights allowing for collective forms of self-provisioning and co-governance. However, state-ownership and control of such lands limited their potential and neoliberal reforms paving the way for the North American Free Trade Agreement (NAFTA) marked a further transition, to private property.

Nevertheless the revolutionary aspect of this fractured and tenuous lineage of Indigenous and collective peasant self-sufficiency and autonomy in Mexico became visible when the Zapatista Army of National Liberation (*Ejército Zapatista de Liberación Nacional*, EZLN), familiarly known as the Zapatistas, strongly resisted the practical imple-mentation of NAFTA beginning on 1 January 1994. As the EZLN took cities across Chiapas and the state responded violently, students and others took to the streets with such an effect that an uneasy truce quickly ensued. This left the Zapatistas bereft of state support as well as state control, but they drew on centuries of Indigenous practical ingenuity and political resistance to colonisation. 'When the EZLN says that they struggle for democracy, justice, freedom, autonomy, and a dignified life', writes human rights activist Dylan Eldredge Fitzwater, 'these terms are spoken and interpreted in the contemporary words and voices of Tsotsil, Tzeltal, Tojolabal, Chol, Mam, Zoque, and a form of Spanish that has been deeply influenced by the cultural referents of these [Indigenous peoples'] languages.'[30]

Not taking power: Autonomy

The Zapatistas represent a peculiarly twenty-first-century movement with a horizontal organisation influenced by Indigenous, Marxist and anarchist thought and practices – as in horizontal autonomy, mutual respect and collective practices – and with global impacts and networks, such as with the food sovereignty, Occupy and alter-globalisation movements.[31] Even as they are challenged by, and resist, the Mexican state militarily – through occupation of land that they have redistributed – Zapatistas hold firm to a revolutionary strategy of *not taking power*, eschewing state forms of hierarchical dominance and control.[32]

Vision and practice centres on grassroots substantive democracy through various forms of autonomous governance, educational, health and media services, and continuous resistance to the Mexican state. Seven guiding principles clarify distinctions between their practices and those of mainstream capitalist economies and polities. Instead of the selfish, individualistic and competitive homo economicus – one serves others, genuinely represents rather than stands in place of others, constructs rather than destructs, obeys rather than rules, proposes rather than forces, convinces rather than conquers, and is humble rather than arrogant.[33]

Different structures of autonomous governance are subservient to the thousands of communities that instruct municipal governance, the *caracoles* and independent good government councils. All these types of institutions are necessarily fluid because they are determined autonomously in distinctive forms. Yet all rotate on the seven principles and Zapatista rights, including women's equality, eschewing the state and the right to defence. The assembly is the beating collective heart of autonomous governance, a forum for proposals, their acceptance or rejection, and evaluation for implementation via monitoring. Agreements in the form of working documents substitute for an ironclad constitution. Injustice is addressed via resolution not punishment, so there is no police force. Equally, the distributed use of force means that 'government does not have a monopoly on the legitimate use of force and no organized armed forces have power over the government.'[34]

In complete contrast to capitalist work for money, tasks of production and governance serve the collective. Work is decolonised, neither hierarchical nor for money but for local people. There is direct collective control of what is produced, how and by whom in the local economies;

collective work in fields of corn, beans and vegetables, and work on the infrastructures on which they rely, such as water supplies, are the material basis for life.[35] Those tasked with governing in rotating positions are supported by food in-kind.[36] It's recognised that too few women are involved in collective governing, mainly because men fail to relieve their *compañeras* of household tasks, so sons and brothers are encouraged to learn 'how to make tortillas'.[37] Yet, it's also acknowledged that within Mexico more generally, a Zapatista woman has 'a much more equal role in decision making than in other indigenous or rural communities'.[38] There are no advantages or perks to governing; it's a chore to properly govern by obeying the people. At the same time, production involves governance and governance involves production.

Zapatista influence

Ecological economist David Barkin's work has highlighted the loss of Mexico's food self-sufficiency in the latter half of the twentieth century and over the last few decades, beyond Zapatista territories, an upsurge of 'millions of Mexicans' who, to varying extents, practice autonomy, self-sufficiency, diverse local and sustainable production of community forests, plant growing and animal caring.[39] Despite ongoing conflicts with capitalist developments Barkin regards such initiatives – that clearly point to postcapitalism – as 'extremely important and encouraging', couched within a hemisphere of actions that might fall short of Zapatista power but do bear its spirit.[40]

Within a few years of its visible existence, Autonomist Marxist Harry Cleaver would write that the Zapatista movement 'set in motion the beginnings of a world-wide discussion about the current state of the class struggle and of a world-wide mobilization aimed at finding new and more effective ways of interlinking both opposition to capitalism and mutual aid in the elaboration of alternatives'.[41] The Zapatistas have made clear the leap necessary to heal the alienation of both Earth and people implicit in capitalist forms of operating. Their solidarity is global, their networks phenomenal: 'we make the pains of the earth our own'.[42] They have drawn on past and current models to create appropriate forms of governance and production for the twenty-first century. As Gottesdiener reported, after staying in Zapatista territory in the mid-2010s, 'The Berlin Wall had fallen. The market had triumphed … yet surging out of the jungles came a movement of people with no market value and the audacity to refuse to disappear.'[43]

A 'zad' (*zone à defender*, zone to defend) is an occupation to deter a planned development. Arguably, the most famous has been at Notre-Dame-des-Landes in France where a proposed international airport was prevented by a coalition of occupiers and their supporters. They fought for around a decade until the state cancelled its plans for the airport. In this zad collective, institutions of interdependency included regular exchange on a 'pay-as-you-want' basis, dedicated spaces to drop off and pick up free unwanted goods for reuse, and 'non-markets'. Facilities and spaces have been shared as commons to allow access to the Internet or to meet, and share food or practices, such as studios and workshops. Resources have been shared on the basis of people's needs and the potential of the local environment to support them. Such spaces of spontaneous eruption of communal living draw from historical trajectories of collective protest to communal occupations that typify anti-capitalist resistance.[44]

In growing networks, zads and similar anti-capitalist communities share knowledge and skills:

After the return of a delegation from the zad from a visit to the Zapatistas in Chiapas in the winter of 2015, occupiers talked about a traditional communality, still alive and transcended by a revolutionary movement, ritualized by festivals, with key functions taken in charge by changing personnel and communal tasks performed collectively – a communality in which each individual is nothing but what connects him or her to the land and others.[45]

KURDS

There are clear similarities between the Zapatista movement and 'Rojava', the Autonomous Administration of North and East Syria. Both have drawn on practices with millennia-long cultural roots, conscious of contemporary anarchist, socialist and feminist philosophies, and both became armed presences under military threat for the last few decades.[46] Around 4 million people, who live within the democratic confederation that declared autonomy in 2014, follow non-hierarchical principles of decentralised co-governance, with hundreds of neighbourhoods and thousands of communes incorporating communities across seven regions. A cooperative economy seeks to meet every resident's basic needs. Inclusion subverts ethnic or religious dominance. People in all their diversity and power are sovereign.

As this manuscript was finalised in mid-2021, a Turkish military campaign to occupy South Kurdistan, which had started months earlier, was still in play. Despite strong resistance from guerrilla fighters defending the Kurdish peoples and their achievements, without strong international support, the Turkish government had extended their project to occupy all Rojava as well as South Kurdistan. Unfortunately, such onslaughts are all too familiar, forming a menacing backdrop and making their revolutionary activities all the more extraordinary.

Background

The Kurds continued to live in mountainous Kurdistan after their forceful division into minorities in Syria, Turkey, Iran and Iraq after the First World War.[47] In the process, weakened and oppressed by various regimes, some 35 million Kurds became the largest stateless 'nation'. Later, the collapse of states such as Iraq and Syria allowed them to regain control of their lives. Nevertheless, they have been continuously distracted from their mission to forge democratic confederalism as pawns in global Middle Eastern politics involving the United States, in a defence against jihadists and ISIS, and treated as terrorists by the Turkish state, losing some 40,000 lives in struggles between 1984 and 1993.

In 1979, Abdullah Öcalan, a leader of the Kurdistan Workers Party (1978–), withdrew to Syria before being captured and imprisoned for life two decades later, in 1999. During exile, and in seclusion, Öcalan has remained active as a strategist, reading prolifically, reflecting on the Kurds' current challenges and experiences, and proposing a radical philosophy and polity for the future of both Kurdish and non-Kurdish peoples. Strongly influenced by Murray Bookchin and social ecology, Öcalan proposed a democratic confederalism and strengthening non-gendered social roles with strong grassroots democracy to replace the nation state. Öcalan's thought informs, and has been informed by, the activities and experiences of revolutionary Kurds.

Revolutionary change

The withdrawal of Syrian forces from western Kurdistan after the 2011 Arab Spring protests offered an opportunity to test social, economic and political forms and processes for living autonomously.[48] The thrust was inclusive and grassroots. Kurdish feminism flourished and the 'Tev-Dem' (*Tevgera Civaka Demokratik* (in Kurdish) – Movement for a Democratic Society) developed to heal divisions heightened by Syrian rule, to embrace both Kurds and a range of non-Kurdish peoples living in Rojava. By August 2011, a considerable proportion of the population were self-organising in community councils and the elected Tev-Dem facilitated the formation of a coherent model of grassroots governance complemented by autonomous institutions.

These experiences informed the development of principles, structures and processes of democratic autonomy, a decentralised confederation, formalised early in 2014 whereby around thirty households form a commune with committees advancing specific interests. People collectively decide, consensually, what they will produce on their land – reminiscent of a traditional village. 'Ecology and feminism are central pillars,' writes Öcalan, backed by a strong critique of the patriarchal family 'as man's small state'.[49] Via one female and one male representative, communes contribute to assemblies governing a locality. Similar representation is replicated within a broader district, a canton and/or region up to the broadest council. Women contribute to committees for conciliation, to policing tasks and to the army.

Not surprisingly, the integration of women and youth face cultural challenges. But the anarchist American anthropologist David Graeber points out stronger tensions within their dual top-down and bottom-up structure. The orientation at the top is driven by a necessary and time-consuming engagement in highly politicised international diplomatic and trading relations, along with military involvements. In contrast, the domestic grassroots system remains internally controlled, potentially more consistent, coherent and radical.[50]

Social economy: Cooperative economy

The social cooperative economy is democratically and communally governed and, as such, both local and generic models are relatively fluid and experimental.[51] The aim is to integrate women fully, to stop male dominance and to gain the benefit of female needs-based and use value-oriented approaches. The social economy is based on ecological harmony and mutuality, eschewing speculation, exploitation and monopoly (as well as feudal practices). Cooperatives are mainly agricultural but encompass craftwork, personal services, hospitality, industry and infrastructural services as well. Water, land and energy are considered communal.

If private enterprises exist and are even protected, their existence is subject to them serving the people. Certain shops are dedicated to selling affordable essentials. Administering within a war emergency, embargos and supporting fighters, the revolutionary administration is the provider of last resort via purchase and distribution. Obtaining industrial technology is a key challenge; import substitution is encouraged, as are activities that satisfy needs in new ways, such as novel crops. The economy is 'eco-industrial' so that the ecological base is highly respected and differentiates their model from both centrally planned and capitalist economies.[52]

In contrast to most cooperatives established within capitalist contexts, various Rojavan cooperatives, based as they are on active assemblies and committees, challenge a wages and incomes model. They are directly linked with democratic control of ecologically sustainable production focusing on basic needs. Some distribute produce in-kind among their members, others according to need, and time is volunteered in cooperative activities. In a standard model, the redistribution of around 70 per cent of a cooperative's monetary income is decided by (and often divided among) cooperative members, with, say, around 25 per cent reinvested in cooperative activities and up to 5 per cent going to the regional union of cooperatives. Products surplus to directly fulfilling local needs are marketed locally or directly passed on to cooperative stores and retailers for cooperative marketing. Still, any such common and ideal principles are differentially applied because they are subject to grassroots decision making.

The flux of a transitional economy is illustrated by an analyst sympathetic to the Rojavan cooperative economy, who engages with Marxist critiques of cooperatives and briefly entertains nonmonetary economies. A 'small-scale experiment' in a Rojavan village 'where money has been abolished as a daily tool' is mentioned, with the point made that 'core principles of a cooperative can also (probably even better) be applied in a system without any wage or even without any money.'[53] However, the analyst concludes, in a rather Hegelian and idealistic way, that 'whether a cooperative is revolutionary or not depends on whether the intention of its members is revolutionary or not.'[54] Moreover, beyond questions around wages, the author eschews questions about the structural problems caused by money.

Indeed, Öcalan's thought is neither fundamentally anti-market nor sceptical of money, instead identifying both the *nation state* and profiteering as the definitive heart and lungs of capitalism.[55] Öcalan writes that economic autonomy 'does not reject the market, trade, product variety, competition and productivity', although they do *minimise* profiteering and accumulation of capital. Consequently, '[f]inance and financial systems are validated only in so far as they serve economic productivity and functionality.'[56] Yet, a short mid-2016 report of the Rojavan economy outlines tensions between cooperative production and market prices, urban and rural production, and weakness in the face of global trade and financialisation – to conclude that 'the market problem is one of the most difficult problems to solve.'[57]

So, why have the market and money not received the wholesale criticism reserved for the state in the works of Öcalan and the practices of the Rojavan social economy, the cooperative economy? Is this due to interruptions and distractions associated with an effective war economy, or a particular stage in the transition? References to revolutionary Spain inform reflections on such questions on money and exchange in revolutionary transformation.

SPAIN, 1936–37

In the Spanish Civil War – triggered by a military coup in July 1936 – organised workers, anarchists, libertarian socialists and peasants sought to bring about broadscale anti-capitalist change by abolishing state institutions, and taking control of industry via councils and collectivising agrarian areas. Here, as Vernon Richards writes, 'the scale on which the collectivist enterprises operated in Spain was such as to silence for once and for all those critics who argue that self-management along anarchist lines is possible on a small scale but quite impractical when applied to large enterprises and urban concentrations.'[58]

Most significantly, Gaston Leval details a variety of experiments with local currencies, ration tokens, vouchers, tickets, barter and 'points', that were all aimed to achieve 'equality of the means of existence' as transactions in quasi-monies were counterbalanced, or infused with, mutual aid.[59] He emphasises that 'the prime movers of the Collective wanted at all costs to avoid a return to the monetary system, to accursed "money".'[60]

Even where local currencies had evolved most, they referred back to the official currency, the peseta. In the event, 'serious inequalities were avoided' by rationing and direct provision in kind of daily needs such as housing, education, medicinal services and goods, roads, nurseries and water supplies.[61]

If the existence of money and interest-free loans proved necessary in the realm of distribution in Aragon, because contributions still included waged labour, a significant change had meant that 'work was not an irksome task.'[62] Most significantly, the political formation of the collective usurped the syndicate, and the future overtook the past.[63] Leval's libertarian democracy in the making saw 'a structuring from the bottom to the top, which corresponds to a real federation and true democracy', in other words 'quite different to what it is or would be in a State apparatus'.[64]

In Naval village, Leval reports, 'No money, not even local money, no rationing. Free consumption from the first day, but supervised consumption.'[65] In Barbastro, 'a rations table was established without *libreta*, without national or local money', but takings were monitored, supervised and recorded, keeping records in kind, such as in weights of grains or meat, and, 'there was never disorder.'[66] This type of 'solidarity bookkeeping', along with audits of local resources, not only informed barter – as practised by CNT (National Confederation of Labour) and UGT (General Union of Workers) collectives and syndicates – but, most significantly, would establish 'mutual aid on a permanent footing'.[67] What becomes distinct here is the conscious, if fleeting, substitution of monetary accounting with in-kind decision making in terms of ecological and social realities and needs.

This grassroots development had greater potential to advance in the direction outlined in Yenomon (Chapter 3) than Soviet experiments of moving away from money – doomed to be superficial and transitory due to their proclivity to calculation and principles of efficiency based on simplifying indicators.[68] In contrast, the revolutionary impulse of satisfying basic needs has the potential to seriously disrupt and compete with monetary values and trade to the point of defeat. Revolutionaries substitute production for trade with production for collective sufficiency. Sharing the collective produce is monitored to ensure that the needs of individuals and households are met within a bigger picture of collective and communal justice. Consequently, there is not only no need for money and trade but both appear counter-intuitive, odd and outdated.

CONCLUSION

A decentralised community mode of production common to non-capitalist and nonmarket-oriented societies is the most direct way to achieve postcapitalism. Here, people consciously and conscientiously relate in terms of their rights to various and non-equivalent needs; they measure what exists and is being planned or possible in terms of their real values; they co-design, co-plan and co-produce what is then distributed on the basis of the needs of local people and the local environment. They can also deliberately produce for, or offer their surplus to, those beyond the locale who live by the same principles.

Targeting the direct needs of people without the unnecessary, indeed confusing, contorting and destabilising, mediation of money is essential. Commoning allows co-production through deliberative and appropriate distribution on the bases of use rights and use values – enabling collective self-provisioning without finance. Indeed, in this context, finance can be seen as an outdated device to assert the dominance of private, and public, property.

The locale is the most immediate, direct and appropriate unit of production to maximise effective and efficient co-governance and distribution, as well as to maintain a balance with the regenerative potential of Earth. Free traffic of ideas and communication of all kinds continue across and between regions in a profusion that is far beyond the interchanges between capitalist firms and states. Capitalist communications over production and distribution are contained and secretive, due to characteristically competitive practices shown, for instance, in the breadth and depth of intellectual property laws and regulations. In contrast, in nonmonetary postcapitalism, a global community of peers can thrive via open communication and learning. But goods and people move to a smaller extent and more slowly, according to ecological and social efficiencies, always respecting Earth's limits.

The propelling and generative force of postcapitalism is highly conscious and conscientious political decision making – way beyond the commodification of capitalism, beyond cooperatives that rely on market exchange, beyond community currencies or community banks. Instead, we need to perceive the world in terms of real social and ecological values, with practices based on direct decision making over existing local conditions and our potential to satisfy the needs of Earth and each and every person simultaneously.

8
Occupy the World!

We have had the good fortune to be born on planet Earth but the misfortune to be born at a point in history when most societies globally are dominated by capitalist practices and monetary dynamics. The extent of Earth managed under capitalist principles – or neglected because capitalist and state forces deem them of no immediate monetary value – has never been greater. It would be counterproductive for anti-capitalist forces to speak with one voice or act as one body. Yet the alliances necessary for transformation require shared understandings of capitalist dynamics and common principles for those diverse yet integrated 'beyonds' to which we all would like to head.

Ecological unsustainability, economic crises and political poverty have continued to deteriorate at more rapid rates in the early 2020s. Precarity, frustrations, dangers and exploitation once defining the disadvantaged are now widespread among classes. Needless and endless commodification, technological 'advances' and debts surround us. Underconsumption is a popular driver of growth while overconsumption transforms Earth into graceless techno-landscapes and adds mountains of waste, impeding our species security. Not only are essential needs unevenly satisfied but our real need to make decisions on how we live is absent. Curbing carbon emissions sinks like a stone in a well, simply leaving ripples. Extinction Rebellion (XR) is but one movement expressing angst at our collective condition and calling for us to act now.

Major factions of other movements, such as ecosocialism, degrowth, ecofeminism and Indigenous peoples' movements highlight socio-political and economic inequalities, social and environmental injustices, and ecological unsustainability. A plethora of campaigns implicitly highlight the critical challenges posed by capitalism, the monetary economy *par excellence*. As such, anthropogenic capitalist dynamics rely on monetary exchanges, calculations and economies that rotate on competition and insecurities cut adrift from critical ecological matters.

This work intervenes in the politics of the 2020s to state that non-monetary practices are a necessary, even if not sufficient, step to forms of postcapitalism that focus on real values of both humans and Earth. To creatively and collectively self-provision and nurture Earth, we need to re-enchant the world with natural and humane values, directly and cooperatively determining production and distribution for our collective needs. Prior to discussing clear and already emergent ways forward, twenty-first-century movements and topics such as nonviolence and commoning, I address so-called 'alternative' monies. You might well have expected to encounter this topic earlier but, due to the particular arc of arguments in this work, its discussion fell most neatly here.

SO-CALLED 'ALTERNATIVE' MONIES

The transition is on everyone's lips. We're experimenting with ways to transform ourselves and our lives beyond inequalities and unsustainability. Where are we going? How will we get there? Market-oriented cooperative structures and community banks are attractive models but offer few benefits beyond being managed by community-oriented and environmentally friendly people and principles. Similarly, universal basic income schemes that rely on monetary re-distribution – rather than working at creating essentials that are distributed on the basis of need – tend to support profit-making business, not only their recipients. Market-oriented models have not offered us successful avenues to postcapitalism. In contrast, models such as an 'unconditional autonomy allowance', which can be delivered wholly in-kind, say through universal basic services, offer more promising pathways.[1]

Among the suite of 'alternative' ways of producing and exchanging, many advocate alternative monies as a transitionary strategy. However, by definition, alternative monies mimic functions of mainstream money, most often operating as a complementary currency, as a relatively informal means of exchange and standard, alongside and within capitalist contexts. As such, alternative money groups either establish a formal exchange rate with legal tender or participants readily refer to mainstream market prices when calculating their exchanges. As a member, since the 1980s, of various Australian LETS (local (or labour) exchange trading system, or local energy transfer system), I have direct experience as well as knowledge of such schemes, which work in various ways. I generally refer to two distinctive models in which such schemes operate and to a departure, which throws the lack of radical potential of LETS into stark relief. Most other alternative currency schemes, such as the Community Exchange System (CES), operate in similar ways and replicate key failings of LETS.

The first and most general LETS model has a local currency linked, through the habits of participants, to legal tender, for example, a dollar or pound. Many exchanges in so-called 'alternative' schemes mirror price equivalences in local markets and, as such, offer little in the way of an alternative system at all. Similar outcomes could, and are, achieved when friends offer credit to one another, except that LETS offers the opportunity of multilateral credit for numerous two-way exchanges. LETS transactions often include a direct legal tender charge for materials or equipment use, which mainstreams exchanges even further. These exchange groups (circles) can bring together like-minded people who, say, reuse and recycle devices and materials, and enable those on low incomes to use direct labour to access goods and services they need. But, simply operating at the level of exchange in ways that mimic mainstream exchanges, LETS fails to change ways that people produce.

However, certain LETS encourage members to exchange on the basis of labour equivalence: a doctor's hour = a gardener's hour = a childminder's hour = a masseur's hour. This introduces a clear alternative to mainstream markets by introducing a principle of equity. Yet, the dominant context of LETS exchanges is a free market of competitive and widely varying standard wage rates that partially reflect the extra costs of developing certain skills and the intensity of certain work (such as qualifying to become a doctor). Contradictions between a mainstream context and LETS exchanges impinge on members' practices, for instance, dissuading those getting higher wages from joining or exchanging their labour. Those on higher wages who do exchange on the basis of time equity generally do not agree with wage differentiation in the first place. So this model allows for acts of radical generosity and, to that extent, offers more in the way of a genuine alternative. At the same time, in the mainstream economy, friends volunteer similar efforts and certain professionals readily make discounts for those on lower incomes as a matter of course. In short, LETS is not necessary to achieve similar outcomes.

The most radical development that I have heard of transformed a relatively small LETS into a voluntary and free gifting system among its few dozen members. This post-LETS system is one of mutual support. Those in need put out a call and those with the capacity or capability to respond do so generously: 'What goes around comes around.' While such practices are akin to familial support, supportive friendships and donating in the mainstream system, a formal dedicated mutual support system is markedly different from completely voluntary and ad hoc charity.[2] That such radicalism was only achieved by transforming away from the alternative currency is the last word on such 'alternatives'.

THE CATALAN INTEGRAL COOPERATIVE

LETS are a simple form of alternative exchange. A range of models, such as the CES, use online platforms to communicate and record their exchanges. Mainly set up in advanced capitalist settings, alternative exchange schemes also exist in locations such as majority-world informal settlements – offering extra ways for those who are politically or economically marginalised to conduct useful exchanges. However, in neither context have such partial economic activities led to substantial social transformation. At the other end of the spectrum from alternative exchange schemes are radical and holistic transitionary experiments, such as the *Cooperativa Integral Catalana*, the Catalan Integral Cooperative (CIC).

Expressions of revolutionary change such as CIC move simultaneously on two legs. In localised, decentralised and networked grassroots movements, so-called 'ordinary' people co-govern and create new forms of economic organisation on modest and localised scales in order to usurp, and practically deconstruct, capitalist economies. They are moved by, and co-create, big-picture ideas and practices of revolutionary change that offer sophisticated forms of networked co-governance and typify the most exuberant transitionary currents.

CIC uses local alternative currencies and a financial network with interest-free loans to promote ecological production and fair distribution of basic needs. In partnership with the P2P Foundation, CIC has been associated with the development and operation of the global digital cryptocurrency FairCoin (with an exchange rate with the euro), FairCoop and other open-source 'Fair' tools.[3] This peer-to-peer (P2P) movement organisation, which advocates commoning, informs and is informed by processes of self-governance within CIC and other such associations and activities. Fortunately, FairCoin has the ecological advantage of operating on a fraction of the energy required for Bitcoin.[4]

Starting in May 2010, by 2014 the scale of CIC was reported as around 300 individual and collective projects of a productive nature; 30 market nodes using community exchange (online accounting) systems (*Ecoxarxes*) with many local currencies; 15 intentional communities (both large and small); 1,700 individual and collective members, and an estimated 4,000–5,000 active participants. In the strongly autonomous and anarchist traditions of the Catalan independence movement and their distinctive language and culture, CIC's democratic practices of open, transparent, direct and participatory deliberation, self-organisation and decentralisation meet practices of permaculture, agroecology, degrowth and ecological sustainability aiming towards 'a communal society'.[5] Moreover, certain CIC activists have always acted to stimulate and incubate a 'worldwide integral revolution'.[6]

By 2017, the umbrella CIC was reported as operating dynamically with ten key committees supporting several dozen committee functionaries with a basic income derived from fees from members and a range of donations and other revenues. Hundreds of semi-autonomous individual and collective members used CIC accounting and reporting systems to operate. Members of local exchange networks totalled more than 2,600, with more than 40 local eco-networks and some 20 pantry-nodes organising extensive food distribution throughout Catalonia. With local governance on the basis of subsidiarity, bioregional assemblies existed in both South and North Catalonia. Some projects nurtured by CIC are semi-autonomous, or autonomous partners. Moreover, CIC economic activities are porous, with perhaps a couple of tens of thousands of non-members engaging in certain exchanges and activities.[7]

Techno-nerdery

When in Barcelona back in mid-2012, I came into contact with CIC activists Didac Sanchez-Costa and Carolina Zerpa, and frequented the rural Calafou, some CIC markets and nodes, and the CIC *AureaSocial* workshop and discussion space in the centre of Barcelona. At that time, the most visible activities of CIC's housing, living and working project Calafou – based on an abandoned textile colony near Vallbona d'Anoia – seemed to be the hacklab[8] and a mechanical workshop for repairing vehicles from motorbikes to trucks.[9]

Another visitor to Calafou, this time in 2016, noted:

> a multitude of productive activities and community infrastructures, including a carpentry, a mechanical workshop, a botanical garden, a community kitchen, a biolab, a hacklab, a soap production lab, a professional music studio, a guest-house for visitors, a social centre with a free shop, as well as a plethora of other productive projects.[10]

This postcapitalist eco-industrial colony with a few dozen dwellings, and communal assemblies every weekend, focuses on making and repairing tools and technological infrastructure, aiming for technological sovereignty based on sharing collectively and situated know-how.[11] Another CIC-initiated but autonomous project, MaCUS (2012–) in Sant Martí, has broad craft and arts, as well as traditional and postmodern technological foci such as a 3D printer.

CIC's scientific techniques and technology network develops appropriate devices and supports copyleft licensing.[12] This technical work dovetails with their collaboration with the P2P Foundation and other global networks. Obviously, this 'smart' and 'brainy' emphasis within CIC over the last decade has had many positive appropriate technology spin-offs.[13] Less constructive consequences include perceiving money and financial processes more as malleable tools that simply require the application of sophisticated digital technologies along with community-based management to advance revolutionary change – rather than appreciate that the fundamental concepts and practices of money and markets produce a dominating exchange value, universal equivalent, and unit of account that is destructive in its social consequences and ecological implications.

The 'alternative' techno CIC economy

The holistic CIC model tends to be politically advanced in its open and decentralised horizontal politicking and networking. Yet CIC is limited to the extent that alternative monetary exchange and financial models mimic market exchange and economies in significant, subtle and obscure ways, even if they are under community management and apply ethical principles. In effect, would-be revolutionaries are creating their own alternative set of technical wands and wizardry, while production and distribution continue to refer back to mystifying and totalising abstract values or indicators rather than the plethora of real, social and ecological, values.

In 2014, CIC founder Enric Duran declared that blockchain technology, on which Bitcoin is based, 'holds the power to make the current banking and financial systems obsolete'. Although acknowledging problems with Bitcoin, Duran saw cryptocurrencies more generally facilitating a postcapitalist transition by freeing the CIC network from capitalist banks and other institutions. This approach shows little suspicion of money or market per se. I conclude that those with a technical or managerial bias seem to be attracted to use money as a managerial unit of apparent technological efficiency. To complicate matters, their efforts towards alternatives are confusingly referred to by certain observers as 'nonmonetary'.[14]

The Integral Community Exchange System (IntegralCES) has a software system distinct from its inspiration, the international South African-born CES. IntegralCES services local exchange groups and connects them with other *Ecoxarxes*.[15] Their online crowd-funding-style CoopFunding offers interest-free cooperative co-financing for CIC projects under members' collective and decentralised control, using their generic 'eco', an inconvertible CIC social currency. Members also operate with euros, cryptocurrencies such as Faircoins and Bitcoins, and other local currencies, including certain LETS ones.[16] Moreover, local markets are based on local, as well as the generic social, currencies.[17]

Thus exchange rates are set, or develop, between such currencies. Meanwhile, barter, time banks and gift exchanges exist as mutual support mechanisms – just as with LETS, and even in the mainstream economy, people with social and ecological ethics engage in informal acts of generosity and solidarity.

As such, CIC members seem to hedge and use all types of exchange according to circumstance. In this context, long-standing CIC member Joel Morist expects the futures of fiat money and various social currencies to sort out of their own accord over time.[18] His views are reminiscent of ecological economist Alf Hornborg's prescriptions for substituting general-purpose money with specially designed and managed local and diverse monies-cum-markets.[19] These approaches hold in common strong critiques of capitalist money, especially for functioning seemingly under monopolistic state control, at a global scale and for selfish profit-making ends. But they seem convinced that local monies and community-based ethics can produce local economies under community control. Yet, in as much as exchange rates exist between the various currencies that CIC members engage in, there is in effect *one* unit of account, a universal equivalent that, for argument's sake, devolves back to the euro.

The 'alternative' techno CIC economy raises further questions. How are digital, open source and techno-systems applied with respect to everyday social reproduction and care, such as with pregnancies, child-rearing and care of the elderly – and daily provisioning as in bioregional farming and food preservation and preparation practices? In short, what do radical Catalan women, including ecofeminists, think of all this? And, what approaches make most sense to those producing in the fields?[20] Where do CIC economic models stand in comparison with, or in contrast to, Indigenous peoples' traditional forms of community modes of production, which take a direct route to managing production on the basis of needs of people and planet using commoning and sharing? How do alternative currency and financing systems deal with the essentially unjust social dynamics of price, and the irreducibility of ecological values to a singular indicator or even a suite of indicators?

As mentioned earlier, the P2P Foundation informs and is informed by the activities of CIC. The P2P Foundation work *Accounting for Planetary Survival* is replete with 'transvestment', a 'thermodynamics of peer production', a 'crypto economy for the common good' with exchange and 'a fair and generative ethical market', all topped up by 'a planning framework that reflects a protection of planetary boundaries, and regulates access to the flows of matter-energy in order to determine the bounds of usage through thresholds and allocations of natural resources, as well as societal priorities'.[21]

Such a paradigm has similarities with market socialist planning, steady-state economy and even mainstream or heterodox – say, Keynesian and neo-Keynesian – models. Moreover, the computational direction aligns with strong currents in the Project Society After Money research led by Jens Schröter (University of Bonn, Germany) – currents that seek to 'substitute' money as we know it with algorithms and other forms of artificial, as if super-human, intelligence.[22] All such attempts seem to be characterised by attraction to an objective measure of efficiency, and assume successful human collaboration and exchange needs to be based on markets and production for trade patterned via indicators that are quasi-units of account or equivalents.[23]

Beyond the state?

Duran has characterised CIC in a state socialist or Polanyian way, framing it as 'an economy "with" a market' but arguing that 'it's not a "market economy"' because 'economic activity is subordinated to political process, or, put another way, the assembly takes precedence over the market.'[24] Clearly, money and market are reduced to tools that can be managed in socio-political ways. In 2021, CIC's community-controlled 'social currency' is still perceived as a useful tool and operates as a unit of account in prices agreed on by buyers and sellers.[25] Local, and let's say 'prosumer', nodes operate via a non-accumulable 'eco-basics' currency.

Why are such currencies problematic? A universal equivalent is essentially the unit of account in which prices are formed, prices that inform decision making by producers, evolving in an *anthropocentric* game distancing both ecological and social values. In as much as models of community-based agriculture create prosumers, they purchase and sell using logic and practices that, through comparison, inevitably refer to the mainstream market and prices in legal tender. The market–money nexus remains a contextual source of alienation, alienation between people, and alienation between people and Earth. Producers tend to market-centricity rather than producing and exchanging along genuine, local, community- and nature-centricity (as in Yenomon).

In certain CIC spheres, such as healthcare, common good resources are pooled, donated to a commons and nonmonetary measures operate in production and distribution. The state has been characterised by Duran as 'better than nothing at all for those who don't want, or know how, to self-organize at a community and mutual aid level', but as an institution the state is considered outdated in the face of sophisticated technology and autonomous initiatives operated on CIC's voluntary principles.[26] Yet, despite the aim of collective provisioning of basic services, this aspect of CIC activities has been contained and restrained because, seemingly perversely, many members prefer to get by using state welfare.[27]

The anti-state sentiment, yet proclivity to recreating monies, warrants interrogation at another level. State theories of the origins of money present a compelling narrative explaining how and why money stands for universal equivalence, as in a unit of account. In a recent work on money, Swiss economic sociologist Axel T. Paul reviews literature on how temples and palaces operated from the seventh century BCE with tokens, or 'receipts' signed off by both deliverer and receiver, in units that stood for a range of substitutable in-kind tributes. In this way, through bureaucratic fiat, issued as payment to Sumerian temple staff, the shekel became 'the first monetary unit we know of that remained valid for thousands of years'. The shekel was a unit of account to the extent that temple administrators identified a series of goods and services as equivalent for the purposes of fulfilling levies for the ruling class, and regulated their quantitative worth in shekel 'prices'. So, along with determining a linear calendar in which to specify contractual times and dates, a restricted market and loans repaid with interest, developed. In short, Paul concludes that, in Mesopotamia, 'central planning gave birth to the market.'[28] All this implies a multi-dimensional universe of fabrications or ways of looking at and dealing with 'the world', Earth and social organisation.

Following Paul, it takes until the fifth century BCE for a society oriented around both market and money to arise in Greece, specifically in Athens and based on the Tetradrachm currency. Coins, which stand for an abstract unit of account, are introduced in the mid-sixth century BCE from Lydia, having arisen in the seventh century BCE in the form of stamped pieces of electrum with which soldiers, and possibly others, were paid. And this, so the theory goes, stimulates a free market via a currency in which taxes are to be paid. As such, by the fourth century BCE, Plato and Aristotle can have their conversation on money as a vital organising tool but with spurious uses for unjust gains.[29] The market and trade cannot arise without associated social roles and relations in which capitalist and worker finally evolve as stereotypes. In the process, money becomes a convincing and significant equivalent.

An intriguing aspect of this narrative of the rise of money is its framing by and of the state – a salutary tale and food for thought for those who are anti-state but neutral with respect to the market, and for those who regard markets and money as malleable and subject to reform. My point is that money is not only the spider sitting in the web, but also the spider spinning the web. Money's unique and all-pervading function is that of a universal equivalent, a unit of account which becomes a dictatorial standard of value and hub from which all spokes of capitalism rotate. Consequently, we need to be deconstructing such monetary practices, not reconstructing them in 'alternative' forms.

REALLY APPROPRIATE APPROACHES

In short, alternative currencies are among a range of models incompatible with postcapitalism because they are hardwired to capitalist imaginaries and practices of markets and trading. Such efforts divert and delay transition to the seamless efficiencies, deeply shared autonomous power and diversities of genuinely glocal community modes of production, as discussed in Chapter 3, Chapter 7 and taken up in the anti-capitalist green materialism discussion below. Alternative currencies, monetary reforms and simplistic ecological indicators are barriers to replacing the entire sphere of exchange value by direct collective governance of localised production and associated distribution, sharing and caring on the basis of transparent needs and real values. Other bridges and avenues to holistic transformation exist, as shown in the following summary description of a practical alternative and embryonic community mode of production, the Twin Oaks Community.[30]

Around a hundred people of all ages live at the rural Twin Oaks Community, which started well before the rise of digital technologies, more than fifty years ago, in central Virginia (US). The internal organisation of this intentional community is income sharing with one purse, everyone working on collective provisioning for direct use and some activities in 'cottage industries' for trade beyond the community. Each week, everyone works around 42 hours – mainly on domestic and self-provisioning activities, as well as some production for trade – unless on holidays or sick, or eligible for reduced hours due to seniority in years of age. Work-exchange programs exist with like communities, such as East Wind (1974–) and Acorn Community (1993–).[31] Some political activities also qualify as work. What constitutes 'work' is determined by the whole community.

The Twin Oaks Community co-governs and self-organises without reference to any particular set of beliefs (religion) but, rather, is based on commons principles and values supporting nonviolent, just, collaborative, cooperative and sharing practices that respect Earth and people. They operate via consensual decision making, assemblies and working groups, as is common among best-practice intentional communities.[32] In the case of Twin Oaks Community, they rotate roles as accountable planners and managers with transparent responsibilities, whose activities (and positions) are open to challenge. They conserve energy, re-use and recycle, use solar power and local firewood, use bikes and make minimal use of a shared fleet of community vehicles. The technologies they use are appropriate, small scale and generally simple and convivial.

In short, Twin Oaks is a living, embryonic version of the types of commoning cells – neighbourhood communities relying on local production and sharing – that could exist as interlinking semi-autonomous networks all over the globe: glocal settlements, open, networked, largely self-sufficient but integrated with one another. They neither need to be intentional communities on an eco-collaborative housing model nor strictly defined ecovillages, but rather deliberative neighbourhoods with a nonmonetary, real value consciousness that co-govern for a transition to genuinely locally sustainable lifestyles with commitments to fulfil the basic needs of all their inhabitants be they people, other animals, plants, water, soil, or rock. Many Indigenous lands are already co-governed by applying such principles and values.

Certain collective provisioning grows out of the plethora of degrowth, food sovereignty and permaculture-inspired housing and self-provisioning initiatives that exist in growing numbers with many commonalties. Clearly, the suggestion has been made that the already impressive CIC might flourish further if enriched with nonmonetary approaches. Other types of radical settlements with ecological ethics include zads (zones to defend) – 'an autonomous collectivity on a scale and duration relatively unknown in the West these last decades' – replete with nonmarkets, shared (collective) tools and pay-what-you-want markets.[33] Beyond a focus on intentionally nonmonetary directions, all such formations require occupation of lands and a steadfast focus on people's and planetary basic needs, to heal people and regenerate Earth.

BACK TO THE FUTURE

In the Hans Christian Andersen rendition of the tale of an imaginary challenged, we find a naked Emperor, whose greatly admired clothes have been so carefully crafted that we can see, feel, and even smell, their materiality. But, look again. It is merely a socially shared intellectual fabric, an imaginary. In fact, the Emperor is an unadorned human. In reality, every commodity and capital asset is merely a naked service or physical good that Earth and humans created – not for direct use, but for trade. The whole monetary fabric of producing for trade develops within market-oriented processes of a socio-political imaginary of 'the economy'. Such imaginaries set to work within human societies exist as institutional practices, relationships and values. Underneath, beyond the imaginary clothing, is the authentic naked process. Money spins an imaginary web that holds market winners in power with anti-social implications and anti-ecological consequences.

We are apt to make neoliberalism a special case; I prefer to talk about our current reality as late stage capitalism. This is the pivot point. The point of no return. We cannot take this imaginary, this madness, any longer. It is killing us humans and our humanity. It is killing Earth. This is the time to share in, and with, Earth by commoning.[34] To occupy that which is ours in a humane rights perspective. To take only what we need and, as living creatures of Earth, to use our creative powers to heal ourselves and Earth together, as one. We are not so much protesters and resisters as we are creators. But we do say no to money and all that stands with the name of capital, so we can create humane relations and livelihoods on the principles of real values of social justice and ecological sustainability.

But, who *are* 'we'?

NEW GREEN MATERIALISM

One characterisation of anti-capitalist factions centres on the traditional left base of trade union and left party organisations, both at a distance from one another and from a youthful, seemingly directionless and disorganised raft of movements that eschew both the so-called 'discipline' of left organisation and its statist and workerist ideologies. Union and left party organisations see few redeeming features in the latter, whom I refer to here as 'young anti-capitalists' – except for their raw energy, which the traditional left would like to capture and control.

Young anti-capitalists of the twenty-first century carry a similar flame as the raw, diverse and emotive 'new left' that arose in the late 1960s in a plethora of guises such as peace activists, women's liberationists and gay activists. The passionate new left made a clear challenge to 'the establishment' and conformist beliefs in 9-to-5 work, military wars and investments in growth that typecast 1950s and 1960s mainstream middle-class culture. Today, young anti-capitalists suffer from lack of visibility, only episodically – as with Occupy – making the headlines, due to the excessive pluralism and chaotic individualism of late stage capitalist media and politicking. Yet young anti-capitalists have made clear advances in terms of entrenching skills of horizontal organisation and networking, and ecological awareness and actions that offer new bases for leftist futures.

On the sidelines, many would-be activists and ex-activists have been disaffected by the worn-out reformist tactics and strategies of the traditional left, yet deem anti-capitalists 'utopian', as in ineffectual dreamers. Frustrated, they critique all sides from the margins or confine themselves to energetically campaigning on single issues. The singularity of separate campaigns within social justice and ecological sustainability spheres leads to competition between social and environmental organisations, objectionable rivalry in which marketing and monetary tactics are employed. All this serves to heighten and deepen fragmentation, another source of hand wringing. The only unity, it seems, is a unity of angry opposition to capitalism, not a hopeful unity set on realising new structures to cradle a complementary suite of futures.

Most significantly, the mainstreams and actions of all three leftist camps – traditionalists, those sidelined and the young anti-capitalists – fail to acknowledge the veritable agency of money as a capitalist tool and weapon.[35] Young anti-capitalists see right through the hierarchical state and readily employ oppositional horizontalist methods. Yet they are much more likely to advocate for increasingly novel ways to manage money in marketplace 'alternatives' – such as cryptocurrency algorithms and community banks – than to campaign for horizontal politics for co-organising localised nonmonetary economies. Hell bent on realising postcapitalism by cobbling together dubious forms, such as market-oriented cooperatives, 'fair' trade, 'social' entrepreneurship and 'sharing' economy initiatives more generally, many fail to acknowledge that money and markets are, by their very nature, capitalist. This caution is crucial as a corrective to naïve experimentation and wasted energy. The time is ripe to make an across-the-board demand for wholly nonmonetary futures through highly conscious and conscientious experimentation and practical implementation.

YOUNG ANTI-CAPITALISTS AS GREEN MATERIALISTS

The 'green materialism' of contemporary anti-capitalist currents offers the bases for replacing the organising principle of our society, money, by direct democracy.[36] A direct democracy based on material production for collective sufficiency, using real values and the principles of social justice and ecological sustainability. Defining characteristics of anti-capitalist movements bear a remarkable correspondence to Marx's 'new materialism', elaborated in his 1845 work *Theses on Feuerbach*, which highlights human agency.[37] Marx's 'new materialism' envisioned scientists and activists perceiving the world without capitalist blinkers or religious distortions, humbly responsible for their collective being, continuously re-aligning their thinking with changes in political, economic and environmental realities.

Akin to Marx's new materialists, young anti-capitalists recognise a world out there that we only partly understand, that we constantly try to understand better in order to improve it. Could replacing money by direct democracy in collectively provisioning locales become the unifying process anti-capitalists need in order to create the integrated beyonds to which all on the left aspire? Clearly, we need to reassert the eminence of real values and manage all Earth's resources as commons. This can only occur if we obliterate monetary values and create socio-political structures for direct democracy and management via real social and ecological values. A tree is a tree, full of qualities and potential; a field is a space for umpteen futures. We, the people, need to embody these understandings and co-govern our futures. Earth and sun as well as human energy determine the number of fruits we have to share between us. Why use money and markets when we can co-decide transparently, directly using real values and direct action?

As both traditional and sidelined lefts lack confidence in young anti-capitalists, pointing to seemingly failed Occupy and arguably failing

XR activities, I see another reality. In the spirit of Marx's philosophy of revolutionary being and practice – a concept of us as active agents – growing numbers of young anti-capitalist activists have become conscious of, and dedicated to, approaches that effectively fulfil his Thesis 10. They are replacing individualistic bourgeois society with collective and creative senses of humanity, concerned with community-based empowerment, relations and self-organisation, creative expression and working at what they like, and feel is socially and environmentally responsible.

In *Anti-Capitalism*, Argentinian Ezequiel Adamovsky distinguishes current anti-capitalists by their focus on operating in ways that are anti-power or counter-power, are autonomous, have immediacy and presence, use horizontalist structures, are de-centred, integrate a multitude of people and causes, strategically respond to specifics, learn through listening rather than laying down a general program, act in glocal rather than national or state-focused struggles against capitalism, use nonviolent direct action and civil disobedience, and develop constructive, creative, rather than 'them–us', cultures.[38] These descriptors show a characteristic unity of purpose and organisation within anti-capitalist movements. They reflect an ecologist's holistic framing of the way nature is interlocking, antagonistic yet balancing, self-sufficient and dynamic. They are remarkably close to Marx's radical view of what it really means to be a social human aware that Earth is our very source of being.

Meanwhile, the culmination of successive appropriations over hundreds of years and all continents has left capitalists in control of Earth and their way of operating is both anti-social and anti-nature. As such, the contemporary social crisis requires us to fulfil everyone's basic needs – no less, no more – rather than continue living in an unequal world of hunger and overconsumption. And ecological crises demand that we take account of the regenerative limits and needs of Earth. Rejecting money – at the hub of the capitalist steering wheel – nonmonetary ways forward allow social and environmental values their natural and significant place in an ecologically sustainable and socially just future.

While cooperatives and commons are often promoted as vehicles to postcapitalism, they are inevitably limited in terms of meeting human and ecological needs to the extent that their decision making and rights of access centre on the market and monetary dynamics. Many activists have learnt through experience to reduce their reliance on the market and monetary ways of operating. The Twin Oaks Community, described above, is substantially self-provisioning and income-sharing. Degrowth households and community-based food activities, and degrowth community-supported agricultural models are other examples where agents often intentionally withdraw from the market.[39] The community of squatters at Can Masdeu on the peri-urban outskirts of Barcelona regard their occupation 'a creative act of disobedience to the world of money, smoke, noise and speed … a recovery of common space and resources re-appropriated from market logic and self-managed by the community'.[40]

Marx's analysis of capitalism was profound, based on a philosophical appreciation of the risks to humanity of being falsely alienated from nature and being forced to work for money and for capitalists. Indeed, Marx appreciated that capitalists were not necessarily intentionally nasty and greedy, but were forced to think and act in particular ways to operate their businesses successfully. Instead, if we ditch the organising principle and power of money on which capitalism is formed, we can engage together directly and respectfully with nature, organising as commoners producing and exchanging for collective sufficiency.

Diving off from Adamovsky's characterisation of young anti-capitalists, imagine a global network of collectively sufficient, cell-like communities, each responsible for the sustainability of the environments that sustain them. Imagine each diverse community empowered, relatively autonomous, present, organised horizontally internally, networked in seamless ways locally and globally, caring for the Earth. Imagine us collectively satisfying everyone's basic needs. In these ways, we would be fulfilling our real human potential as creative active beings.

In short, the defining characteristics of anti-capitalist currents offer the democratic and materialist bases for replacing money as the organising principle of society. The agenda is in front of us. This is what needs to be built on. This is what needs to be done.

ACTIONS: ASSEMBLIES AND COMMONING

Clearly, to achieve this vision of direct democracy and collective self-provisioning in locales various changes need to take place simultaneously, as in the mantra of 'the moneyless man' Mark Boyle: 'Resist, revolt, rewild'.[41] First steps include passive resistance, consciously and conscientiously disengaging from capitalist activities, such as replacing full-time with part-time work, consuming as little as possible of mainstream market-produced and traded goods and services, while encouraging, contributing to and increasingly using locally grown, produced and crafted provisions.

Local collective provisioning and ecological regeneration, creative and convivial production and consumption pursued in neighbourhoods involves active and practical development of more attractive, convivial and workable ways of collectively producing, exchanging and working with nature. This requires applying appropriate technologies; access to, and associated caring for, Earth via commoning use rights, and collective planning to fulfil residents' basic needs through social *compacts* rather than monetary *contracts*. Access occurs through agreements to use erstwhile state or private property, or by squatting/occupying public or private property, and using and managing such Earth via direct democratic co-governance.

To withstand state and private violence and to drive the cultural transformation necessary, we need to explain why monetary values, relations and calculations can never deliver our aims of satisfying the basic needs of people and planet. Conversely, in didactic ways, we need to challenge capitalists to tell and show us how they produce to satisfy needs, no more or less, and without or with few social and ecological disadvantages – so as to point out the holes in their logic and case studies. Advocating for passive resistance to the market and active reclamation of land and associated means of production to contribute, instead, to commoning models, requires rationalisation. We need to persist with a persuasively monetary critique of capitalist activities, assertively proclaiming and defending nonmonetary direct democracy to fulfil all, and only, the basic needs of people and planet.

Powerful and entrenched resistance, enriched by nonmonetary cultures, actions and rhetoric is necessary. The intellectual and cultural shift already under way – discussed in previous chapters and in movements such as food sovereignty, radical ecological democracy and degrowth – must be made more highly visible and replicated. Political assemblies and other forms of horizontal organising must become more familiar ways of achieving livelihoods through commoning. The community mode of production – commoning – is at the basis of postcapitalism where Earth and people are free from private property, which fragments ecological systems and pits human against human in everyday life.

NONVIOLENCE: DEFENCE AND (RE)CREATION

If only because Earth and people are so damaged by capitalist practices, we must act as much as is humanly possible in nonviolent ways, making necessary an overt and strident cultural shift in terms of monetary and real value consciousness. Our aim is to substitute capitalist practices with just and sustainable practices based on real values.

Real value production uses ecologically sustainable processes to derive and create goods and services by applying principles and values that centre on satisfying people's needs. Work is collective or delegated to individuals as a result of collective participatory decision making and volunteering. Within commoning, producers work an obligatory number of hours or are delegated specific tasks. They supply direct orders of products, orders made in terms of particular quantities of specific necessities. Real value exchange is direct supply as a result of production on demand, resulting from participatory decision making regarding the basic needs of identified people. Surplus is stored or directed to others, according to need. Environmental considerations are accounted for in all decision making. Thus real values are the basic qualities, quantities and indicators in real value production, the community mode of production.

We need to turn degraded landscapes into rich ecosystems that sustain all our lives in environmentally light ways and support as much other life as possible. If we all act locally, which is the quickest way these principles can be instituted globally, the grassroots will become a glocal force. Doing-it-together, mutually supporting Earth and humanity, we can multiply skills and activities in regenerative, productive and consumptive practices that enable planetary sustainability. This logic and genuine efforts are already under way in all these directions.

We might engage in sabotage and ecotage, say, where disabling and decommissioning sophisticated technologies that cannot support a sustainable future is calculated to halt the violent destruction of forests and other lands, oceans and other waters. Examples are coal mines and non-renewable electricity power plants. But we cannot be so weighed down by resistance that we do not celebrate our creativity by making claim to commons, through commoning. Let us directly occupy spaces, embedding renewable energy systems and emphasising low energy-use lifestyles, consumption and production. We need to share and care, and concentrate on fulfilling our essential needs. Again, many sustainability activists from a range of movements are doing just this. But let us act proudly with explicit statements that monetary capitalist economies do not and cannot be sustainable and fulfil everyone's needs, but our types of efforts can and, therefore, must.

To strike and to sabotage or ecotage in ways that simply damage the capitalist process and property expresses free will and freedom of choice, and shows that the capitalist system cannot work without us and that we are changing. In such proactive ways, we seek to manage the collapse that already surrounds us. We increasingly adopt new practices of collective self-provisioning and consumption, of politicking, of exercising our bodies and minds, and of creative endeavours. If capitalists insist on us playing their game, then we call it what it is – unacceptable domination. If we say 'No' and they try to force us – by denying us access to property for food, clothing and sheltering ourselves – that is violence, and we must resist and defend ourselves against such violence.[42] We have a right to claim Earth for shared sustenance. They have no right to defile Earth and reproduce rich and poor.

In as much as the state violently addresses protesters and dissidents – typically ignoring us up to a point then legally busting, arresting and punishing, even imprisoning us – they have no right to keep us in their system at the point of a gun. Simultaneously, we embrace ex-capitalists prepared to transform their daily practices, providing for them as they will provide for us and as we all will provide for ourselves. But capitalist, monetary, reproduction must end. The alternative is to continue to allow the exploitation of Earth and ourselves under the domination of money and capital, through capitalist practices. If we take the latter course, Earth will endure but our species will not.

Strategically, creation and defence trumps victim-making protest and blindly violent destruction of capitalist forces. A creative and embracing strategy is a practical, material necessity, because capitalism has been so socially violent and so ecologically destructive. Our impulse must be to heal, to restore, to regenerate, to re-enchant the world. Only defensive 'violence' is admissible and must be minimised because we represent, and need to continuously show, the life-full side in this struggle. Here our rejection of monetary logic, values and relations is powerful.

Capital must answer for its destructive practices. Monetary ways of thinking cannot be efficient in a holistic sense, if they are effectively socially and ecologically destructive. We must insist that everything is judged, instead, in terms of real social and environmental values. Our discourse is in terms of people and their needs, the planet and its regenerative needs, the fact that another world is possible and that money, markets and capital represent an inefficient and unjust past. This line embeds social justice and ecological sustainability as principles and values of the future.

We are a collaborative animal, a species that perceives patterns in everything around us, recognising connections and playing with them.[43] We plan collaboratively, and follow patterns. We follow plans intelligently, recognising the need to adapt and to innovate to achieve the primary principles of fulfilling regenerative and reproductive needs of people and Earth. We identify conflicts and sit with the trouble till an optimal solution arises through a collaborative forum. We act in nurturing ways toward one another and Earth. We need to end private property, which cannot exist without money and trade and, instead, embrace the principles and values of commoning and sharing on the basis of co-governed use rights.

The logic of all our discourse needs to be infused by real values and processes, nonmonetary values and processes. This way we can address our crises and manage collapse as degrowth activists advocate. The radical left and many movements already do what is suggested here by promoting social values and communal relations, ecological values and Earth-centred relations. But let us drop the economic contortions and statist dead ends. Money is the weapon that must be put aside.

CONCLUSION

Our societies are wrought by inequalities globally and we face major ecological challenges that threaten the future of our species. Both ecological challenges and social inequities are exaggerated by monetary activities, specifically capitalism.

I have argued that we need to see monetary values and activities as the key stumbling block to us achieving socio-political and economic justice and sustainability on Earth. Monetary dynamics separate us as people, you and me, and our species from the rest of Earth. Identifying monetary activities as a strong barrier between us and postcapitalist justice for people and planet gives us a common focus.

Withdrawing our support for monetary activities must go hand-in-hand with creating nonmonetary, socially fair and just, and ecologically sustainable postcapitalisms. The strategy of co-creating workable and effective nonmonetary economies rules out capitalist activities in one stroke. Consequently, we can act quickly, constructively and deeply at a time when urgent action is crucial. We can act right now, directly, in both directions simultaneously, all around us, altogether.

Still, I am neither a preacher nor a dogmatist. I encourage you to engage with the ideas and arguments presented in this book in creative, challenging and didactic ways.

I hope that we can move beyond the conflicts of capitalism, consciously, in concert, collectively. The future is not mine but, rather, ours.

Notes

1 CAPITAL AND CRISES

All URLs current as of 15 August 2021

1. Juliet B. Schor and Andrew K. Jorgenson, 'Is it too late for growth?', *Review of Radical Political Economics*, 51(2), 2019: pp. 320–329, esp. p. 323.
2. Thomas Piketty, *Capital in the Twenty-First Century*, Cambridge, MA: Harvard University Press, 2014, p. 554.
3. Ibid., p. 475.
4. Immanuel Wallerstein, *The Modern World System*, Vols I–IV, Oakland: University of California Press, 2011.
5. Piketty, *Capital in the Twenty-First Century*, pp. 108–109.
6. Ibid., p. 241.
7. Seth Donnelly, *The Lie of Global Prosperity: How Neo-Liberals Distort Data to Mask Poverty and Exploitation*, New York: Monthly Review Press, 2019, p. 7.
8. Ibid., p. 46.
9. Jason Hickel, 'The true extent of global poverty and hunger: Questioning the good news narrative of the Millennium Development Goals', *Third World Quarterly*, 37(5), 2016: pp. 749–767, cited in Donnelly *The Lie of Global Prosperity*, pp. 48–49.
10. Anitra Nelson, 'The poverty of money: Marxian insights for ecological economists', *Ecological Economics*, 36, 2001: pp. 499–511. Even 'in-kind accounting' as considered by Eric Magnin and Nikolay Nenovsky in 'Calculating without money: Theories of in-kind accounting of Alexander Chayanov, Otto Neurath and the early Soviet experiences', *European Journal of the History of Economic Thought* 28(3), 2021: pp. 456–477, is based on 'calculation' via indicators of efficiency within the spectre of technical, top-down control rather than community-based decision making, allowing unique criteria and principles to be applied to deciding what to produce and how to produce it. I discuss Neurath in Chapter 4.
11. See 'World' within 'Country Trends' accessed at Global Footprint Network – https://data.footprintnetwork.org/
12. See Earth Overshoot Day, which approximates the day in the year when we breach our one Earth's regenerative potential, at Global Footprint Network – www.footprintnetwork.org/our-work/earth-overshoot-day/
13. These comments relate to the common ecological footprint National Footprint Accounts, as critically assessed by David Lin, L. Hanscom, A. Murthy, A. Galli, M. Evans, E. Neill, M.S. Mancini, J. Martindill, F.-Z. Medouar, S. Huang and M. Wackernagel, 'Ecological footprint accounting

for countries: Updates and results of the national footprint accounts, 2012–2018', *Resources* 7(58), 2018: p. 15.

14. According to data derived from Global Footprint Network – https://data.footprintnetwork.org/#/

15. Sivan Kartha, Eric Kemp-Benedict, Emily Ghosh, Anisha Nazareth and Tim Gore, *The Carbon Inequality Era: An Assessment of the Global Distribution of Consumption Emissions among Individuals from 1990 to 2015 and Beyond*, Stockholm: Stockholm Environment Institute and Oxfam International, 2020, p. 8.

16. Institute for Economics and Peace, *Global Peace Index 2019: Measuring Peace in a Complex World*. Sydney, June 2019, p. 45 – http://visionofhumanity.org/reports

17. David Spratt, 'At 4°C of warming, would a billion people survive? What scientists say', Climate Code Red, 18 August 2019 – www.climatecodered.org/2019/08/at-4c-of-warming-would-billion-people.html#more

18. David Spratt, 'What would 3 degrees mean?', Climate Code Red, 1 September 2010 – www.climatecodered.org/2010/09/what-would-3-degrees-mean.html

19. Ibid.; James Hansen, 'Tipping point', in *2008–2009 State of the Wild* [magazine]: pp. 6–15 (fn pp. 258–259), p. 9, 2009 – http://www.columbia.edu/~jeh1/2008/StateOfWild_20080428.pdf; William E. Rees, 'Yes, the climate crisis may wipe out six billion people', *The Tyee*, 18 September 2019 – https://thetyee.ca/Analysis/2019/09/18/Climate-Crisis-Wipe-Out/

20. NYDF Assessment Partners, *Protecting and Restoring Forests: A Story of Large Commitments yet Limited Progress*, New York Declaration on Forests Five-Year Assessment Report, Climate Focus (coordinator and editor), 2019, pp. 25–27 – https://forestdeclaration.org

21. Ibid., pp. 13, 29.

22. United Nations, Sustainable Development Goals, 'UN Report: Nature's dangerous decline "unprecedented"; Species extinction rates "accelerating"', Paris: UN SDG, 6 May 2019 – www.un.org/sustainabledevelopment/blog/2019/05/nature-decline-unprecedented-report/

23. See 'Most endangered' at OneKindPlanet — https://onekindplanet.org

24. Kenneth V. Rosenberg et al., 'Decline of the North American avifauna', *Science* (19 September 2019) – www.nytimes.com/2019/09/19/opinion/crisis-birds-north-america.html

25. Erik Olin Wright, *How to be an Anti-Capitalist in the 21st Century*, London: Verso, 2019, p. xiv.

26. L. Randall Wray, 'Conclusion: The credit money and state money approaches', in L. Randall Wray (ed.), *Credit and State Theories of Money: The Contributions of A. Mitchell Innes*, Cheltenham/Northampton, MA: Edward Elgar Publishing, 2004, pp. 223–262, esp. p. 231.

27. Genevieve Vaughan, 'Introduction: A radically different worldview is possible', in Genevieve Vaughan (ed.), *Women and the Gift Economy: A Radically Different Worldview is Possible*, Toronto: Inanna Publications and Education Inc., 2007, p. 12.

28. For a discussion as to why 'barter' is such a controversial term, see David Graeber, *Debt: The First 5,000 Years*, Brooklyn, NY: Melville House, 2011, pp. 21–41.
29. Barry L. Isaac, 'Karl Polanyi', in James G. Carrier (ed.) *A Handbook of Economic Anthropology*, Cheltenham/Northampton, MA: Edward Elgar, 2005, pp. 14–25, esp. p. 16.
30. Karl Polanyi, 'The economy as instituted process', in Karl Polanyi, Conrad M. Arensberg and Henry W. Pearson (eds), *Trade and Markets in the Early Empires: Economics in History and Theory*, Glencoe, IL: The Free Press, 1957, p. 264.
31. Polanyi, 'The economy as instituted process'.
32. Maximilien Rubel and John Crump (eds), *Non-Market Socialism in the Nineteenth and Twentieth Centuries*, Houndmills: Macmillan, 1987.

2 MONEY: THE UNIVERSAL EQUIVALENT

All URLs current at 15 August 2021

1. John F. Henry, 'The social origins of money: The case of Egypt', in L. Randall Wray (ed.), *Credit and State Theories of Money: The Contributions of A. Mitchell Innes*, Cheltenham/Northampton, MA: Edward Elgar Publishing, 2004, pp. 79–98.
2. The classic work is Georg Friedrich Knapp, *The State Theory of Money*, London: Macmillan and Company Ltd, 1924 [1904 in German, this translation based on 4th edn, 1923]. See also Randall Wray (ed.), *Credit and State Theories of Money*.
3. For credit theories of money, and money as a claim, see Joseph A. Schumpeter, *History of Economic Analysis*, London: Allen & Unwin, 1986, pp. 62–64, 279–299. See too Randall Wray (ed.), *Credit and State Theories of Money*. For Marx's unique theory of the money-commodity, which does not fit neatly into either main stream of thought as a commodity or credit theory of money, see Anitra Nelson, *Marx's Concept of Money: The God of Commodities*, Abingdon: Routledge, 1999/2014, pp. 1–4. See also Anitra Nelson, 'Marx's theory of the money commodity', *History of Economics Review 33*, 2001: pp. 44–63.
4. A useful source is Pierre Vilar, *A History of Gold and Money: 1450–1920*, London: Verso, 1991.
5. Karl Marx, *A Contribution to the Critique of Political Economy*, Moscow: Progress Publishers, 1977 [1859, German], p. 125.
6. Immanuel Wallerstein, *The Modern World System*, Vols I–IV, Oakland: University of California Press, 2011.
7. Nelson, *Marx's Concept of Money*, pp. 23–29, 54–57.
8. Part V in Keith Hart, Jean-Louis Laville and Antonio David Cattani (eds), *The Human Economy: A Citizen's Guide*, Cambridge/Malden, MA: Polity Press, 2010, pp. 301–360; Mary Mellor, *Money: Myths, Truths and Alternatives*, Bristol: Policy Press, 2019, esp. pp 143–46; Steven Hall, 'Explainer: What

is modern monetary theory?', *The Conversation*, 31 January 2017 – https://theconversation.com/explainer-what-is-modern-monetary-theory-72095

9. Nelson, *Marx's Concept of Money*, pp. 48–50, 155–159.

10. Karl Marx, *Capital: A Critique of Political Economy*, Volume III, Harmondsworth: Penguin, 1981, p. 911.

11. Karl Marx, *Economic and Philosophic Manuscripts of 1844*, Moscow: Progress Publishers, 1977, pp. 72–73, original emphasis.

12. For an introduction see the *Capitalism Nature Socialism* journal site — www.tandfonline.com/toc/rcns20/current

13. Anitra Nelson and Frans Timmerman (eds), *Life Without Money: Building Fair and Sustainable Economies*, London: Pluto Press, 2011; Maximilien Rubel and John Crump, *Non-Market Socialism in the Nineteenth and Twentieth Centuries*, London: The Macmillan Press, 1987.

14. See democratic socialists Erik Olin Wright, *How to be an Anti-Capitalist in the 21st Century*, London/New York: Verso, 2019, and Hans Baer, *Democratic Eco-Socialism as a Real Utopia: Transitioning to an Alternative World System*, New York/Oxford: Berghahn Books, 2019. On Polanyi, see Peadar Kirby, *Karl Polanyi and the Contemporary Political Crisis: Transforming Market Society in the Era of Climate Change*, London/Oxford: Bloomsbury, 2020.

15. Marx, *Economic and Philosophic Manuscripts of 1844*, pp. 129–132.

16. Georg Simmel, *The Philosophy of Money* (3rd enlarged edn), London: Routledge, 2004 [1900].

17. Graeber emphasises the violence of monetised debtor agreements and 'money's capacity to turn morality into a matter of impersonal arithmetic – and by doing so, to justify things that would otherwise seem outrageous or obscene': David Graeber, *Debt: The First 5,000 Years*, Brooklyn, NY: Melville House, 2011, esp. p. 14.

18. Andrew Phillips and J.C. Sharman, *Outsourcing Empire: How Company-States Made the Modern World*, Princeton, NJ: Princeton University Press, 2020.

19. Henry, 'The social origins of money', p. 83.

20. The Economist Intelligence Unit, *Democracy Index 2020: In Sickness and in Health*, London/New York/HongKong: The Economist Intelligence Unit, 2021, p. 3.

21. Christian Dorningera, Alf Hornborg, David J. Abson, Henrik von Wehrden, Anke Schaffartzik, Stefan Giljum, John-Oliver Engler, Robert L. Fellera, Klaus Hubacekh and Hanspeter Wieland, 'Global patterns of ecologically unequal exchange: Implications for sustainability in the 21st century', *Ecological Economics* 179, 2021, DOI: 10.1016/j.ecolecon.2020.106824; John Brolin, *The Bias of the World: Theories of Unequal Exchange in History*, Lund, Sweden: Lund University, 2007.

22. In particular for those unfamiliar with his works, the explanation in this section owes much to Karl Marx's general approach and analyses of capitalism.

23. Jane Gleeson-White, *Double Entry: How the Merchants of Venice Shaped the Modern World and How their Invention Could Make or Break the Planet*, Sydney: Allen & Unwin, 2012, esp. pp 10–25.

24. Ibid., p. 174.

25. Mary Poovey, *A History of the Modern Fact: Problems of Knowledge in the Sciences of Wealth and Society*, Chicago, IL/London: University of Chicago Press, 1998, pp. xii, 29.

26. Ibid., pp. 30, 36–38, 54.

27. Derrick Jensen, *The Culture of Make Believe*, White River Junction, VT: Chelsea Green Publishing, 2004, p. 439.

28. See discussion and details on references associated with this problem identified by Rosa Luxemburg and resolved by Samir Amin in Nelson, *Marx's Concept of Money*, pp. 190–191.

3 YENOMON: COMMONING

All URLs current at 15 August 2021

1. Karl Marx and Friedrich Engels, *The Communist Manifesto*, in *Marx/Engels Selected Works* Volume I, Progress Publishers: Moscow, 1969 [February 1848], pp. 98–137 – www.marxists.org/archive/marx/works/1848/communist-manifesto/index.htm; Paresh Chattopadhyay, *Marx's Associated Mode of Production: A Critique of Marxism*, New York: Palgrave Macmillan, 2016; Erik Olin Wright, *How to be an Anti-Capitalist in the 21st Century* London/New York: Verso, 2019.

2. An initial brief summary of key themes in this chapter appeared in Anitra Nelson, "'Your money or your life": Money and socialist transformation', *Capitalism Nature Socialism* 27(4), 2016: pp. 40–60, esp. pp 55–57. A more elaborate yet shorter sketch than the one here, was presented as 'Nonmarket socialism. What is it?' at the 11th Australian International Political Economy Network (AIPEN) Conference in Sydney, University of Sydney, 6–7 February 2020 in a joint session with Terry Leahy – 'Nonmarket socialism. What is it? How will we get there?'. Moreover, this chapter draws on many living and working 'experiments' that I have observed or experienced, for instance, when I lived in the early 1990s at Commonground Cooperative (Seymour, Victoria, Australia) – www.common-ground.org.au/. The development of this working and living cooperative was influenced by a community which I stayed in for several weeks, in 2012, Twin Oaks Community (Virginia, United States) – www.twinoaks.org/ – which has a small tofu-producing factory and a labour system similar to the one described here. The ecological bent is partly influenced by living in the late 1990s at Round the Bend Conservation Cooperative (Christmas Hills, Victoria, Australia), a community with which I am still associated – www.roundthebend.org.au/. Also see Anitra Nelson, *Small is Necessary: Shared Living on a Shared Planet*, London: Pluto Press, 2018, and David Barkin and Alejandra Sánchez, 'The communitarian revolutionary subject: New forms of social transformation', *Third World Quarterly* 41(84), 2020: pp. 1421–1441.

4 SYSTEM CHANGE, NOT CLIMATE CHANGE

All URLs current at 15 August 2021

1. Here, as in other discussions in this book, 'carbon emissions' stands for not only for carbon dioxide but also five other major greenhouse gases: methane, nitrous oxide, hydrofluorocarbons, perfluorocarbons and sulphur hexafluoride.

2. Anthony D. Barnosky, 'Preventing the sixth mass extinction requires dealing with climate change', *Huffington Post*, 18 January 2015 update – www. huffingtonpost.com/news/generation-change. On heat impacts, David Wallace Wells, 'The uninhabitable earth', *New York Magazine*, 9 July 2017 – https://nymag.com/intelligencer/2017/07/climate-change-earth-too-hot-for-humans.html

3. International Union for Conservation of Nature, *The IUCN Red List of Threatened Species*, version 2021-1, 2021 – www.iucnredlist.org

4. John Woinarski, Andrew Burbidge and Peter Harrison, 'Ongoing unraveling of a continental fauna: Decline and extinction of Australian mammals since European settlement', *PNAS* (*Proceedings of the National Academy of Sciences*) 112(15), April 2015: pp. 4531–4540.

5. BZE, *Zero Carbon Communities: Guide 2020*, Melbourne: Beyond Zero Emissions, 2020 – https://zerocarboncommunities.org.au/

6. Don Driscoll, Bob Pressey, Euan Ritchie and Noel D. Preece, 'Research reveals shocking detail on how Australia's environmental scientists are being silenced', *The Conversation*, 9 September 2020 – https://theconversation. com/research-reveals-shocking-detail-on-how-australias-environmental-scientists-are-being-silenced-140026; Lisa Hymas, Nicholas Beuret, Martin Lukacs, Amantha Perera and Jenni Monet, 'How are the media covering the climate change threat?', *The Listening Post* (Al Jazeera), 15 November 2017 – www.aljazeera.com/programmes/listeningpost/2017/11/media-covering-climate-change-threat-171111125020532.html; Alexandra Wake and Michael Ward, 'Latest $84 million cuts rip the heart out of the ABC, and our democracy', *The Conversation*, 24 June 2020 – https://theconversation. com/latest-84-million-cuts-rip-the-heart-out-of-the-abc-and-our-democracy-141355

7. Corey J.A. Bradshaw, 'Little left to lose: Deforestation and forest degradation in Australia since European colonization', *Journal of Plant Ecology* 5(1), March 2012: pp. 109–120, esp. pp. 109–110.

8. David Bellamy in Michael Feller, 'Old-growth forests – imperilled in Victoria', *Park Watch*, Victorian National Parks Association, 2020 – https://vnpa.org.au/old-growth-forests-imperilled-in-victoria/

9. Lisa Cox, '"Unprecedented" globally: More than 20% of Australia's forests burnt in bushfires', *Guardian*, 25 February 2020 – www.theguardian.com/australia-news/2020/feb/25/unprecedented-globally-more-than-20-of-australias-forests-burnt-in-bushfires

10. Beverly Law and William Moomaw, 'Keeping trees in the ground where they are already growing is an effective low-tech way to slow climate

change', *The Conversation*, 23 February 2021 – https://theconversation.com/keeping-trees-in-the-ground-where-they-are-already-growing-is-an-effective-low-tech-way-to-slow-climate-change-154618

11. Lesley Hughes, Annika Dean, Will Steffen and Martin Rice, *This is What Climate Change Looks Like*, Potts Point (NSW): Climate Council of Australia, 2019, p. 3 – www.climatecouncil.org.au/resources/ecosystems-report/; Katri Uibu and Michael McKinnon, 'Queensland Government isn't enforcing law aimed at protecting Great Barrier Reef from fertiliser run-off, documents show', *ABC News*, 11 October 2018 (updated version) – www.abc.net.au/news/2018-10-11/laws-not-stopping-fertilser-runoff-to-reef/10348718

12. Lorena Allam and Calla Wahlquist, 'More than 100 Aboriginal sacred sites – some dating before the ice age – could be destroyed by mining companies', *Guardian*, 28 August 2020 – www.theguardian.com/australia-news/2020/aug/28/more-than-100-aboriginal-sacred-sites-some-dating-before-the-ice-age-could-be-destroyed-by-mining-companies

13. Mike Szabo, 'World's carbon markets grow 34% in value to $215 billion in 2019 – report', *Carbon Pulse*, 22 January 2020 – https://carbon-pulse.com/90631/

14. Umair Irfan, 'Can you really negate your carbon emissions? Carbon offsets, explained', *Vox*, 27 February 2020 – www.vox.com/2020/2/27/20994118/carbon-offset-climate-change-net-zero-neutral-emissions

15. Tamra Gilbertson, *Carbon Pricing: A Critical Perspective for Community Resistance*, 2017, Climate Justice Alliance and Indigenous Environmental Network – https://climatejusticealliance.org/workgroup/energy-democracy/

16. Irfan, 'Can you really negate your carbon emissions?'.

17. Kevin Smith, *The Carbon Neutral Myths: Offset Indulgences for Your Climate Sins*, Amsterdam: Transnational Institute (Carbon Trade Watch), 2007, pp. 5, 14ff and, final quote, p. 7 – www.tni.org/en/publication/the-carbon-neutral-myth-0

18. Mirabelle Muûls, Jonathan Colmer, Ralf Martin and Ulrich J. Wagner, *Evaluating the EU Emissions Trading System: Take it or Leave it? An Assessment of the Data after Ten Years*, Grantham Institute Briefing Paper No. 21, October 2016 – www.imperial.ac.uk/grantham/publications/energy-and-low-carbon-futures/

19. Danika Drury, 'Resources for a better future 6. Offsetting', *Uneven Earth*, 17 August 2020 – http://unevenearth.org/2020/08/offsetting/

20. Larry Lohmann, 'Ecosystem service trading', in Ashish Kothari, Ariel Salleh, Arturo Escobar, Federico Demaria and Alberto Acosta (eds), *Pluriverse: A Post-Development Dictionary*, New Dehli: Tulika Books, 2019, pp. 47–50.

21. On ice melting, Wallace Wells, 'The uninhabitable earth'. For the rest of the paragraph, Jonathan Watts, 'Water shortages could affect 5bn people by 2050, UN report warns', *Guardian*, 18 March 2018 – www.theguardian.com/environment/2018/mar/19/water-shortages-could-affect-5bn-people-by-2050-un-report-warns. On nature-based solutions, World Rainforest Movement, *WRM Bulletin 255*, March/April 2021.

22. Ian Lowe, *A Big Fix: Radical Solutions for Australia's Environmental Crisis*, Melbourne: Black Inc., 2009; MDBA, 'Water markets and trade', Murray–Darling Basin Authority, 2021 – www.mdba.gov.au/managing-water/water-markets-and-trade

23. Michael Slezak, Mark Doman, Katia Shatoba, Penny Timms and Alex Palmer, 'The mystery of the Murray-Darling's vanishing flows', *ABC News*, 3 September 2020 – www.abc.net.au/news/2020-09-03/the-mystery-of-the-murray-darlings-vanishing-flows/12612166?nw=0. On rice, see Peter Hannam, '"Don't export our rivers": Push for export ban on cotton', *Sydney Morning Herald*, 4 February 2019 – www.smh.com.au/politics/federal/push-for-export-ban-on-cotton-to-save-sick-rivers-20190204-p50vgv.html

24. Calla Wahlquist, 'Droughts can affect river flows permanently, Australian study suggests', *Guardian*, 14 May 2021 – www.theguardian.com/australia-news/2021/may/14/drought-affected-rivers-face-reduced-flows-even-after-droughts-break-study

25. Slezak et al., 'The mystery of the Murray-Darling's vanishing flows'; Ella Archibald-Binge, 'Indigenous groups in Murray-Darling Basin fight to have their voices heard over water rights', *ABC 7.30 Report*, 26 May 2021 – www.abc.net.au/news/2021-05-26/indigenous-water-rights-murray-darling-basin-730/100166380

26. Archibald-Binge, 'Indigenous groups in Murray-Darling Basin fight to have their voices heard over water rights' (which includes Brad Moggridge and the extract from the South Australian Royal Commission 2019).

27. Adam Morton, 'Australian scientists warn urgent action needed to save 19 "collapsing" ecosystems', *Guardian*, 26 February 2021 – www.theguardian.com/environment/2021/feb/26/australian-scientists-warn-urgent-action-needed-to-save-19-collapsing-ecosystems

28. ABS, 'South Australian Murray-Darling Basin NRM region', in 4632.0.55.001 *Discussion Paper: From Nature to the Table: Environmental-Economic Accounting for Agriculture, 2015–16*, Canberra: Australian Bureau of Statistics, 2017 – www.abs.gov.au/

29. Robert Costanza, Rudolf de Groot, Leon Braat, Ida Kubiszewski, Lorenzo Fioramonti, Paul Sutton, Steve Farber and Monica Grasso, 'Twenty years of ecosystem services: How far have we come and how far do we still need to go?', *Ecosystem Services* 28, 2017: pp. 1–16, esp. p. 3.

30. Jane Gleeson-White, *Double Entry: How the Merchants of Venice Shaped the Modern World and How their Invention Could Make or Break the Planet*, Sydney: Allen & Unwin, 2012, p. 249.

31. Adam Smith, *The Wealth of Nations*: Books I–III, London: Penguin Books, Penguin Classic edn, 1986 [1776], pp. 132ff.

32. Costanza et al., 'Twenty years of ecosystem services', p. 13.

33. Anitra Nelson, *Marx's Concept of Money: The God of Commodities*, London/New York: Routledge, 1999/2014, pp. 48–50, 155–159.

34. E.P. Thompson, 'The moral economy of the English crowd in the eighteenth century', *Past and Present* 50, February 1971: pp. 76–136.

35. Órlan Ryan, *Chocolate Nations: Living and Dying for Cocoa in West Africa*, London: Zed Books, 2012; Laurens Ankersmit, *Green Trade and Fair Trade: In and With the EU Process-based Measures within the EU Legal Order*, Cambridge: Cambridge University Press, 2017.
36. XR VIC News: 1 June 2020 (email to subscribers: https://ausrebellion.earth/local-groups/)
37. Joe Ament, 'Toward an ecological monetary theory', *Sustainability* 11, 2019: pp. 923ff, esp. pp. 924, 937.
38. Kristofer Dittmer, 'Alternatives to money-as-usual in ecological economics: A study of local currencies and 100 percent reserve banking', PhD thesis, Institute of Environmental Science and Technology, Autonomous University of Barcelona, September 2014, pp. 26–27.
39. Tim Harford, 'How the world's first accountants counted on cuneiform', 50 Things That Made the Modern Economy podcast, *BBC World Service*, 12 June 2017 – www.bbc.co.uk/programmes/p04b1g3c; David Graeber, *Debt: The First 5000 Years*, London: Melville House Publishing, 2011.
40. Alf Hornborg, *Nature, Society, and Justice in the Anthropocene: Unraveling the Money-Energy-Technology Complex*, Cambridge: Cambridge University Press, 2019, p. 46, original emphasis.
41. Ibid., p. 149.
42. Ibid., p. 231.
43. Critiques of such approaches include Louis Larue, 'The ecology of money: A critical assessment', *Ecological Economics* 178, 2020: 106823.
44. Hornborg, *Nature, Society, and Justice in the Anthropocene*, pp. 231–247.
45. Ibid., esp. pp. 39, 44, and for 'ecologically unequal exchange', pp. 56–59.
46. Jairus Banaji, *A Brief History of Commercial Capitalism*, Chicago, IL: Haymarket Books, 2020; see too the 'Money orientation' section of Chapter 5, this volume.
47. Christian Dorninger and Alf Hornborg, 'Can EEMRIO analyses establish the occurrence of ecologically unequal exchange?', *Ecological Economics* 119, 2015: pp. 414–418, esp. p. 415, original emphasis.
48. Rikard Warlenius, *Asymmetries: Conceptualizing Environmental Inequalities as Ecological Debt and Ecologically Unequal Exchange*, Lund, Sweden: Lund University, 2017.
49. Jason Hickel, Dylan Sullivan and Huzaifa Zoomkawala, 'Plunder in the post-colonial era: Quantifying drain from the Global South through unequal exchange, 1960–2018', *New Political Economy*, Online 30 March 2021, DOI: 10.1080/13563467.2021.1899153
50. Dorninger and Hornborg, 'Can EEMRIO analyses establish the occurrence of ecologically unequal exchange?', p. 417.
51. Sam Bliss, 'The case for studying non-market food systems', *Sustainability* 11, 2019: pp. 3224ff, esp. p. 3230.
52. John Brolin, 'The bias of the world: A history of theories of unequal exchange from mercantilism to ecology', PhD thesis, Human Ecology Division, Lund University, 2007 – https://lup.lub.lu.se/search/ws/files/4378178/26725.pdf

53. Howard T. Odum, 'Energy, ecology and cconomics', Royal Swedish Academy of Science, *Ambio* 2(6), 1973: pp. 220–227; Howard T. Odum and Elisabeth C. Odum, *Energy Basis for Man and Nature*, New York: McGraw-Hill Book Company, 1981 (2nd edn) [1976].
54. Brolin, 'The bias of the world', p. 349.
55. Anitra Nelson, 'The poverty of money: Marxian insights for ecological economists', *Ecological Economics* 36, 2001: pp. 499–511, esp. pp. 505–508.
56. Brolin, 'The bias of the world', pp. 245ff.
57. Ibid., pp. 259–264.
58. Josh Ryan Collins, Ludwig Schuster and Tony Greenham, *Energising Money: An Introduction to Energy Currencies and Accounting*, London: New Economics Foundation, 2013, p. 18.
59. Ibid., p. 60.
60. Ibid., p. 6.
61. Dittmer, 'Alternatives to money-as-usual in ecological economics', p. v.
62. Mathis Wackernagel and Bert Beyers, *Ecological Footprint: Managing our Biocapacity Budget*, Gabriola Island, BC, Canada: New Society Publishers, 2019, pp. 2–3, original emphasis.
63. Ibid., p. 18.
64. Ibid., p. 4.
65. Global Footprint Network research team, *Footprint: Limitations and Criticism: Ecological Footprint Accounting: Limitations and Criticism*, 2020 – www.footprintnetwork.org/content/uploads/2020/08/Footprint-Limitations-and-Criticism.pdf
66. ABS, 'Accounting for the environment in the national accounts', 5206.0 – *Australian National Accounts: National Income, Expenditure and Product, September 2002*, Belconnen (ACT): Australian Bureau of Statistics, January 2003 – www.abs.gov.au/ausstats/abs@.nsf/featurearticlesbytitle/5A0A96EF9E45D3B8CA256CAE0016E525?
67. Wackernagel and Beyers, *Ecological Footprint*, pp. 4, 15.
68. Axel T. Paul, *Money and Society: A Critical Companion*, London: Pluto Press, 2020, pp. 42–43.
69. Camila Moreno, Daniel Speich Chassé and Lili Fuhr, *Carbon Metrics, Global Abstractions and Ecological Epistemicide*, Ecology 42, Berlin: Heinrich Böll Foundation, 2015, p. 52.
70. John O'Neill and Thomas Uebel, 'Analytical philosophy and ecological economics', in Joan Martínez-Alier and Roldan Muradian (eds), *Handbook of Ecological Economics*, Cheltenham/Northampton, MA: Edward Elgar, 2015, pp. 48–73, esp. pp. 48–56.
71. Otto Neurath, 'Physicalism, planning and the social sciences: Bricks prepared for a discussion v. Hayek', 26 July 1945, *The Otto Neurath Nachlass in Haarlem* 202 K.56, cited in O'Neill and Uebel, 'Analytical philosophy and ecological economics', pp. 56–63, quote p. 61.
72. Eric Magnin and Nikolay Nenovsky, 'Calculating without money: Theories of in-kind accounting of Alexander Chayanov, Otto Neurath and the early

Soviet experiences', *European Journal of the History of Economic Thought* 28(3), 2021: pp. 456–477, esp. pp. 463–464 and 470.

73. John O'Neill, *Life Beyond Capital*, Guildford: University of Surrey Centre for the Understanding of Sustainable Prosperity, 2017, pp. 5–6.

74. Ibid., p. 12.

75. A North American ecosocialist network is known by this rallying call – https://systemchangenotclimatechange.org

76. Anitra Nelson, 'Moneyfree economies and ecosocialism' in Salvatore Engel-Di Mauro, Leigh Brownhill, Michael Löwy, Ana Isla, Terran Giacomini and Terisa Turner (eds), *Routledge Handbook on Ecosocialism*, New York: Routledge, forthcoming.

77. Anitra Nelson, 'Eco-socialism from a post-development perspective', in Samuel Alexander, Sangeetha Chandra-Shekeran and Brendan Gleeson (eds), *Post-Capitalist Futures*, Singapore: Palgrave Macmillan, 2021.

78. Zone à Défendre ('ZAD') translates as 'deferred development area'; Maxime Combes and Nicolas Haeringer, 'The airport project of Notre Dame des Landes is dead! Long live the ZAD!', *Radical Ecological Democracy*, 10 April 2018 – www.radicalecologicaldemocracy.org/the-airport-project-of-notre-dame-des-landes-is-dead-long-live-the-zad/

5 WOMEN'S LIBERATION: EQUALITY AND VALUES

All URLs accessed 15 August 2021

1. Françoise D'Eaubonne, *Le Féminisme ou la Mort*, Paris: Pierre Horay, 1974.

2. Carolyn Merchant, *Science and Nature: Past, Present and Future*, New York: Routledge, 2018, quote from pp. 287–288.

3. Maximilien Rubel and John Crump (eds), *Non-Market Socialism in the Nineteenth and Twentieth Centuries*, London: Palgrave Macmillan, 1987.

4. See, for instance, Susan Ferguson, *Women and Work: Feminism, Labour, and Social Reproduction*, London: Pluto Press, 2020.

5. Margaret Benston, 'The political economy of women's liberation', *Monthly Review* 21(4), September 1969: pp. 13–27, (republished by *Monthly Review*, 1 September 2019 – https://monthlyreview.org/2019/09/01/the-political-economy-of-womens-liberation/).

6. Juliet Mitchell, 'Women: The longest revolution', *New Left Review* 40, 1966.

7. On earlier works on the same topic, see Ferguson, *Women and Work*, esp. pp. 40–41.

8. Eric Bogle, 'Singing the spirit home', on the album *Singing the Spirit Home*, Greentrax Records, 2005; Maria Mies, *Patriarchy and Accumulation on a World Scale*, London/Melbourne: Zed Books/Spinifex, 1998 [1986], p. 223.

9. Benston, 'The political economy of women's liberation'.

10. Ibid.; Mies, *Patriarchy and Accumulation on a World Scale*, pp. 4, 223.

11. Silvia Federici, 'Wages for housework', in Ashish Kothari, Ariel Salleh, Arturo Escobar, Federico Demaria and Alberto Acosta (eds), *Pluriverse:*

A Post-Development Dictionary, New Dehli: Tulika (and Authorsupfront), 2019, pp. 329–332.

12. Silvia Federici and Arlen Austin (eds), *Wages for Housework: The New York Committee 1972–1977: History, Theory, Documents*, Brooklyn, NY: Autonomedia, 2018, p. 18.

13. Clare Coffey, Patricia Espinoza Revollo, Rowan Harvey, Max Lawson, Anam Parvez Butt, Kim Piaget, Diana Sarosi and Julie Thekkudan, *Time to Care: Unpaid and Underpaid Care Work and the Global Inequality Crisis*, Oxford: Oxfam International, January 2020, p. 10.

14. Ferguson, *Women and Work*, p. 9.

15. Brendan Churchill, 'No one escaped COVID's impacts, but big fall in tertiary enrolments was 80% women. Why?', *The Conversation*, 23 November 2020 – https://theconversation.com/no-one-escaped-covids-impacts-but-big-fall-in-tertiary-enrolments-was-80-women-why-149994

16. Silvia Federici, 'Women, money and debt: Notes for a feminist reappropriation movement', *Australian Feminist Studies* 33 (96), 2018: pp. 178–86, esp. pp. 184–85.

17. Simon Black, *Social Reproduction and the City: Welfare Reform, Child Care, and Resistance in Neoliberal New York*, Athens, GA: University of Georgia Press, 2020.

18. Echoing conceptual connections highlighted in German Marxist Rosa Luxemburg's work, the 'women of Bielefeld' – Veronika Bennholdt-Thomsen, Maria Mies and Claudia von Werlhof – wrote *Frauen, die Letzte Kolonie: Zur Hausfrauisierung der Arbeit*, Rowohlt: Reinbek bei Hamburg, 1983, appearing in English as *Women: The Last Colony*, London: Zed Books, 1988.

19. Claudia von Werlhof, 'On the concept of nature and society in capitalism', in Bennholdt-Thomsen et al., *Women: The Last Colony*, p. 97.

20. Ibid., p. 104.

21. Mies, *Patriarchy and Accumulation on a World Scale*, p. 210.

22. Ibid., p. 205.

23. Ibid., p. 212.

24. Maria Mies, 'Preface to new edition', in ibid. [1986], p. xvii.

25. Ibid., p. 212.

26. Bennholdt-Thomsen et al., *Frauen: Die Letzte Kolonie*.

27. Mies, *Patriarchy and Accumulation on a World Scale*, 'Preface to new edition' [1986], p. x.

28. OECD, 'LMF2.5: Time use for work, care and other day-to-day activities', in *OECD Family Database*, Organisation for Co-operation and Development: Social Policy Division; Directorate of Employment, Labour and Social Affairs, 2014 – www.oecd.org/social/family/database

29. John Bellamy Foster and Brett Clark, 'The robbery of nature: Capitalism and the metabolic rift', *Monthly Review* 70(3), 2018 – https://monthlyreview.org/2018/07/01/the-robbery-of-nature/; John Bellamy Foster and Brett Clark, *The Robbery of Nature: Capitalism and the Ecological Rift*, New York: Monthly Review, 2020.

30. Mies, *Patriarchy and Accumulation on a World Scale*, p. 213.

31. Ibid., esp. pp. 211–216.

32. Ibid., p. 215.

33. See interpretations by Autonomist Marxist Harry Cleaver, esp. pp. 128–135, in the most useful introduction, *Capital – Thirty-Three Lessons on Capital: Reading Marx Politically*, London: Pluto Press, 2019.

34. Ibid., p. 157; first section of Silvia Federici, 'The reproduction of labour-power in the global economy, Marxist theory and the unfinished feminist revolution', at *Caring Labour: An Archive* – https://caringlabor.wordpress. com/2010/10/25/silvia-federici-the-reproduction-of-labour-power-in-the-global-economy-marxist-theory-and-the-unfinished-feminist-revolution/

35. Silvia Federici, *Re-Enchanting the World: Feminism and the Politics of the Commons*, Oakland, CA: PM Press, 2019, p. 155.

36. Lest you interpret my main argument in this section as an apologetic defence of Marx, please note that I critically interrogate and challenge Marx's relations with key women in his life – namely Helene Demuth 'Lenchen', the Marx family housekeeper for most of their married lives, his wife Jenny (née von Westphalen) and daughter Tussy (Eleanor Marx) – in creative non-fiction play *Servant of the Revolution* (available in German translation) – https://anitranelson.info/servant-of-the-revolution/. See also Anitra Nelson, 'Servant of the Revolution: The creative art of serving history and the imagination', *Hecate: An Interdisciplinary Journal of Women's Liberation* 36(1&2), 2017: pp. 137–152.

37. Mies, *Patriarchy and Accumulation on a World Scale*, p. 228.

38. Ibid., pp. 218–223, esp. pp. 218, 221.

39. Vandana Shiva, *Who Really Feeds the World?*, London: Zed Books, 2015, pp. 26, 124.

40. Ibid., p. 137.

41. Veronika Bennholdt-Thomsen, 'What really keeps our cities alive?', in Veronika Bennholdt-Thomsen, Nicholas Faraclas and Claudia von Werlhof, *There Is an Alternative: Subsistence and Worldwide Resistance to Corporate Globalization*, North Melbourne/London/New York: Spinifex Press/Zed Books, 2001, pp. 217–218, 230.

42. Veronika Bennholdt-Thomsen, *Money or Life: What Makes Us Really Rich*, Bonn: Women and Life on Earth e.V., 2011, pp. 15–16.

43. Maria Mies and Veronika Bennholdt-Thomsen, *The Subsistence Perspective: Beyond the Globalised Economy*, London/New York: Zed Books/Room 400, 1999, p. 20.

44. Ibid., p. 17.

45. Bennholdt-Thomsen, *Money or Life*, p. 15.

46. Ibid., p. 22.

47. Mies and Bennholdt-Thomsen, *The Subsistence Perspective*, pp. 111–113.

48. Ibid., p. 119.

49. Ibid., p. 114.

50. Ibid., p. 116.

51. Maria Mies, '"Moral economy": A concept and a perspective', in R Rilling, H Spitzer, O. Green, F. Hucho and G. Pati (eds), *Challenges: Science and*

Peace in a Rapidly Changing Environment, Schriftenreihe Wissenschaft und Freiden, Vol. I, Marburg: BdWi, 1992; Mies and Bennholdt-Thomsen, *The Subsistence Perspective*, p. 116.

52. Mies and Bennholdt-Thomsen, *The Subsistence Perspective*, pp. 109–111.
53. Bennholdt-Thomsen, 'What really keeps our cities alive', p. 225
54. Mies and Bennholdt-Thomsen, *The Subsistence Perspective*, p. 63.
55. Ibid., p. 133.
56. Ibid., pp. 133–134.
57. Bennholdt-Thomsen, *Money or Life*, p. 30, see also p. 28.
58. Bennholdt-Thomsen, 'What really keeps our cities alive', pp. 224, 228.
59. Friederike Habermann, 'The post-capitalist feminism cookie: The main course – A commons-creating peer production as a possible future', Project Society After Money, *Society After Money: Dialogue*, London: Bloomsbury, 2020, pp. 285–300, esp. p. 290.
60. Ariel Salleh, 'The value of a synergistic economy', in Anitra Nelson and Frans Timmerman (eds), *Life Without Money: Building Fair and Sustainable Economies*, London: Pluto Press, 2011, pp. 94–110.
61. Mies, *Patriarchy and Accumulation on a World Scale*, pp. 228ff, esp. p. 229.
62. Petr Daněk and Petr Jehlička, 'Food self-provisioning in Central Europe', in Anitra Nelson and Ferne Edwards (eds), *Food for Degrowth: Perspectives and Practices*, Abingdon: Routledge, 2020, pp. 33–44, esp. p. 36.
63. For publications and projects of J.K. Gibson-Graham and community economies, see – www.communityeconomies.org/people/jk-gibson-graham
64. Joan. C. Tronto, *Moral Boundaries: A Political Argument for an Ethic of Care*, New York: Routledge, and Chapman & Hall, 1993, p. 103.
65. Anna Coote, Jane Franklin and Andrew Simms, *21 Hours: Why a Shorter Working Week Can Help Us All to Flourish in the 21st Century*, London: New Fconomics Foundation, 2010, pp. 1, 2 and 30–31.
66. Nancy Fraser, interviewed by Jo Littler, 'An astonishing time of great boldness: On the politics of recognition and redistribution', *Soundings* 58, 2014.
67. Cäcilie Schildberg (ed.), *A Caring and Sustainable Economy: A Concept Note from a Feminist Perspective*, Berlin: Friedrich-Ebert-Stiftung/Global Policy and Development, 2014.
68. Christa Wichterich 'Contesting green growth, connecting care, commons and enough', in Wendy Harcourt and Ingrid L. Nelson (eds), *Practising Feminist Political Ecologies: Moving Beyond the 'Green Economy'*, London: Zed Books, 2015, pp. 67–100, esp. p. 72.
69. Ibid., esp. p. 75.
70. Ibid., esp. pp. 75 and 81.
71. Ibid., esp. pp. 87–88, 92.
72. Feminisms and Degrowth Alliance, *Feminist Degrowth: Collaborative FaDA reflections on The COVID-19 Pandemic and the Politics of Social Reproduction*, short version in tweet (accessed at Twitter, 1 November 2020) – https://twitter.com/fem_degrowth/status/1253403063987159041

73. According to Friederike Habermann (personal correspondence, 8 May 2021): Gabriele Winker, *Solidarische Care-Ökonomie: Revolutionäre Realpolitik für Care und Klima*, Bielefeld: transcript Verlag, 2021.
74. Bennholdt-Thomsen, *Money or Life*, p. 25.
75. Habermann, 'The post-capitalist feminism cookie', p. 298. Friederike Habermann, Stefan Meretz and Christian Siefkes, 'Trialogue: Implicit and explicit views of human nature', in Project Society After Money, *Society After Money: Dialogue*, London: Bloomsbury, pp. 300–321.
76. Tobi(as) Rosswog in interview by Katherina Moebus, 'Participatory spaces for social change/Mitmachräume für den Wandel', in *Economies of Common/ing – Ökonomien des Gemeinschaffens*, Interview Reader #1/ Gesammelte Gespräche #1, Berlin: Agents of Alternatives, 2020, pp. 29–40 – www.economiesofcommoning.net/interviews/
77. Katherina Moebus, 'Economies of commoning – New frameworks for citizen participation?', XVI Biennial IASC Conference Practising the Commons: Self-governance, cooperation and institutional change, Utrecht, 10–14 July 2017.
78. Friederike Habermann, *Ecommony: UmCARE zum Miteinander*, Sulzbach am Taunus: Ulrike Helmer Verlag, 2016.
79. Habermann, 'The post-capitalist feminism cookie', p. 290.
80. This summary description of Habermann's work draws from personal conversations and the following: Katherina Moebus, '*Ecommony. Turn to Togetherness*' (2016) [review of Friederike Habermann *UmCARE zum Miteinander*], undated – http://economiesofcommoning.net/ecommony-turn-to-togetherness/, and Katherina Moebus, 'About absence of barter-logics, feminist commons and "basic material caring"', July 2017 – http://economiesofcommoning.net/about-absence-of-barter-logics-etc/
81. International Feminists for a Gift Economy, *Position Statement for a Peaceful World*, presented at World Social Forum, Porto Alegre (Brazil), 2002 – http://gift-economy.com/international-feminists-for-a-gift-economy-position-statement-for-a-peaceful-world/
82. Genevieve Vaughan, 'Reciprocity' in *For-Giving: A Feminist Criticism of Exchange*, 1997 – http://gift-economy.com/for-giving/; Genevieve Vaughan, 'Introduction: A radically different worldview is possible' in Genevieve Vaughan (ed.) *Women and the Gift Economy: A Radically Different Worldview is Possible*, Toronto: Inanna Publications and Education Inc., 2007, pp. 1–40, esp. p 20.
83. Terry Leahy, 'A gift economy', in Anitra Nelson and Frans Timmerman (eds), *Life Without Money: Building Fair and Sustainable Economies*, London: Pluto Press, 2011, pp. 111–135. Terry Leahy site – https://gifteconomy.org.au/
84. Federici, *Re-Enchanting the World*, pp. 102–115, esp. p. 110.
85. Ibid., p. 167.
86. Silvia Federici and George Caffentzis, 'Common against and beyond capitalism' [originally 2013] in Federici, *Re-Enchanting the World*, pp. 85–98, esp. p. 89.

87. Ibid., pp. 85–98, esp. pp. 93–96.
88. Federici, *Re-Enchanting the World*, pp. 102–115.
89. Federici and Caffentzis, 'Common against and beyond capitalism', pp. 88–89 and 96.

6 TECHNOLOGY, AND THE REAL DEBT CYCLE

All URLs current at 15 August 2021

1. Chelsea Schelly, *Dwelling in Resistance: Living with Alternative Technologies in America*, New Brunswick, NJ: Rutgers University Press, 2017.
2. On degrowth futures and transitionary strategies blending nonmonetary decision making and in-kind sharing of collective provisioning, see Vincent Liegey and Anitra Nelson, *Exploring Degrowth: A Critical Guide*, London: Pluto Press, 2020, pp. 116–153 and 157–169.
3. Ibid., pp. 62–67.
4. The essential concept of capital as asset co-evolving with the notion of money saved becoming capital is elaborated in works such as Karl Marx, *Grundrisse: Foundations of the Critique of Political Economy (Rough Draft)*, Harmondsworth: Penguin Books, 1973, pp. 239ff, and Karl Marx, *Capital: A Critique of Political Economy*, Vol. I, Harmondsworth: Penguin Books, 1976, pp. 247–257.
5. On so-called 'alternative' monies and financing, see Chapter 8. On Alf Hornborg's complementary currencies proposal, see Chapter 4. On public money, see Mary Mellor, *Debt or Democracy: Public Money for Sustainability and Social Justice*, London: Pluto Press, 2016.
6. Robert Ostertag, *Facebooking the Anthropocene in Raja Ampat: Technics and Civilization in the 21st Century*, Oakland, CA: PM Press, 2021, p. ix.
7. Ibid.
8. Lewis Mumford, *Technics and Civilization*, London: Routledge, 1934, esp. pp. 14–15.
9. Ostertag, *Facebooking the Anthropocene in Raja Ampat*, p. 130.
10. Lewis Mumford, *The City in History: Its Origins, Its Transformations and Its Prospects*, London: Martin Secker & Warburg, 1961, pp. 364–365.
11. Ibid., pp. 363–367, 410ff.
12. Global Forest Coalition, *Forest Cover 63: Circular Economy or Vicious Cycle? How Corporate Capture of Policy-Making and Perverse Incentives are Driving Deforestation*, December 2020 – http://globalforestcoalition.org/
13. Robert Frank, 'Elon Musk is now the richest person in the world, passing Jeff Bezos', *CNBC*, 8 January 2021 – www.cnbc.com/2021/01/07/elon-musk-is-now-the-richest-person-in-the-world-passing-jeff-bezos-html
14. *Bloomberg Billionaires Index*, 11 January 2021 – www.bloomberg.com/billionaires/
15. See, for instance, Karl Marx, *Capital: A Critique of Political Economy*, Vol. II, Harmondsworth: Penguin Books, 1978, pp. 299–300.

16. Eduardo Galeano, in Jonah Raskin,'Saying more with less: Eduardo Galeano interviewed by Jonah Ruskin', *Monthly Review* 61(5), October 2009 – http://monthlyreview.org/2009/10/01/saying-more-with-less-eduardo-galeano-interviewed-by-jonah-raskin

17. E.F. Schumacher, *Small is Beautiful: Economics as if People Mattered* – 25 *Years Later ... with Commentaries*, Vancouver: Hartley & Marks, 1999, p. 5 (including Paul Hawken note).

18. Marx, *Grundrisse*, p. 693.

19. Ibid., p. 700.

20. Ibid.

21. Ibid.

22. Ibid., p. 694.

23. Ibid., p. 703.

24. Ibid., p. 694.

25. Ibid., pp. 694–695, original emphasis.

26. Karl Marx, *Capital: A Critique of Political Economy*, Vol. III, Harmondsworth: Penguin Books, 1981, pp. 317–344.

27. Riccardo Bellofiore, 'The monetary aspects of the capitalist process in the Marxian system: An investigation from the point of view of the theory of the monetary circuit', in Fred Moseley (ed.), *Marx's Theory of Money*, London: Palgrave Macmillan, 2005, pp. 124–139.

28. Paul Mattick, *Business as Usual: The Economic Crisis and the Failure of Capitalism*, London: Reaktion Books, 2011; Anitra Nelson, 'COVID-19: Capitalist and postcapitalist perspectives', *Human Geography* 13(3), 2020: pp. 305–309.

29. *The Socialist Party of Great Britain*, see esp. 'How the SPGB is different' –www.worldsocialism.org/spgb/how-spgb-different/; Ecommony and commons in Chapter 5 (this volume) for Friederike Habermann on 'no-exchange communities'.

30. David Graeber, *Debt: The First 5,000 Years*, Brooklyn, NY: Melville House Publishing, 2011, pp. 102–108.

31. Kristin Ross, *Communal Luxury: The Political Imaginary of the Paris Commune*, London/Brooklyn, NY: Verso, 2015, p. 142.

32. Axel T. Paul, *Money and Society: A Critical Companion*, London: Pluto Press, 2020; V.A. Zelizer, *The Social Meaning of Money*, New York: Basic Books, 1995; Mark Granovetter, 'Economic action and social structure: The problem of embeddedness', *American Journal of Sociology* 91, 1985: pp. 481–510.

33. Marcel Mauss, *The Gift: The Form and Reason for Exchange in Archaic Societies*, London: Routledge, 2002 [French edn, 1925]; Kevin Hart and Wendy James, 'Marcel Mauss: A living inspiration', *Journal of Classical Sociology* 14(1), 2014: pp. 3–10; Yunxiang Yan, 'The gift and gift economy', in James G. Carrier (ed.), *A Handbook of Economic Anthropology*, Cheltenham/Northampton, MA: Edward Elgar, 2005, pp. 246–261.

34. For utopian currents see, for instance, Terry Leahy's site, *The Gift Economy: Anarchism and Strategies for Change* – http://gifteconomy.org.au/

35. Yunxiang Yan, 'The gift and gift economy', esp. p. 249.
36. Marx, *Capital: A Critique of Political Economy*, Vol. II.
37. Fred Block, 'Rethinking capitalism', in N.W. Biggart (ed.), *Readings in Economic Sociology*, Malden, MA: Blackwell, 2002, p. 224.
38. Karl Polanyi, 'The economy as instituted process', in Karl Polanyi, Conrad M. Arensberg and Harry W. Pearson (eds), *Trade and Markets in the Early Empires*, Glencoe, IL: Free Press, 1957, pp. 243–269.
39. Jukka Gronow, *Deciphering Markets and Money: A Sociological Analysis of Economic Institutions*, Helsinki: Helsinki University Press, 2020.
40. Mary Poovey, *A History of the Modern Fact: Problems of Knowledge in the Sciences of Wealth and Society*, Chicago, IL/London: University of Chicago Press, 1998, p. 29.
41. Ibid., p. 62.
42. Ibid., pp. 68, 74.
43. Ibid., p. 78.
44. Marx, *Capital: A Critique of Political Economy*, Vol. II, pp. 180–190.
45. This fact accounts for the perverse ways that workers with superannuation and home ownership integrate within capitalism with mainly working-class self-interests but also, typically increasing as they age, concerns as rentiers.
46. Zoya Teirstein, 'Science dishes out an answer on the old handwashing vs. dishwasher debate', *Grist*, 18 February 2020 – https://grist.org/climate/science-dishes-out-an-answer-on-the-old-handwashing-vs-dishwasher-debate/; Gabriela Porras, Gregory Keoleian, Geoffrey Lewis and Nagapooja Seeba, 'Corrigendum: A guide to household manual and machine dishwashing through a life cycle perspective', *Environmental Research Communications* 2(2), 2020 – https://iopscience.iop.org/article/10.1088/2515-7620/ab716b; Melissa Goodwin, 'How to wash dishes without wasting water', *Frugal and Thriving: Enjoy Good Living for Less*, 20 October 2020 version – www.frugalandthriving.com.au/how-to-hand-wash-dishes-using-minimal-water/
47. Liegey and Nelson, *Exploring Degrowth*, pp. 34–35.
48. Aaron Bastani, *Fully Automated Luxury Communism: A Manifesto*, London/New York: Verso Books, 2019, p. 12.
49. Richard Maxwell, 'High-tech consumerism, a global catastrophe happening on our watch', *The Conversation*, 11 September 2015 – https://theconversation.com/high-tech-consumerism-a-global-catastrophe-happening-on-our-watch-43476
50. Bastani, *Fully Automated Luxury Communism*, p. 119.
51. Ibid., pp. 159–181.
52. Nick Srnicek and Alex Williams, *Inventing the Future: Postcapitalism and a World Without Work*, London/New York: Verso Books, 2015, pp. 69–70.
53. Ibid., pp. 178–183, esp. p 178.
54. Adam Greenfield, *Radical Technologies, The Design of Everyday Life*, London/New York: Verso, 2017, esp. pp. 88–114.
55. Srnicek and Williams, *Inventing the Future*, pp. 113–114.

56. Maria Mies, *Patriarchy and Accumulation on a World Scale*, London/Melbourne: Zed Books/Spinifex, 1998 [1986], p. 217.

57. Ibid., p. 218.

58. Ibid., p. 212.

59. Silvia Federici, in Jane Elliott and Seb Franklin, "'The Synthesis is in the Machine": An interview with Silvia Federici', *Australian Feminist Studies* 33(96), 2018: pp. 172–177, esp. p. 174.

60. Silvia Federici, 'Feminism and the politics of the commons in an era of primitive accumulation', in Silvia Federici, *Re-Enchanting the World: Feminism and the Politics of the Commons*, Oakland, CA: PM Press, 2019, pp. 102–115, esp. pp. 110–111.

61. Friederike Habermann, 'The post-capitalist feminism cookie: The main course – A commons-creating peer production as a possible future', in Project Society After Money, *Society After Money: Dialogue*, London: Bloomsbury, pp. 285–300, esp. p, 287.

62. Tyson Yunkaporta, *Sand Talk: How Indigenous Thinking Can Save the World*, Melbourne: Text Publishing, 2019, p. 224.

63. Ross, *Communal Luxury*, p. 140.

64. Ibid., p. 142.

7 INDIGENOUS PEOPLES, REAL VALUES AND
THE COMMUNITY MODE OF PRODUCTION

All URLs current at 15 August 2021

1. Indigenous peoples have tenure rights and/or manage up to one-quarter of the land surface of Earth, spanning some two-fifths of protected and/or ecologically intact landscapes (such as forests) – Stephen T. Garnett et al., 'A spatial overview of the global importance of Indigenous lands for conservation', *Nature Sustainability* 1, July 2018: pp. 369–374. Indigenous peoples continue to protect environmental services that are integral with community forest management and provide widespread social, cultural and ecological benefits – FAO and FILAC, *Forest Governance by Indigenous and Tribal Peoples*, Santiago: FAO América Latina y el Caribe, 2021. The ICCA Consortium offers a rich hub of information on ICCAs, 'territories and areas conserved by indigenous peoples and local communities' or 'territories of life' (see, especially, ICCA annual reports – www.iccaconsortium.org), and Ashish Kothari, 'Territories of life: The past, present, and future of conservation on earth', *Wall Street International Journal*, 13 June 2021 – https://wsimag.com/economy-and-politics/66065-territories-of-life

2. Eduardo Galeano, 'The blue tiger and the promised land', *NACLA Report on the Americas* 24(5), February 1991: pp. 13–17, esp. p. 13.

3. Hannah Devlin, 'Indigenous Australians most ancient civilisation on Earth, DNA study confirms', *Guardian*, 22 September 2016 – www.theguardian.com/australia-news/2016/sep/21/indigenous-australians-most-ancient-civilisation-on-earth-dna-study-confirms

4. Geoffrey Blainey, *Triumph of the Nomads: A History of Ancient Australia*, South Melbourne: Macmillan, 1975, pp. 225–229.

5. Bill Gammage, *The Biggest Estate on Earth: How Aborigines Made Australia*, Crows Nest, NSW, Australia: Allen & Unwin, 2012, back cover.

6. Marshall Sahlins, *Stone Age Economics*, Abingdon/New York: Routledge Classics, 2017, p. 2.

7. NMA, 'Cook claims Australia', *National Museum of Australia*, 9 April 2021 update – www.nma.gov.au/defining-moments/resources/cook-claims-australia

8. The Common Ground Team, 'Massacres', 19 March 2021, *Common Ground* – www.commonground.org.au/learn/massacres-2

9. Sophie Russell and Chris Cunneen, 'As Indigenous incarceration rates keep rising, justice reinvestment offers a solution', *The Conversation*, 11 December 2018 – https://theconversation.com/as-indigenous-incarceration-rates-keep-rising-justice-reinvestment-offers-a-solution-107610

10. F. Markham and N. Biddle, *Income, Poverty and Inequality*, 2016 Census Paper 2. Canberra: Centre for Aboriginal Economic Policy Research, Australian National University, 2018.

11. The Common Ground Team, '2019 – The year of indigenous languages', 19 March 2021, *Common Ground* – www.commonground.org.au/learn/2019-the-year-of-indigenous-languages

12. Tyson Yunkaporta, *Sand Talk: How Indigenous Thinking Can Save the World*, Melbourne: Text Publishing, 2019, p. 41.

13. Calla Wahlquist, 'Leaked tape reveals Rio Tinto does not regret destroying 46,000-year-old Aboriginal rock shelter to expand mine', *Guardian*, 17 June 2020 – www.theguardian.com/australia-news/2020/jun/16/rio-tinto-repeats-apology-for-blasting-46000-year-old-rock-shelter-to-expand-mine. In 2021, the Chair announced he would leave Rio Tinto, acknowledging responsibility for deciding to blow up the sacred caves, but the company remained a solid player earning billions of dollars of profits, taxes and royalties.

14. Calla Wahlquist, 'Rio Tinto blames "misunderstanding" for destruction of 46,000-year-old Aboriginal site', *Guardian*, 5 June 2020 – www.theguardian.com/business/2020/jun/05/rio-tinto-blames-misunderstanding-for-destruction-of-46000-year-old-aboriginal-site

15. Sarah Holcombe and Bronwyn Fredericks, '"Destruction by a thousand cuts": the relentless threat mining poses to the Pilbara cultural landscape', *The Conversation*, 25 February 2021 – https://theconversation.com/destruction-by-a-thousand-cuts-the-relentless-threat-mining-poses-to-the-pilbara-cultural-landscape-155941

16. Clare Wright, 'Friday essay: Masters of the future or heirs of the past? Mining, history and Indigenous ownership', *The Conversation*, 29 January 2021 – https://theconversation.com/friday-essay-masters-of-the-future-or-heirs-of-the-past-mining-history-and-indigenous-ownership-153879

17. James Cowan, *Letters from a Wild State: An Aboriginal Perspective*, Longmead: Element Books, 1991, p. xiii.

18. David Suzuki with Amanda McConnell, *The Sacred Balance: Rediscovering Our Place in Nature*, St Leonards: Allen & Unwin, 1997.

19. Cowan, *Letters from a Wild State*, p. 93.

20. Yunkaporta, *Sand Talk*, pp. 158–159, 255.

21. Eduardo Galeano, *Open Veins of Latin America: Five Centuries of the Pillage of a Continent*, trans Cedric Belfrage, London/New York: Monthly Review Press, 1973.

22. Eduardo Galeano, *Days and Nights of Love and War*, trans Judith Brister, New York: Monthly Review Press, 1983, p. 130. Most of this section is drawn from Anitra Nelson, 'The political economy of space and time in Eduardo Galeano', *Progress in Political Economy*, 20 February 2018 – www.ppesydney. net/political-economy-space-time-eduardo-galeano/

23. Eduardo Galeano, *We Say No: Chronicles 1963–1991*, New York: W.W. Norton & Co., 1992, pp. 241, 244.

24. Galeano, 'The blue tiger and the promised land', p. 13.

25. Eduardo Galeano, in M. Potosi (2003) 'Interview with Eduardo Galeano', *The Progressive*, 13 July 2003, p. 7 – www.mail-archive.com/ugandanet@ kym.net/msg05039.html

26. Eduardo Galeano, *Upside Down; A Primer for the Looking-Glass World*, New York: Metropolitan Books, 1998.

27. Eduardo Galeano, *Genesis (Memory of Fire Part I)*, London: Methuen, 1987, p. 225.

28. Galeano, 'The blue tiger and the promised land', p. 13.

29. Galeano, in Potosi, 'Interview with Eduardo Galeano'.

30. Dylan Eldredge Fitzwater, *Autonomy is in Our Hearts: Zapatista Autonomous Government Through the Lens of the Tsotsil Language*, Oakland, CA: PM Press, p. 45.

31. Enlace Zapatista (pages include English translations) – http://enlacezapatista. ezln.org.mx/

32. John Holloway, *Change the World Without Taking Power: The Meaning of Revolution Today*, London/New York: Pluto Press, 2002, pp. 20–21.

33. Fitzwater, *Autonomy is in Our Hearts*, p. 2.

34. Information in this paragraph draws from ibid., pp. 90, 157–158, 160–161.

35. Ibid., pp. 104, 106, 161.

36. Ibid., p. 134.

37. Ibid., pp. 148–155.

38. Will Grant, 'Struggling on: Zapatistas 20 years after the uprising', *BBC News*, 1 January 2014 – www.bbc.com/news/world-latin-america-25550654

39. David Barkin, 'Principles for constructing alternative socio-economic organizations: Lessons learned from working outside institutional structures', *Review of Radical Political Economics*, 41(3), 2009: pp. 372–379, esp. p. 378; Erin Araujo, 'Moneyless economics and non-hierarchical exchange values in Chiapas, Mexico', *Journal des Anthropologues*, 152–3, 2018: pp. 147–170, esp. p. 165.

40. David Barkin and Banca Lemus, 'Third world alternatives for building post-capitalist worlds', *Review of Radical Political Economics*, 48(4), 2016: pp. 569–576, esp. p. 574.
41. Harry Cleaver, 'The Zapatistas and the international circulation of struggle: Lessons suggested and problems raised', written for conferences in 1998, posted 10 August 2015 at *Libcom.org* – http://libcom.org/library/zapatistas-international-circulation-struggle-cleaver
42. Palabra del Ejército Zapatista de Liberación Nacional, 'Part One: A declaration … For life', *Enlace Zapatista*, 1 January 2021 – http://enlacezapatista.ezln.org.mx/2021/01/01/part-one-a-declaration-for-life/
43. Laura Gottesdiener, 'Now you see me: A glimpse into the Zapatista movement, two decades later', *TomDispatch*, 23 January 2014 – https://tomdispatch.com/laura-gottesdiener-visiting-a-revolution-that-won-t-go-away/
44. Mauvaise Troupe Collective, *The Zad and NoTAV: Territorial Struggles and the Making of a New Political Intelligence*, London/Brooklyn, NY: Verso, 2018, p. 160.
45. Ibid., p. 167. See too, Schools for Chiapas – https://schoolsforchiapas.org/
46. For general information, see Rojava Information Center – https://rojavainformationcenter.com/ and Women Defend Rojava – https://womendefendrojava.net/en/ and ANF News – https://anfenglishmobile.com/
47. Unless indicated otherwise, this section is informed by Dor Shilton, 'Rojava: The radical eco-anarchist experiment betrayed by the West, and bludgeoned by Turkey', *Ecologise*, 27 October 2019 – https://ecologise.in/2019/10/27/rojava-the-eco-anarchist-experiment/
48. Ibid.
49. Abdullah Öcalan, *The Political Thought of Abdullah Öcalan: Kurdistan, Woman's Revolution and Democratic Confederalism*, London: Pluto Press, 2017, pp. 39 and 76–80, esp. p. 78.
50. David Graeber via interview, in Shilton, 'Rojava'.
51. Unless otherwise indicated, information in this section is drawn from Anonymous, *Revolution and Cooperatives: Thoughts about my time with the economic committee in Rojava Cooperatives as a Revolutionary Strategy – Facing Capitalist Modernity*, Internationalist Commune of Rojava, 9 October 2020 – https://internationalistcommune.com/revolution-and-cooperatives-thoughts-about-my-time-with-the-economic-committee-in-rojava/
52. Cooperativa Integral Catalana, 'Economic self-governance in democratic autonomy: The example of Bakûr (Turkish Kurdistan)', *Cooperativa.cat*, 9 July 2016 – https://cooperativa.cat/economic-self-governance-in-democratic-autonomy-the-example-of-bakur-turkish-kurdistan/
53. Anonymous, *Revolution and Cooperatives*, p. 16.
54. Ibid., p. 19.
55. Öcalan, *The Political Thought of Abdullah Öcalan*, pp. 82–85.
56. Ibid., p. 129.
57. Cooperativa Integral Catalana, 'Economic self-governance in democratic autonomy'.

58. Vernon Richards, 'Foreword', in Gaston Leval, *Collectives in the Spanish Revolution*, Oakland: PM Press, 2018 [1975], pp. 7–15, esp. p. 14.

59. Leval, *Collectives in the Spanish Revolution*, p. 76.

60. Ibid., p. 133.

61. Ibid., p. 110.

62. Ibid., pp. 95–96, 108–109, 110, 117.

63. Ibid., p. 115ff.

64. Ibid., p. 204.

65. Ibid., p. 193.

66. Ibid., p. 196.

67. Ibid., p. 202.

68. Eric Magnin and Nikolay Nenovsky, 'Calculating without money: Theories of in-kind accounting of Alexander Chayanov, Otto Neurath and the early Soviet experiences', *European Journal of the History of Economic Thought* 28(3), 2021: pp. 456–477.

8 OCCUPY THE WORLD!

All URLs current at 15 August 2021

1. Vincent Liegey and Anitra Nelson, *Exploring Degrowth: A Critical Guide*, London: Pluto Press, 2020, esp. pp. 133–145, 163–169.

2. On mutual aid, see Marina Sitrin and Colectiva Sembrar (eds), *Pandemic Solidarity: Mutual Aid During the Covid-19 Crisis*, London: Pluto Press, 2020.

3. Xavier Balaguer Rasillo, 'Alternative economies, digital innovation and commoning in grassroots organisations: Analysing degrowth currencies in the Spanish region of Catalonia', *Environmental Policy and Governance*, 2020, doi.org/10.1002/eet.1910; elleflane, 'Understand Faircoin, the real economy of common people', *El Poblet Cooperativa*, 11 January 2018 – https://cooperativa.cat/understand-faircoin-the-real-economy-of-people/; *FairCoop* – https://git.fairkom.net/faircoop/MediaCommunication/-/wikis/welcome-to-faircoop

4. Nic Carter, 'How much energy does Bitcoin actually consume?', *Harvard Business Review*, 5 May 2021 – https://hbr.org/2021/05/how-much-energy-does-bitcoin-actually-consume

5. Michel Bauwens, Neal Gorenflo and John Restakis, 'Integral revolution: An interview to Enric Duran about CIC', 29 March 2014, *El Poblet Cooperativa* – https://cooperativa.cat/integral-revolution/

6. Ibid.

7. George Dafermos, *The Catalan Integral Cooperative: An Organizational Study of a Post-Capitalist Cooperative*, P2P Foundation and Robin Hood Coop, October 2017, esp. pp. 8–9, 27, 30.

8. A 'hacklab' or 'hackerspace' offers a hub and workspace for people interested in digital technologies to work, to share knowledge and skills, and to socialise.

9. Anitra Nelson, *Small is Necessary: Shared Living on a Shared Planet*, London: Pluto Press, 2018, pp. 234–237.
10. Dafermos, *The Catalan Integral Cooperative*, p. 22.
11. Learn more here – https://calafou.org/en/
12. Copyleft, contra copyright, signals conditional free use. Copyleft licences permit free use on the condition that derivative works are also copyleft. See, for example, GNU General Public License – www.gnu.org/licenses/gpl-3.0.en.html
13. Alberto Cottica, 'Catalan Integral Cooperative: A closer look', *Edgeryders Platform*, 19 November 2020 – https://edgeryders.eu/t/catalan-integral-cooperative-a-closer-look/14799
14. Eric Duran in Bauwens et al., 'Integral revolution'; Prapimphan Chiengkul, 'The degrowth movement: Alternative economic practices and relevance to developing countries', *Alternatives: Global, Local, Political*, 43(2), 2018: pp. 81–95, esp. pp. 81–82, 91.
15. *Integral Community Exchange System* – https://integralces.net/
16. *CoopFunding* – https://coopfunding.net/
17. *Ecoxarxes* – https://ecoxarxes.cat/
18. Joel Morist in Cottica, 'Catalan Integral Cooperative: A closer look'.
19. Alf Hornborg, *Nature, Society and Justice in the Anthropocene: Unraveling the Money-Energy-Technology Complex*, Cambridge: Cambridge University Press, 2019.
20. I'm pointing to something along the lines of this: Gung Hoe Growers/ Harcourt Farming Co-op, 'Learning true value', *Harcourt Organic Farming Coop News*, 26 February 2021 – https://hofcoop.com.au/2021/02/26/learning-true-value/
21. Michel Bauwens and Alex Pazaitis, *Accounting for Planetary Survival: Towards a P2P Infrastructure for a Socially Just Circular Society*, P2P Foundation, Guerrilla Foundation and Schoepflin Foundation, June 2019, see esp. pp. 28–29 and 49 – http://commonstransition.org/p2p-accounting-for-planetary-survival/
22. Project Society After Money, *Society After Money: A Dialogue*, New York/ London: Bloomsbury Academic, 2019.
23. See the top-down approach and development in Chavanov's thought – taking an arc away from money only to return to it – in Eric Magnin and Nikolay Nenovsky, 'Calculating without money: Theories of in-kind accounting of Alexander Chayanov, Otto Neurath and the early Soviet experiences', *European Journal of the History of Economic Thought* 28(3): pp. 456–77, esp. pp. 462, 466–470.
24. Bauwens et al., 'Integral revolution: an interview to Enric Duran about CIC'.
25. Cottica, 'Catalan Integral Cooperative: A closer look'.
26. Bauwens et al., 'Integral revolution: an interview to Enric Duran about CIC'.
27. Dafermos, *The Catalan Integral Cooperative*, p. 30.
28. Axel T. Paul, *Money and Society: A Critical Companion*, London: Pluto Press, pp. 42–43.
29. Ibid., pp. 47–51.

30. For more details, see Twin Oaks Community – www.twinoaks.org/; Kat Kincade with the Twin Oaks Community, 'Labour credit – Twin Oaks Community', in Anitra Nelson and Frans Timmerman (eds), *Life Without Money: Building Fair and Sustainable Economies*, London: Pluto Press, 2011, pp. 173–191.

31. Eastwind Community – www.eastwindblog.co/; Acorn Community – www.acorncommunity.org/

32. Nelson, *Small is Necessary*, pp. 214–237.

33. Mauvaise Troupe Collective, *The Zad and NoTAV: Territorial Struggles and the Making of a New Political Intelligence*, London/Brooklyn, NY: Verso, 2017, esp. pp. 155, 160, 199.

34. On commons and commoning, see Massimo de Angelis, *On the Commons and the Transformation to Postcapitalism*, London: Zed Books, 2017. While I agree that in capitalism 'money is for money's sake', I cannot fathom any postcapitalism where 'commons are for commons' sake (and money at most is an instrument for the reproduction of the commons)' (ibid., p. 313). This notion seems to be based partly on misinterpretations of Marx (ibid., pp. 173–197). A preferred interpretation of Marx appears in Paresh Chattopadhyay, *Marx's Associated Mode of Production: A Critique of Marxism*, New York: Palgrave Macmillan/Springer Nature, 2016, esp. pp. 64–65, 150–153, 161–188, 205–209.

35. Harry Cleaver's work is essential here, such as *Rupturing the Dialectic: The Struggle Against Work, Money and Financialization*, Chico, CA/Edinburgh: AK Press, 2017, esp. pp. 228–234.

36. This section draws heavily on Anitra Nelson, 'New and green materialism', *Progress in Political Economy*, 29 July 2015 – www.ppesydney.net/new-and-green-materialism/; Anitra Nelson, 'New materialism is green materialism', Historical Materialism Australasia 2015: Reading Capital, Class & Gender Today conference, University of Sydney, NSW, Australia, 17–18 July; and is worked up with reference to work in Anitra Nelson, 'Changing ourselves: Marx on work', in Joe Collins (ed.), *Applying Marx's Capital to the 21st Century*, London: Palgrave Macmillan, forthcoming.

37. Karl Marx, *Theses on Feuerbach*, translated by Cyril Smith, 1845 (2002, trans.) – www.marxists.org/archive/marx/works/1845/theses/ My 'green materialism' here is a contemporary variant of the philosophical and political essence of Marx's 'materialism', as such distinct from and opposed to ever-increasing production and consumption of purportedly earth-friendly goods and services, green consumerism and 'green' growth.

38. Ezequiel Adamovsky, *Anti-Capitalism: The New Generation of Emancipatory Movements*, New York: Seven Stories Press, 2011, pp. 89–124.

39. For examples, see chapters in Anitra Nelson and François Schneider (eds), *Housing for Degrowth: Principles, Models, Challenges and Opportunities*, Abingdon/New York: Routledge, 2018. Likewise, chapters in Anitra Nelson and Ferne Edwards (eds), *Food For Degrowth: Perspectives and Practices*, Abingdon/New York: Routledge, 2021, esp. Chapters 2 and 7 by Patrick

Jones and Meg Ulman, and Silvio Cristiano et al., respectively, pp. 19–32 and 90–99.

40. Can Masdeu, 'Who are we', *Vall de Can Masdeu* – www.canmasdeu.net/who-are-we/?lang=en

41. Mark Boyle, *Drinking Molotov Cocktails with Gandhi*, East Meon: Hyden House, 2015. For details on types of activities referred to in this section, see Liegey and Nelson, *Exploring Degrowth*, esp. pp. 49–85, 116–153.

42. John Holloway, *Crack Capitalism*, London/New York: Pluto Press, 2010, esp. pp. 17–20, and John Holloway, *Change the World Without Taking Power: The Meaning of Revolution Today*, 2nd edn, London: Pluto Press, 2010 [2002].

43. Peter Kropotkin, *Mutual Aid: A Factor of Evolution*, London: Freedom Press, 2011 [1891].

Annotated Select Reading List and Links

This select reading list is not comprehensive. Beyond references that can be gleaned from endnotes in the text, this sample offers starting points for journeys of thought and action.

ART, MONEY AND POSTCAPITALISM

Max Haiven – https://maxhaiven.com/ – for publications such as
——, *Art after Money, Money after Art: Creative Strategies Against Financialization*, London: Pluto Press, 2018 and
——, *Revenge Capitalism: The Ghosts of Empire, the Demons of Capital, and the Settling of Unpayable Debts*, London: Pluto Press, 2020.

COMMONS, COMMONING

Camille Barbagallo, Nicholas Beuret and David Harvie (eds), *Commoning with George Caffentzis and Silvia Federici*, London: Pluto Press, 2019.

George Caffentzis, see '[Tribute to] The Work of George Caffentzis', 17 June 2020, at *The Commoner* – https://thecommoner.org/tribute/tribute-to-the-work-of-george-caffentzis/ and articles at the libcom.org site – http://libcom.org/tags/george-caffentzis

The Commoner: The Web Journal for Other Values, edited by Massimo de Angelis – https://thecommoner.org/ and Massimo de Angelis – www.researchgate.net/profile/Massimo-De-Angelis/research

The Deep Commons: Cultivating Ecologies of Solidarity and Care beyond Capitalism, Patriarchy, Racism and the State curated by the Deep Commons collective visioning project – www.deepcommons.net/

Gustova Esteva, bio and publications at – http://gustavo-esteva.blogspot.com/ and Unitierra Oaxaca (University of the Earth, Oaxaca, Mexico) in Multi-Sense Media, *Re-learning Hope: A Story of Unitierra* (documentary) – https://vimeo.com/172681670

Friederike Habermann, *Ecommony: UmCare zum Miteinander*, Sulzbach: Ulrike Helmer Verlag, 2016.

Jineolojy, thinking of and publications by the Women's Movement of Kurdistan – https://jineoloji.org/en/

DEBT

The Belgian-based international Committee for the Abolition of Illegitimate Debt (CADTM) offers a useful clearing house for exploring debt from radical perspectives in multiple languages and you can subscribe to newsletters – http://cadtm.org/English

The Global Debt Syllabus: Capital, Violence, and the New Global Economy is a public syllabus generated by the Unpayable Debt: Capital, Violence, and the New Global Economy working group at Columbia University – https://debt-syllabus.com/

David Graeber, *Debt: The First 5000 Years*, London: Melville House Publishing, 2011.

DEMONETIZE IT!

Demonetize it! – *Planet demonetization* is a site with news and resources on money-free activism and scholarship where you can subscribe to the *Demonetize Digest* and e-list – https://demonetize.it/

ECOLOGICAL ECONOMICS AND ENVIRONMENTAL JUSTICE

For an online glossary of relevant terms regularly used by the environmental justice movement and in ecological economics see the Environmental Justice Organisations, Liabilities and Trade project site – www.ejolt.org/section/resources/glossary/

MONEY IN ECONOMICS, SOCIETY AND HISTORY

Michell Aglietta, *Money: 5000 Years of Debt and Power*, London: Verso, 2018.

Constantine George Caffentzis, *Clipped Coins, Abused Words, and Civil Government: John Locke's Philosophy of Money*, London/New York: Pluto Press, 2021 [1989].

——, *Exciting the Industry of Mankind George Berkeley's Philosophy of Money*, Heidelberg: Springer Netherlands, 2000.

——, *Civilizing Money: Hume, his Monetary Project, and the Scottish Enlightenment*, London/New York: Pluto Press, 2021.

Geoffrey Ingham, *The Nature of Money*, Cambridge: Polity, 2004.

——, *Money: Ideology, History, Politics*, Cambridge: Polity, 2020.

Costas Lapavitsas, *Social Foundations of Markets, Money and Credit*, London: Routledge, 2003.

——, *Profiting without Producing: How Finance Exploits Us All*. London: Verso, 2013.

Midnight Notes Collective – https://web.archive.org/web/20090416180149/http://www.midnightnotes.org/

Anitra Nelson, *Marx's Concept of Money: The God of Commodities*, London: Routledge, 1999/2014.

Bertell Ollman (ed.), *Market Socialism: The Debate Among Socialists*, New York: Routledge, 1999.

Joseph A. Schumpeter, *History of Economic Analysis*, edited by Elizabeth Boody Schumpter, London/Boston, MA/Sydney: Allen & Unwin, 1986 [1954] edn – I highly recommend using the index to extract relevant material.

Pierre Vilar, *A History of Gold and Money: 1450–1920*, London: NLB, 1969.

MONEY AND ALTERNATIVE NONMONETARY/REAL-VALUE FUTURES

Adam Buick, see articles at the libcom.org site – https://libcom.org/tags/adam-buick

Harry Cleaver, *Rupturing the Dialectic: The Struggle Against Work, Money, and Financialization*, Chico, CA/Edinburgh: AK Press, 2017.

——, *Thirty-Three Lessons on Capital: Reading* Capital *Politically*, London: Pluto Press, 2019.

Harry Cleaver site – https://la.utexas.edu/users/hcleaver/

Gilles Dauvé and Karl Nesic, *Communisation* (English version), 2011 – www.troploin.fr/node/24

Andreas Exner, 'Degrowth and demonetization: On the limits of a noncapitalist market economy', *Capitalism Nature Socialism* 25(3), 2014: pp. 9–27.

——, Justin Morgan, Franz Nahrada, Anitra Nelson and Christian Siefkes, 'Demonetize: The problem is money', in Corinna Burkhart, Matthias Schmelzer and Nina True (eds), *Degrowth in Movements(s): Exploring Pathways for Transformation*, London: Zero Books, 2020, pp. 159–171.

Friederike Habermann, *Ecommony: UmCare zum Miteinander*, Sulzbach: Ulrike Helmer Verlag, 2016.

——, *Ausgetauscht: Warum Gutes Leben für alle Tauschlogikfrei sein Muss*, Roßdorf: Ulrike Helmer-Verlag, 2018.

Friederike Habermann site – www.friederike-habermann.de

John Holloway, 'Read *Capital*: The first sentence – or, capital starts with wealth, not with the commodity', *Historical Materialism* 23(3), 2015: pp. 3–26.

——, 'No', *Historical Materialism* 13(4), 2005: pp. 265–284.

——, 'Now is the moment to learn hope' (video), 28 September 2016 – www.youtube.com/watch?v=VxKXd5BjchI

John Holloway site – www.johnholloway.com.mx

Terry Leahy, in particular his work on prefigurative hybrids, transformations towards nonmonetary economies at his site *The Gift Economy: Anarchism and Strategies for Change* – http://gifteconomy.org.au/

Anitra Nelson, 'The poverty of money: Marxian insights for ecological economists', *Ecological Economics*, 36, 2001: pp. 499–511.

——, '"Your money or your life": Money and socialist transformation', *Capitalism Nature Socialism* 27(4), 2016: pp. 40–60.

Anitra Nelson – http://anitranelson.info/
——, and Frans Timmerman, *Life Without Money: Building Fair and Sustainable Economies*, London: Pluto Press, 2011. Contributors: Adam Buick, Claudio Cattaneo, Harry Cleaver, Kat Kinkade and the Twin Oaks Community, Terry Leahy, Mihailo Marković, Anitra Nelson, John O'Neill, Ariel Salleh and Frans Timmerman.
John O'Neill, see Publications page – www.research.manchester.ac.uk/portal/en/researchers/john-oneill(f38c5bc2-3fab-4956-b865-9320310f4481).html
Project Society After Money, *Society After Money: Dialogue*, London: Blooms-bury Academic, 2019. Contributors: Ernest Aigner, Peter Fleissner, Friederike Habermann, Stefan Heidenreich, Lars Heitmann, Jasmin Kathöfer, Tobias Kohl, Ernst Lohoff, Stefan Meretz, Hanno Pahl, Annette Schlemm, Jens Schröter and Christian Siefkes.
Hans Widmer (aka P.M.), and initiatives with which he is associated:

- https://theanarchistlibrary.org/library/p-m-bolo-bolo
- https://newalliance.earth/
- http://0500.org/

RADICAL ECOLOGICAL DEMOCRACY

For an introduction, and allied developments in the Global South, see:

- *Global Tapestry of Alternatives* – https://globaltapestryofalternatives.org/
- *Radical Ecological Democracy* – www.radicalecologicaldemocracy.org/
- Ashish Kothari, 'Radical ecological democracy: Reflections from the South on degrowth', in Corinna Burkhart, Matthias Schmelzer and Nina True (eds), *Degrowth in Movements(s): Exploring Pathways for Transformation*, London: Zero Books, 2020, pp. 258–271.

SOCIALIST PARTY OF GREAT BRITAIN

The Socialist Party of Great Britain (SPGB) 'claims that socialism will, and must, be a wageless, moneyless, worldwide society of common (not state) ownership and democratic control of the means of wealth production and distribution' – www.worldsocialism.org/spgb/how-spgb-different/ and browse the rest of the site. An SPGB associated publication is Philoren, *Money Must Go!*, London: J. Phillips, 1943 – https://libcom.org/library/money-must-go

VIDEOS (ONLINE) OF INTENTIONAL GRASSROOTS NO-MONEY INITIATIVES

Artist as Family You Tube (Patrick Jones and Meg Ulman) – www.youtube.com/channel/UC90Jv6gBc7mf4dyfTyWj4tQ
——especially note the 45-minute 'Replacing growth with belonging economies'.

Mark Boyle, 'The man living in off-grid cabin without technology! Foraging & growing own Food!', *Smooth Gefixt*, 1 December 2019 – www.youtube.com/watch?v=tkZoUuAqRhk

See also

———, *The Way Home: Tales from a Life Without Technology*, London: One World, 2019/2020.

———, *The Moneyless Man: A Year of Freeconomic Living*, Re-issue, London: One World, 2019 [2010].

———, *The Moneyless Manifesto: Live Well, Live Rich, Live Free*, East Meon (Hampshire, UK): Permanent Publications, 2012 and free online – www. moneylessmanifesto.org/why-free/

———, *Drinking Molotov Cocktails with Gandhi*, East Meon: Hyden House, 2015.

El Cambalache, Departamento de Economía Decolonial (2015–), based in San Cristobal de las Casas, Chiapas (Mexico) for sharing knowledge and skills towards moneyless economies, as follows:

- Erin Araujo, 'Moneyless economics and non-hierarchical exchange values in Chiapas, Mexico', *Journal des Anthropologues*, 152–3, 2018: pp. 147–170 – https://doi.org/10.4000/jda.6907 – http://journals.openedition.org/jda/6907
- https://cambalache.noblogs.org/
- Inter-Change Value (2016) video on sharing and swapping as *internal change* — https://vimeo.com/159060233
- You Tube channel – www.youtube.com/channel/UCslgLGj8VoLFxSa DnL8iYQg/videos

Index

Thanks to our Patreon subscriber:

Ciaran Kane

Who has shown generosity and
comradeship in support of our publishing.